The Continuum Guide to
Media Education

PAT BRERETON

continuum
LONDON • NEW YORK

Continuum

The Tower Building   15 East 26th Street
11 York Road   New York
London SE1 7NX   NY 10010

www.continuumbooks.com

First published in 2001

This edition published in 2005
Reprinted 2005

British Library Cataloguing-in-Publication Data

A catalogue record for this book is available from the British Library.

ISBN: 0–8264–5397–X (hardback)
          0–8264–7773–9 (paperback)

Designed and typeset by Ben Cracknell Studios
Printed and bound in Great Britain by Antony Rowe Ltd., Chippenham, Wiltshire

The Continuum Guide to
Media Education

Also available:

Joanna Baker and Heather Westrup: *The English Language Teacher's Handbook*

Martin Blocksidge (ed.): *Teaching Literature 11–18*

Graham Butt: *Continuum Guide to Geography Education*

John Eggleston (ed.): *Teaching and Learning Design and Technology*

Andrew Goodwyn: *English in the Digital Age*

Richard Hickman (ed.): *Art Education 11–18*

Helen Nicholson (ed.): *Teaching Drama 11–18*

John Lello: *The Resourceful History Teacher*

Marilyn Nickson: *Teaching and Learning Mathematics: A Teacher's Guide to Recent Research*

Adrian Oldknow and Ron Taylor: *Teaching Mathematics with ICT*

Peter Taylor: *The Agricultural Science Teacher's Handbook*

Anne Watson and Mike Ollerton: *Inclusive Mathematics 11–18*

Contents

Introduction

This guide to media education aims to provide the reader with a collection of references and definitions encompassing this broad interdisciplinary subject area. It must be noted initially that the study of media draws heavily on film, communications, social science and cultural studies in particular. The purpose of producing a guide of this sort is to afford media educators at all levels quick access to a wide range of media education information. The information contained within this book is specifically focused on understanding and appreciating the processes of teaching and learning media and provides a concise overview of contemporary issues, terms and debates in media education.

Entries within this guide often proceed beyond the mere definition of words to provide the reader with a fuller contextual or analytical understanding of terms. This is particularly pertinent for media education, which strives constantly to subvert and problematize simplistic meanings and definitions. Often the meanings of related concepts can be explained more easily when they are collected together. Furthermore, entries will sometimes be associated with specific media writers who have written about such terms within the context of debates in media education generally. The theoretical underpinning of the discipline together with major core concepts can be correlated within clusters of media terms that will be cross-referenced where appropriate. Examples of such primary clusters include **audience, genre, ideology, narrative**.

This book also includes a number of longer discussion pieces that focus on those core concepts or issues which benefit from a fuller coverage than that provided within a simple definition. It is important to provide a rationale for the choice of terms used, which is somewhat biased by my particular interests in film and TV and my priorities with regard to the relative importance of a range of terms. The media references chosen for this guide echo terms found in a number of popular media readers and classic media texts used at post-primary and undergraduate level, which are included in the Bibliography.

Throughout this book the term 'media studies' together with the more preferred notion of 'media education' are used interchangeably across all forms of media expressions. However, it must be noted that for some critics in the UK particularly, media studies has evoked negative connotations of being a vague catch-all subject and therefore not a legitimate and worthwhile area of study. Because of such negative associations many university courses have avoided and often distanced themselves from using the term in their degree titles. Nevertheless it is difficult to avoid such a generic term in this guide.

It is hoped that this book will prove useful to a wide range of readers who have an interest both in media and in higher education. Much of its curricular success up to recently has occurred in the further education (FE) sector in the UK alongside the larger sixth form colleges. A major factor for its growth in popularity is the influence of other discipline areas, particularly English literature, and keen teachers who actively developed the study of media to augment their discipline area and thereby tap into students' more popular media pleasures and interests. Teachers trained in English, history, politics as well as other areas have often become most active in promoting the study of media as an extension of their own discipline. Consequently students engaged in Initial Teacher Training (ITT) in any related subject may find it valuable; while those who are pursuing education degrees which contain a media component at Masters, B.Phil., or even M.Phil. and Ph.D. levels, may consider it useful for providing a quick overview of terms and concepts. The guide also includes a small number of references to media education, associations, societies, legislation and journals in other English-speaking countries.

Throughout the text, words which are presented in **bold** print also occur within the alphabetical listing of terms, thus making cross-referencing possible. A continuing difficulty with such a project is how to maintain a 'language register' which is readily understandable yet also able to appropriate the technical media jargon used in academic texts and which must be understood if a deeper appreciation of the subject is to be developed. Getting this balance right is always difficult.

For example, the danger of reducing ideological analysis to crude conspiracy theories or simple platitudes remains ever-present within such a guide. Also, because of the language register required, the entries and definitions try to be jargon-free, which is not always possible. There is a continuing danger of not articulating the full complexity of the range of ideas expressed in this guide. Such difficulties occur more often with extremely complex and often ambiguous concepts like ideology or postmodernism for example. It must also be remembered that concepts dealt with in this text are defined by their particular application within media education, yet such terms often have contradictory meanings both within and outside the multidisciplinary area of media.

The eclectic nature of the discipline is also augmented by its wide-ranging influences, drawing directly from very many areas of study. These include sociology, art history, literary theory, politics, history, anthropology, geography and even philosophy. Media education incorporates the study of various media, including radio, press, TV and film, together with 'new media' such as the internet.

Experts in the field find it difficult to agree on the most suitable methods and approaches for the study of mass media. For example, should methods be discursive, analytical and purely theoretical, or must more practical applications inform an appropriate methodology for study. Such issues become most pertinent when considering the vocational requirements of the media industries, whose standards keep changing and adapting to new circumstances and new technology. This issue has become more pointed with the growing percentage of undergraduate students in Great Britain who at one level appear to be attracted to the subject because of its glossy surface and in addition believe its study will put them on the fast track towards a successful career. Nonetheless **Skillset**, the official government-financed agency, affirms that 60 per cent of media and communications students get jobs in media-related areas within six months of graduating (cited in the *Journal of Media Practice* 1(1), pp. 53–4). Numbers doing journalism and media-related courses in higher education in the UK rose from around 6,000 in 1990 to nearly 35,000 by 2000, according to the current *Media Guide*. These figures must be appreciated in the context of around 1.2 million undergraduate students in total in the UK. The government 'Creative Industries Task Force' predicted a growth in employment in this sector of 50,000 jobs in the UK over the following three years. (See *Guardian* article by Harriet Marsh, Saturday 16 January 1999.)

This correlation between media education and jobs is often undermined by barbed comments from professional attitude-formers in media and education, such as the former Chief Inspector of Schools, who glibly announced on a BBC radio interview on 1 March 2000 that he did not accept a connection between media degrees and employment in the industry.

In spite of a growing emphasis being placed on the vocational applicability of media education, a majority of undergraduate courses are designed to be 'generalist' rather than following on the road of purely vocational training. It is somewhat difficult to envisage a purely vocational approach without direct industrial underpinning and validation, except for more specific job-centred practical media courses (see **media education versus media studies**). Yet this ever-present vocational justification for the subject and the corresponding functions of media education generally has continued within the academic establishment since the subject evolved in the UK back in the 1970s. Nevertheless, in spite of the many criticisms, the subject has endured and grown in stature and importance ever since. As we start a new century, the only safe prediction is that media studies/education, in whatever form, will continue to develop within all levels of education establishments, with students wanting to become more and more 'media literate'.

A Level (Advanced Level). Examinations providing more able pupils in England, Wales and Northern Ireland with an academic General Certificate of Education (GCE). They are usually studied as part of a two-year course, after the age of 16. During the 1990s media attracted around 7,000 A Level students in the UK and was a popular A Level choice for candidates from within a wide range of possible subjects to study. A Levels have been criticized for apparent over-specialization. However, while they might maintain their status as the 'gold standard' qualification for university entrance, the situation is more complex especially for new curricular areas like media which includes a wide range of A Levels, GNVQ and more practical BTEC media courses. Such courses are recognized as acceptable entry qualifications, particularly for more practical-based degree courses.

Curricular choice in the UK is continuing to change, particularly with the announcement of the creation of a new two-year vocational degree programme which will require lower overall entry points. Equally significant is the announcement of new vocational A Level courses intended to unify practical studies and presumably overtake BTECs and possibly GNVQs. Such changes will, according to the government, help break down prejudices between so-called academic and vocational qualifications. Critics, however, have already raised objections to this possible break-up of the hard-earned legitimacy of vocational programmes, which will have to be reconstituted all over again. There are signs of a very slow take-up of these new courses, however, which may jeopardize their future.

aberrant decoding. Infers that audiences take meanings in different ways from what was intended by the producers of the mediated message in the first place. Consequently audiences are not necessarily controlled by the so-called inherent meaning in the text. This debate ranges on all fronts, with ideological/post-**Marxist** and **postmodernist** positions placing audiences in varying relations to the text.

In general terms it can be argued that the dominance of a 'conventional' ideological and Marxist reading of the media, while remaining embedded within the core of the discipline, is becoming more contentious and problematic. Nevertheless, media studies as a discipline could not exist without the bedrock of Marxist theory and analysis which has permeated the whole discipline and has influenced a majority of writers on the subject.

ability. The capacity to perform given tasks or skills. Students within many systems have traditionally been educated according to their age, aptitude and related ability. This divisive issue was very influential in the early days of media education debates. An assessment of academic ability used to select pupils in the UK for different forms of secondary education is now largely stopped by the advent of comprehensive schools. Ability as an educational indicator continues to be applied, some argue, with regard to practical work, which is sometimes stereotyped as providing a suitable curricular strategy for 'less able students'. This has particular relevance to media education, which seeks to connect theory with practice, especially in the more practical A Level syllabi, GNVQ, BTEC, HND and many degree-level media courses.

accent. One component of dialect, it encompasses the emphasis given to vowels, for instance. The meaning of a broadcast media message is strongly affected by the regional/national accent of the mediated voice. For example the official voice of BBC (up to the 1960s at least) projected an upper-class, Queen's English, accent which is often described as 'received pronunciation'. More recently this uniform style of presentation has been considered dated and stilted, with more regional variations now actively encouraged. **Linguists** who analyse speech connections in the media and elsewhere often focus on how racial/regional **stereotyping** is particularly affected by accent.

access course. An alternative route of entry into university for UK mature students who do not possess the 'standard' entry qualifications of two Advanced Levels (A Levels), or the vocational equivalent. By successfully completing an access course students may satisfy a university that they have met the standards of entry equivalent to those provided by A Levels. Further education (FE) colleges usually offer access courses and typically contain more than one subject discipline. Media and film studies are often popular choices for mature students.

Curzon, L. B. (1989) *Teaching in Further Education: An Outline of Principles and Practice.* Holt Education.

access TV. Television programmes or even whole channels which provide direct and unedited entry for ordinary people to get their voice/message recorded and broadcast for the general public. Access TV has become a major phenomenon particularly in America, which provides facilities of 'uncensored' public access to the broadcasting medium and has led to numerous debates concerning freedom of expression, for example. The ethos of **public service broadcasting** (PSB) also encourages access but not always in such an unedited and uncontrolled way.

active learning. Motivates pupils to take a proactive role in the learning process, rather than being passive recipients of information. It acknowledges that for learning to occur a student must be fully involved in the learning process rather than passively receiving knowledge from the teacher. Media education has developed a firm belief in active learning, especially through the growth of vocational courses such as BTEC in media and communication, which encourages high levels of interaction between pupils and teachers. Teachers often function as 'facilitators' allowing students to do primary research and develop their questioning and problem-solving skills helped by the guidance of the teacher. The **'key concepts'** approach to media education encouraged the avoidance of rote learning and unhelpful, undigested 'knowledge banking' as it is called, by articulating the interrelationship between subjects and concepts as well as the range of often conflicting meanings which need to be negotiated to allow active learning to take place.

Buckingham, D. (1983) *Reading Audiences: Young People and the Media*. Manchester University Press.

active reading. A term which suggests that rather than passively consuming mediated products, audiences contribute to and often take a wide range of meanings when reading texts. Such readings are dependent on their wishes, desires and other personal attributes which they bring to the communication process. See also **uses and gratification theory** as well as **popular culture** and **audience research**.

adaptation. When a text in one medium is translated into another medium. In particular film and TV adaptation have had a long history with a large number of media products beginning as a short story, novel or play before becoming reconstituted, using the conventions of an audiovisual medium. The study of the cross-fertilization between literature and film has been aided by a tradition of literary studies teachers applying their skills to subsequent adaptations. The **codes** and **conventions** of these interrelated media provide appropriate case study materials to teach the skills of reading and even creating artefacts within either medium. Adaptation is a good way to teach the 'grammar' of both film and literature while at the same time improving various forms of literacy. Many educationalists assert that popularized TV/ film adaptation of plays helps to increase awareness and understanding of such texts, though some purists worry that the study of classic texts is being 'dumbed down' by this.

Colin **MacCabe** persuasively wrote in the 1970s *Screen* journal how the novelistic narrative structure embedded within Hollywood film draws heavily from the narrative conventions of the nineteenth-century novel. As a result the study of film became more closely connected to literature.

Adapting theatre and plays to film has also become a growing study, especially with many Shakespeare plays and other theatrical masterpieces being adapted to film.

Dollimore, J. and Sinfield, A. (1985) *Political Shakespeare*. Manchester University Press.

Eisenstein, S. (1988) *Writings*, vol. 1: 1911–1934. Indiana University Press.

Esslin, M. (1987) *The Field of Drama.* Methuen.

Izod, J. (1989) *Reading the Screen.* Longman.

Naremore, J. (1988) *Acting and the Cinema.* University of California Press.

address. A term used to explore how media **texts** speak to their audiences. It can be described as the mode of communication, like the way the news is delivered on TV or on radio. While the 'addressee' is the person(s) to whom the message is intended, the 'addressor' is the person(s)/author(s) who sent the message. Media theorists try to work out how the style and approach of the media text constructs a relationship between its content and intended audience. Texts are examined to discover how they help to 'construct' and address their audiences (see also **discourse** analysis).

addresses. The best and most up-to-date addresses for all media organizations in the UK and elsewhere are contained in the following yearly publications:

Guardian Media Guide. Fourth Estate.

BFI Year Book. BFI.

These publications are essential, for all students doing practical projects in particular and who wish to work in the media, and even for looking towards future work experience.

If you need to access video material you can contact the following addresses:

BBC Educational Publishing, PO Box 234, Wetherby, West Yorks, LS23 7EU
BBC Education Information, White City, 201 Wood Lane, London, W12 7TS
Channel 4, 124 Horseferry Road, London, SW1P 2TX
Granada Television, Granada TV Centre, Quay Street, Manchester, M60 9EA
ITV Association, Knighton House, 56 Mortimer Street, London, W1N 2AN

advertising. Providing space in some medium to directly promote or sell some product or service. All commercial media are directly affected by their endless desire to attract advertisers to pay for time/space. The advertising business is often described as the 'handmaiden of capitalism' by **Marxists**, since it remains the lifeblood of all commercially run media from print, to radio and TV and even product placements in films as well as more conventional advertisements shown before films in cinemas. Whereas business studies analysis focuses on the advertisement's power as a marketing and advertising tool, media studies often questions its function and examines how advertisements represent reality and create pleasures for audiences to engage with. To be successful, advertisements usually fulfil various aims which ensure they connect with their target audience. These include:

• attracting attention,

• arousing interest,

• creating desire,

• providing information,

• inspiring confidence and, most importantly of all,

• stimulating action.

The study of advertising, especially in print and TV, has become a practical focus for teaching **semiotics** together with looking at changing historical attitudes to **gender** representations. Because of the ease of access and source material, teachers are able to use cuttings from newspapers/ magazines or contemporary off-air recordings of adverts which guarantee topicality and relevance. **Feminist** decodings of adverts, in particular, often concentrate on the 'objectification' and '**commodification**' of females as conventional objects of the '**male gaze**'. Similar arguments have more recently been applied to male models. Because of the highly constructed nature of advertisements, which often draw on many other media texts and **intertextual connotations**, it is relatively easy to unpack their meaning and display how audiences are positioned, **addressed** and implicated by the pleasures they produce and call upon.

Barthes, R. (1957) *Mythologies*. Paladin.

Berger, J. (1972) *Ways of Seeing*. Penguin.

Cook, G. (1992) *The Discourse of Advertising*. Routledge.

Dyer, G. (1982) *Advertising as Communication*. Routledge.

Goddard, A. (1998) *The Language of Advertising*. Routledge.

Lévi-Strauss, C. (1969) *The Raw and the Cooked*. Harper and Row.

Packard, V. (1957) *The Hidden Persuaders*. Longman.

Young, B. (1990) *Television Advertising and Children*. Clarendon.

Advertising Standards Authority (ASA). A British organization which oversees professional and ethical standards in advertising. It was established in 1962 to oversee self-regulation in the industry. The ASA ensures that everyone who commissions, prepares and publishes advertisements in non-broadcast media within the UK observes the British codes of advertising.

The organization handles, according to its own figures, 12,000 complaints a year, which have to be tested against the all-encompassing criteria of 'legal, decent, honest and truthful'. Also advertisements must not cause serious or widespread offence. Particular care should be taken to avoid causing offence on the grounds of race, religion, sex or disability.

mail: 2 Torrington Place, London WC1E 7HW. See also their monthly reports, which provide full information on complaints and the official judication.
Research on advertising archives can be done at 45 Lyndale Avenue, London NW2 2QB, where you can for example access British and American press advertisements and magazine covers from 1890 to the present.
website: www.asa.org.uk

aesthetics. The study of 'beauty' and the creation of a 'visual style' in art. This remains highly relevant to media education, especially since film and other media aspire to the level of 'art'. Appreciation of beauty can of course end up as an elitist exercise for those who have so-called 'good taste' and can therefore appreciate 'good' art. Media studies, however, takes a much broader approach to aesthetics and looks for the beauty in every genre of media analysis focusing on audience pleasure rather than determining some objective and abstract criteria. However, when it comes to valuation and defining the relative value of different genres, then difficulties occur which cannot be easily resolved. For example **auteur theory** of film proposed a hierarchy of value and of 'great' filmmakers, which has been shunned ever since as an elitist and ultimately subjective exercise. Nonetheless aesthetic criteria for the study of media texts is becoming more prevalent of late within media criticism.

Sim, S. (ed.) (1995) *The A/Z Guide to Modern Literary and Cultural Studies*. Prentice Hall.

Affective Fallacy. The Affective Fallacy theory critiques the notion that texts only support the emotional effect produced in the audience. **Psychoanalytical** critics for example put great emphasis on emotions of all types in their readings in their critical analysis.

Grodal, T. (1997) *Moving Pictures: A New Theory of Film Genres, Feelings and Cognition*. Clarendon.

affective learning. The area of education that deals predominantly with emotions, feelings, beliefs, values and attitudes. It aims to foster the emotional growth and development of pupils and may involve aspects of education not normally linked to cognitive development, such as socialization skills, self-esteem, and acceptable behaviour. Media studies is uniquely tied into such learning since students often study the most popular programmes, like **soaps**, which are predicated on dramatizing a wide range of emotions and social/ethical values in particular.

Bloom. B (1956) *Taxonomy of Educational Objectives*. Longman.

age. One of the primary determinants in the study of **representations** and **audiences** and a major factor within many media production assignments. Students are often asked to complete assignments aimed at particular age-groups. On a practical level, with regard to **censorship** and film classification or the 9 o'clock watershed, age is used to categorize audiences. **Schedulers** of TV programmes and producers of all media texts have to be fully aware of the intended audience for their products so that they can avoid censure and a mismatch with poor audience returns.

Student assignments often concentrate on audience research and statistics on gender, race and class, as well as age breakdowns, when researching and producing products for a range of audience profiles. Matching media products with the age categories of its intended audience remains an important element in many practical assignments.

agencies. Any groups which affect the development of societies; the word can most certainly apply to all major media organizations. The notion of agency, which is more commonly used in social science, is used to analyse the effects of human performances and organizations on the outcome of events in which they are implicated. Film theorists, for example, might use the term to analyse a chief protagonist's role in film. Such agents often effect radical change and progress the narrative forward.

agenda-setting. Occurs when a media news organization for example decides priorities and the level of importance of any news item as well as determining what is news in the first place. Many media theorists suggest that mass media news programmes in particular set the standard and criterion for what is news at any given time by highlighting and foregrounding certain stories above other ones. Both the order and importance of news stories are decided in advance of broadcast and indicated by the time given to the story and its relative position in the broadcast. Professional media **gatekeepers** including media owners often apply various unwritten rules to determine the priorities of such programmes. Stories at the start of the news have been given greater importance than those later on, which is similar to the relative position of newspaper news which privileges the front page.

Also, so called '**spin-doctors**' are employed by political parties and other organizations to manipulate what appears in the news and provide a favourable image. They do this by feeding particular information to their sources within the media so that their partisan agenda is hopefully adopted. See also **news values**.

agents. Representative characters/protagonists who use their skills to try to effect some form of change with the help of their position in society. For example ideological critics like **Althusser** would suggest that teachers are agents of cultural reproduction who assist in the maintenance of the dominant ideology of **capitalism**. Sociologists use the concept of agency to denote major institutional influences on society. However, the concept is also becoming more popular within cultural and media studies in the reappraisal of the potency of human protagonists within representational contexts.

alienation. A term which implies being separated from a benevolent force or from within society generally. **Marxist** theory in particular has adapted the term to mean the removal of workers from the means of production, since they are only a small cog in the big capitalist wheel of production/consumption. Rather than finding 'true fulfilment', Marxist critics argue how the mass media encourage audiences to become like commodities unable to express their true individuality. **Advertising** in particular encourages audiences to define themselves by the products and services they consume. In crude terms, the general public is potentially repressed and simply defined by what they consume rather than finding their 'true selves' beyond the influences of the media.

There are philosophical and sociological permutations of the term also which feed into media education. In particular Jean-Paul Sartre's take on the term, as central to existentialism, was very popular in the 1960s, among radical counter-cultural students who felt left outside the power structures of bourgeois society. Sociologists also use related terms like **anomie** which signal the breakdown of order and feelings of marginalization, disorientation and anxiety which often occur in Western society.

Althusser, Louis. A highly influential ideological thinker for media who has refined **Marxist** ideas most succinctly by defining the power structures that make up Western society. The two interrelating power strata that maintain a modern capitalist society, he declared, are: the **repressive state apparatus**, which consists of police, army and the judiciary; together with **ideological**

state apparatus, consists of the family, religion and education as well as the media.

Describing the institutional apparatus of education as essentially 'ideological' became very influential, particularly in the run-up to the 1968 student revolt in Paris and elsewhere and has permeated academic discourse. Such a theory would contest the apparatus of an educational system which maintains the status quo by disseminating rules and codes of behaviour rather than radical critical and independent thinking. In particular, critical analysis of the media, especially in 1970s, was framed by this ideological agenda.

Althusserian analysis of education can be broken down into various areas of discussion, including:

- Structural organization of the school as a hierarchical system;
- Daily classroom relationships;
- Principles which serve to structure the curriculum;
- Attitudes of school staff to students in particular;
- The form and content of classroom material (hence the move towards 'politically correct' representations, thereby avoiding racist and sexist representations, for instance);
- Discourse and practice of even those who 'penetrate this logic'.

(Cited in *The Continuum Guide to Geography Education*. Continuum, 2000.)

That the mass media supports/promotes an ideological construct has remained a key premise of the study of media. Many now feel that Althusser's apparatus model remains overly pessimistic and reductive, allowing little scope for change or transformation in society. An ideological state apparatus like the media can only serve to reproduce the dominant ideology. Consequently, there can be little hope of change since the media will always serve to reproduce the dominant ideology.

Price, S. (1997) *The Complete A–Z Media and Communication Handbook*. Hodder and Stoughton.

American Culture Association (ACA). Promotes the study of American culture in the broadest sense of the term, from elite to popular and folk culture. They produce a journal four times a year called the *Journal of American Culture*, published by Bowling Green University, USA.

American mass media. Key dates

1455	Gutenberg invents printing press
1844	Morse invents telegraph
1876	Bell invents telephone
1877	Edison demonstrates the phonograph
1894	America's first movie (Kinetoscope house opens)
1895	Lumière introduces single-screen motion picture
1922	First commercial announcement broadcast on radio
1926	NBC begins broadcasting
1938	Orson Welles's *War of the Worlds* broadcast (see **radio**)
1939	First public broadcast on TV

1947   Hollywood calls the famous 10 before HUAC (see **Cold War**)
1948   Cable TV invented
1958   Murrow challenges McCarthy on TV
1960   Kennedy and Nixon meet in Great Debate (see **radio**)
1960   80% of American homes have a television
1963   President John F. Kennedy is assassinated.
1973   Watergate hearings broadcast live
1991   Gulf War – CNN emerges as major news provider

Baran, S. and Davis, D. (1995) *Mass Communication Theory: Foundations, Ferment and Future.* Wadsworth Press.

anchorage. Particularly, the way written captions are placed alongside a photograph in a newspaper story to tie down its meaning. **Barthes** in particular affirms that such anchorage makes an image less open to differing interpretations. Often captions help to skew meaning in a certain way which is highly **ideological** as Barthes and others have explained. For example after recent scandals, a happy-looking President Clinton is very much subverted if some sexual reference is made in the caption alongside his image.

animation. Involves the use of either stop-motion photography and/or computer-generated imagery to produce movement in **cartoons** etc. According to Stuart Price, the first animated short was Winsor McCay's *Gertie the Dinosaur,* made in 1914. Walt **Disney** is probably the most successful studio to produce animated entertainment.

Price, S. (1997) *The Complete A–Z Media and Communication Handbook.* Hodder and Stoughton. See also Paul Wells's essay, in Nelmes, J. (ed.) (1996) *An Introduction to Film Studies.* Routledge.

anomie. A state of mind caused by the breakdown of social norms. It was first used in a social science context by Emile Durkheim. While less frequently used within a media context, nonetheless it is becoming more popular as a term to explore a new form of **alienation** within **postmodern** human agency.

anthropology. Traditionally has involved the study of so-called 'primitive' peoples to learn about their culture and general social practices. Famous practitioners include: **Lévi-Strauss**, Malinowski (how 'primitive' myths strengthen traditions and cultural norms) and van Gennep (rites of passage and stages of growth from childhood to old age, specifically adolescence). Often such **ethnographic** research has been interpreted to reflect all human cultures and has been applied especially within **myth** study, which is used in film analysis, and within media studies generally.

anthropomorphism. A style of representation where non-humans are endowed with the attributes of humans through **animation**, for example. In particular the term is most frequently used when studying **Disney** and other types of animation films where animals speak and act like humans.

aperture. The size of opening of a lens which lets in light onto the film stock. For a fuller explanation see **F-stop**.

AS Level (Advanced Subsidiary Level). Examinations designed to be completed in just one year, as they contain only half the content of a traditional A Level. Like A Levels, the AS Levels are available in linear or modular form and are accepted as an entry qualification by most higher education institutions. Any AS Level qualification represents the first half of a full A Level. This level is aimed to provide greater breadth of choice for post-16 study and a worthwhile qualification for those choosing not to complete a full A Level.

New developments introduced for the academic year 2000 in the UK include the radical extension of the breadth of study for post-GCSE education. The normal curricular choice of three often related A Level subjects to specialize in has been widened to encourage the breadth of study which is the norm within a large percentage of other Western educational systems. In future, therefore, many students will now choose four or five subjects and complete an AS Level in these. Then in the second year of A Levels, students will complete their three chosen A2 Level subjects. It is probable that this will lead to a greater increase in students choosing at least an AS Level media course.

An example of one of the newly amalgamated **awarding bodies** which offers A Level media is Oxford, Cambridge and RSA (OCR). Its syllabus continues to cite the key conceptual areas of media studies as:

- Media forms and conventions;
- Media institutions (participants and their roles in the process, institutions they represent);
- Media audiences (individuals/social groups involved in consumption of media texts);
- Media representations (relations between people, places, events, ideas, values and beliefs and their representation in media, and issues and debates arriving out of this relationship).

The OCR syllabus focuses on three media areas:

- audiovisual – film, TV, radio, video, photography and music;
- print based – newspapers, magazines, comics;
- ICT based – digital technologies – software and hardware, including internet, CD-Roms, DVD and interactive/multimedia. (This emphasis on new technology, including mobile phones, computer games and use of new media technology generally, is a new focus at this level of media education.)

assessment. The measurement of the extent of an individual's learning, or an evaluation of their performance or a particular aspect of their attainment. An assessment must take into account the validity, reliability and fitness for purpose of the assessment methods used.

Good assessment should seek to improve the learning of pupils, and of course its aims and methods should be clear to those undergoing the assessment process. As a consequence, the relative newness of media studies as a discipline has encouraged a wide range of traditional and relatively 'new' assessment tools; from conventional exams and essays to more interactive forms of presentations, reports and productions and even interactive computer assessments.

What in particular is media education assessment for? There are a number of equally valid answers to this question; however, the following may provide a helpful overview:

* to enhance pupils' learning;

* to measure, even raise standards;

* to check teaching objectives against learning outcomes;

* to place pupils against different descriptors of achievement;

* to discover what pupils know, understand and can do;

* to help plan future learning objectives;

* to help pupils to devise personal targets;

* to motivate both pupils and teachers.

(Cited in *The Continuum Guide to Geography Education.* Continuum, 2000.)

There have been strong debates in early media curricula over the efficacy of rigid assessment systems and specifically their role in encouraging 'true learning'. Whereas **Masterman** *et al.* sought to break down assessment barriers, others felt this served to de-legitimize the subject's credibility and seriousness.

Assessment should of course always be a major factor considered at the start of a process of designing a curriculum. Problems invariably occur when assessment is considered as an afterthought: it should therefore be integral to curriculum construction and delivery.

But how to avoid the domination of the curriculum by what is often referred to as the assessment 'tail' wagging the curriculum 'dog' remains a problem. This is a difficulty regularly experienced in General Certificate of Secondary Education (GCSE) and Advanced Level (A Level) courses, where the 'high stakes' assessment at the end of the course can dominate the pace and practice of teaching and learning throughout the year.

Black, P. and Wiliam, D. (1998) *Inside the Black Box: Raising Standards through Classroom Assessment.* King's College, London.

assessment criteria. Statements that describe educational objectives accurately enough for valid and reliable assessment to take place against them.

For example, the aims and objectives of a level-3 degree-level module on German cinema devised by Julia Knight as part of the media degree at the University of Luton include:

[A rationale which states that this module aims to explore the role that audiovisual culture plays in creating national and cultural identities, using

West German cinema from the 1960s through to the late 1980s as a case study.]

- To provide an opportunity for students to analyse what factors, including national myths, contribute to creating a sense of national identity.

- To introduce students to theories of national identity, to relate these to theories of myth and examine how audiovisual culture can be viewed as one site where national identity is articulated.

- To enable students to analyse cinema films in particular as a manifestation of national and cultural identity.

- To facilitate an understanding of social, cultural, political and economic factors that helped shape and develop West Germany's national cinema during the 1960s through to the late 1980s.

- To explore the notion of German identity/ies as it is/were articulated in West German films during the above-mentioned period.

See Julia Knight's chapter on German cinema, in Nelmes, J. (ed.) (1999) *An Introduction to Film Studies*. Routledge.

assessment opportunities. Occasions when evidence of what pupils know, understand and can do can be gathered, either informally or formally, to be used by teachers for assessment purposes. In media studies especially with the growth of modular courses, the opportunities for gathering such evidence and knowledge are available through a range of predetermined skills that are assessed.

attainment. An individual's grasp of different skills, information and understanding within a certain, specified area of learning. Attempts at defining attainment targets in media are at an early stage of development. Also because of the range of courses and breadth of the subject discipline – including practical as well as theoretical – attainment has been a difficult issue to negotiate. The GNVQ experiment in particular sought to harmonize and develop more prescriptive standards of levels of attainment. But this process is far from concluded.

Attainment targets (AT) were introduced by the Education Reform Act (1988) within specific subject areas and include the knowledge, skills and understanding which pupils of different abilities and maturities are expected to have by the end of each key stage of the National Curriculum. Each attainment target was originally divided into ten levels, which were reduced to eight following the Dearing Report (1994), with one level for exceptional performance, as defined by the level descriptions.

attitude. A disposition to behave in a certain way towards a particular person, object or event. Attitudes are often linked to emotional, social and cognitive development and their promotion and is an important aspect of study for media education. For example **textual analysis** often involves detecting attitudes of main protagonists with a range of texts, and **audience** analysis often involves detecting changes in attitude, values and beliefs.

audience (general). Technically, the aggregate pooling together of a range of readers/listeners who receive the media product transmitted. Audiences are further broken down into categories, most usually: gender, race, age, social and economic groups, which are the primary categories of study in media education. Matching media products with types of audiences who consume them is essential for understanding media in general. Audience figures in particular are very important for media organizations who seek to quantify audiences for certain programmes. Such figures are used to determine the **advertising** revenue gained and serve to legitimize the cost of producing media products. Especially within commercial media organizations, audience figures directly determine the profitability and future media production direction of that organization.

Nightingale, V. (1996) *Studying Audiences: The Shock of the Real.* Routledge.

Morley, D. (1992) *Television, Audiences and Cultural Studies.* Routledge.

audience ratings. Audience research and ratings analysis have become indispensable for the functioning of many strands of mass media, especially since good ratings results are the agreed criteria for effective communication between commercial media and the audience. Consequently broadcasters are often concerned less with individual 'viewers', according to Ien Ang (1991), than with aggregated audiences to justify their programme decisions. Unfortunately for television schedulers who seek to control and maintain loyal audiences, new technology like the video cassette recorder (VCR) can disrupt conventional methods of determining and controlling audiences for TV through **scheduling**. Viewers can time-shift programmes on their VCR recorders to be viewed at their convenience and therefore need not be influenced by scheduling structures and timetables which attempt to keep audiences faithful to a given channel. Even more significantly from an advertiser's perspective, audiences can fast-forward through advertising slots or avoid them altogether, which raises serious questions regarding the mass media's ability to deliver audiences to the advertisers.

Even non-commercial media are strongly affected by ratings, since strong ratings provide legitimacy and justifications for affirming the value of the media provider which might be getting funded from government or other non-commercial sources.

Abercrombie, N. and Longhurst, B. (1998) *Audiences.* Sage.

Ang, I. (1991) *Desperately Seeking the Audience.* Routledge.

Dickinson, R. et al. (1998) *Approaches to Audiences: A Reader.* Arnold.

Kent, R. (ed.) (1994) *Measuring Media Audiences.* Routledge.

Lewis, J. (1991) *The Ideological Octopus: An Exploration of Television and Its Audience.* Routledge.

audience research. Audience research has become very important throughout media studies in general and is focused on what has come to be regarded as

effects theory. This is probably the most recognizable debate within media studies and has garnished extensive research funding since the 1950s. At one extreme there is what is called the **hypodermic needle model**, which is often linked to high/low cultural debates and perceives the potency of the mass media as analogous to a needle-injected drug. Most notably back in the 1940s, Sigfried Kracauer argued that Hitler's rise to power was partly due to his successful use of the media. Kracauer became preoccupied with the effects of various cultural industries, particularly the mass media, on society which helped initiate a critical approach to the mass media in general.

Such a model of media effects has been used extensively by agencies who set out to 'prove' the harmful effects of the filmic representations of sex and violence – especially with regard to young innocent minds. Various reports, most notably by the **Payne Fund** in America, set out to prove this thesis in an attempt to validate ideological fears of the effects of such technology on the general public.

However, as techniques became more sophisticated and analysis more rigorous and less partisan, new research began to suggest that perhaps such a direct correspondence between products and effects was less probable than first thought. It was more likely that audiences were influenced by the wider reality of society as well as the mass media. It became less common for social analysts to seek crude direct causal links between social phenomena and media texts. Increasingly such interrelationships were considered to involve complex interconnections. Nonetheless these often crude 'common-sense' links helped to scapegoat the media and promote **moral panics** of various kinds. Often such panics were perpetuated by rival media industries themselves.

How to analyse audience pleasures, especially if little primary research is carried out, remains a major difficulty with audience analysis. Especially problematic is the question of how historical audiences read and interpret media within their time and place. Without extensive research of these audiences such questions cannot be convincingly answered. But as Adorno and many other critics affirm, theoretical reflections upon society as a whole cannot be completely realized by empirical findings alone. American media research is constantly criticized for its blind faith in so-called scientific empirical research, whereas much British media analysis often questions empirical assumptions implicit in statistical analysis. So-called 'objective research testing' is most certainly far from objective.

Australian media. See **media literacy/education (Australia)** and note that for media education, Australia is probably the most developed of all English-speaking media nations.

Frow, J. and Morris, M. (1993) *Australian Cultural Studies: A Reader.* University of Illinois Press.

auteur theory. Began with French critics in the 1950s (many of whom later became filmmakers and part of the French New Wave) who critically elevated the 'best of' Hollywood product to the realms of 'art'. It remains essentially a romantic theory which sought to find the individual signature of the creator (notably the film director) from within the mass production of filmic output. Directors like Ford, Hitchcock and Welles were eulogized both for their thematic exploration and more especially for their unique signature and style in constructing their films. The French critics particularly admired the existentialist themes and content embedded in the Western genre which glorified human nature in opposition to the bourgeois restrictions of social convention. This conformed with their wish to dismantle the restrictions of the old order that continued to dominate the post-war period.

In 1962 the American film critic Andrew Sarris transformed this auteurist idea into a critical tool by naming a number of auteurs as opposed to mere 'craftsmen' who were well capable of applying the ingredients of filmmaking but did not finally have the original spark of genius. However, the nagging difficulty of determining value and deciding who was on the A list, or not, has continued up to the present day. (The best film of a so-called craftsman could never be favourably compared with even the most pedestrian film of an auteur.) In spite of Peter **Wollen**'s seminal structuralist application of the theory, which initially saved the theory from becoming overtly iconoclastic, individualistic, elitist and subjective, it has nevertheless fallen out of academic favour.

In particular, auteur theory has to contend with questions raised in response to the **Intentionalist Fallacy**, which critiques the assumption that a close analysis of the biographical details and social background of the 'author' will finally unlock the secret voice of the text. But, it is argued, biographical details are often irrelevant to the meaning of the films produced. Yet the artist behind the art remains a centre of attention and continues to be a media preoccupation for critics and public alike. Even with so-called **postmodernist** film directors like David Lynch; audience pleasure is nonetheless closely tied into auteurial notions of engagement and pleasure.

With the growing dominance of ideological and audience analysis, and the communal nature of film production, media critics have tended to agree that there is no all-embracing theory to understand or decode a text outside of the socio-temporal considerations of the period from which the text is produced. **Barthes** proposes the symbolic and radical notion of the 'death of the author', which is designed to allow the birth of the 'active' audience/ viewer. In spite of all these criticisms, auteur theory has remained important, within film consumption, funnelling viewers' pleasures as they seek out directors/stars to identify with and provide pleasurable continuity and satisfaction within the cacophony of media output.

Caughie, J. (1981) *Theories of Authorship*. BFI.
Cook, P. (ed.) (1999) *The Cinema Book*. BFI.

avant-garde. A term applied to the experimental use of media forms which tend to break down conventional codes and conventions of established genres. They are often not driven by commercial success and the profit motive. In film, for example, avant-garde filmmakers include those who often subvert conventional Hollywood forms of filmmaking and consider themselves artists who happened to use the medium of film. However, cultural historians suggest that from the 1960s onwards there was much more cross-fertilization between the apparently radical alternative forms of the avant-garde and the mainstream Hollywood product. (See Peter **Wollen**'s **structuralist** model, which exaggerates the positive aspects of the avant-garde style of filmmaking perpetuated by the French master Jean Luc Godard in particular, compared with Hollywood cinema.)

awarding bodies (UK). External examinations such as the General Certificate of Secondary Education (GCSE), Advanced and Advanced Subsidiary Level (A and AS Level) and General National Vocational Qualification (GNVQ) are currently administered by awarding bodies (previously called examination boards and groups). The creation of national criteria for GCSE in each subject, monitored by the Joint Council, meant not only greater central control over examination boards but also a clearer standardization of examination practice.

Fewer, but more powerful awarding bodies now exist in the UK and have changed their titles to reflect their amalgamation with vocational bodies. They are currently reducing the numbers of syllabi they offer in an attempt to clarify **standards** and reduce duplication of awards.

- AQA (Assessment and Qualification Alliance; made up from AEB, SEG and NEAB): www.aqa.org.uk
- EDEXEL (made up of ULEAC and BTEC) is the leading provider of A Level courses and has over 40,000 candidates achieving BTEC certificates every year as well as providing a majority of the GNVQs in the UK: www.edexcel.org.uk
- OCR (Oxford, Cambridge and RSA; made up from UCLES and RSA): www.ocr.org.uk
- WJEC/CBAC (Welsh Joint Education Committee)
- City & Guilds

B

back to basics. Describes attempts to return education to a more basic diet of subjects, with a strong emphasis on reading, writing and arithmetic (the so-called 'three Rs'). This debate at first sight appears to be irrelevant to media education, which is not part of the core curriculum. Some educationalists and media studies critics seek to use this to dismiss the subject as wallowing in 'cheap pleasures' and 'knowledge' of the mass media rather than promoting a serious and rigorous academic subject. But such critics often fail to appreciate that what pleases also teaches most effectively. Media education can be used to improve and complement general literacy by using recognizable and pleasurable media stimuli which students actively consume in their personal leisure time. Finding such a pleasurable focus for study is in many ways half the battle within education, which often has major difficulties in motivating students to learn.

In recent years, however, politically motivated campaigns have continued to attack so-called progressive teaching methods and curriculum design, claiming that they are responsible for declining educational standards. Those who believe in taking the school curriculum back to a more basic form usually support the return to an educational system which prioritizes the teaching of conventional literacy, numeracy and possibly ICT/technology. Media educators similar to other marginalized disciplines argue that a 'back to basics' approach to the curriculum creates dangers of squeezing out broader subjects like media studies which are denied a firm foothold on the curriculum. There is a danger of students' overall diet becoming severely impoverished. However, this criticism may be superseded by a recent UK initiative to widen the number of AS subjects students should do, to at least four or five.

BARB (Broadcasters' Audience Research Board). Used for audience measurement, which is very important in the competitive market of TV, it is owned jointly by BBC and ITV. Weekly audience figures provide an invaluable resource for students of the media who need such statistics to evaluate and develop research projects.

For example, in the week ending 14/5/2000 the following programmes achieved a range of audiences quoted in millions in the UK.

Programme	Channel	Audience
EastEnders	BBC1	13m
Coronation Street	ITV	14m
Brookside	C4	3.8m
Six O'Clock News	BBC1	5.5m
Gardeners' World	BBC2	4.3m
Friends	C4	2.7m
X Certificate	C5	1.9m

See www.barb.co.uk/weekly

As well as providing the top 30 on all channels, BARB also cites the day and time of each programme. This information is invaluable for all forms of research within media education.

bardic TV. The term suggests that the act of watching TV is similar to a primitive Celtic custom, before TV was invented. Back then communities would sit around a camp fire and listen to a storyteller called a bard, narrating exciting stories of interest and relevance to their audience. John Fiske and John Hartley have used this to suggest that the act of communal TV-watching as a family and in conjunction with a community of other families has a very close affinity with such an ancient system of storytelling. They suggested that the TV has replaced the bard as a site of communal storytelling for the modern mass media society. Critics, however, speak of the growth of fragmented audiences for television which is aided by a 'narrow casting' approach promoted by the proliferation of new channels.

Fiske, J. and Hartley, J. (1978) *Reading Television*. Routledge.

Barker, Martin. A prolific writer on **audiences** and the effects of media on children in particular. He is a scathing critic of so-called **moral panic** said to be created by **video nasties**, which can be traced back to the 'penny dreadfuls' in previous centuries, where it was always the poor/working classes which were considered to be at risk of corruption by such media artefacts. At present new technology such as video games and the **internet** are receiving similar treatment.

In a recent book *From Ants to Titanic: Reinventing Film Analysis,* Barker lays down the gauntlet against elitist preoccupations – particularly **psychoanalysis/ideological** and **structuralist** criticism – which has been carried out at the expense of more robust and empirically validated audience investigations. His reappraisal of the centrality of audience effects, while appreciating the emotional as well as the cognitive aspects of film, is both warranted and provocative.

Barker, M. (1989) *Comics: Ideology, Power and the Critic*. Manchester University Press.

Barker, M. *et al.* (1993) *Reading into Cultural Studies*. Routledge.

Barker, M. and Austin, T. (2000) *From Ants to Titanic: Reinventing Film Analysis*. Pluto Press.

Barker, M. and Brooks, K. (1998) *Knowing Audiences: Judge Dredd, its Friends, Fans and Foes*. University of Luton Press.

Barker, M. and Petley, J. (ed.) (1997) *Ill Effects: The Media Violence Debate*. Routledge.

Barthes, Roland. Has been a profound influence on media education, particularly with regard to **semiotics**, **myth**, **ideology** and **discourse** theory. John **Fiske** provides a basic overview of his ideas, particularly concerning semiotics. Barthes speaks of the first order of signification as being that of **denotation**, which is described as 'the common sense, obvious meaning of the sign'. While the second order of signification is called **connotation** – comprising associations produced by the denotative order reflected in the understanding of the person who interacts with the sign. Barthes uses the example of a red rose, which may connote romance, and the presentation of red roses by one person to another, which may act as a specific attempt at signifying romantic affection. However, such connotations can change over time and within different cultures.

Barthes was particularly interested in culturally deconstructing his native France. For example, he analysed the significance and **codes** of meaning of a black soldier saluting the French flag on the cover of a magazine. He has been highly influential in promoting **textual analysis** and the 'reading' of all mediated stimuli, over authorial intentions, with his famous essay 'The Death of the Author' (1968).

Barthes, R. (1972) *Mythologies*. Jonathan Cape.

Barthes, R. (1975) *S/Z*. Jonathan Cape.

Barthes, R. (1976) *The Pleasure of the Text*. Jonathan Cape.

Barthes, R. (1977) *Image-Music-Text*. Collins.

base. The term used by Marx to describe the fundamental economic determinant of society and culture. This term is often coupled with what is called the 'superstructure', the major institutional structures which control systems, particularly Western industrial society. For more details see **ideology** and **Marxism** entries.

baseline assessment. Data gathered on students before a period of study, for example before the start of their primary education. From September 1998 all children in English, Welsh and Northern Irish schools were assessed in language and literacy, maths and personal and social development before they entered compulsory schooling. The aim was for teachers to be able to match their educational programmes to the particular needs of the children they were to teach, to demonstrate evidence of progress.

BBC. The British Broadcasting Corporation, which was originally a private company set up in 1923 and became one of the most famous TV and **radio** organizations in the world. Its first most influential Director General was Lord Reith, who helped construct the **public service broadcasting (PSB)** ethos of the organization which has remained so central in the development of UK television and radio ever since. Over the years, the organization has continued to change and face new challenges. Various committees in particular helped to determine the future of the organization.

The *Sykes* committee in 1923 declared that the BBC should not be a commercial monopoly and later produced a charter for the organization.

The *Beveridge* committee in the post-war period wanted the organization to remain outside of direct government control. However, possibly the most significant influence on the BBC occurred in 1954 with the Television Act and the creation of the Independent Television Authority. The first competitor to the BBC was very successful, especially through importing 'cheap' American programming. But later the *Pilkington* committee in 1962 was critical of the quality of broadcasting overall and awarded the BBC another channel to develop more 'high quality' programming.

Other important committees included the *Peacock* in 1986, which continued to look into the role of public service broadcasting and the growing issue of finance. The BBC was finding it increasingly difficult to survive on the government-controlled licence fee which is paid by all households who have televisions. Trying to increase the licence fee above inflation figures has always been highly contentious and part of a party political debate. Pressure groups argued over the legitimacy of all households having to pay a compulsory licence fee, particularly as audiences were more and more opting for other commercial channels which were paid for through advertising.

In November 1992 the Conservative government, which was in favour of greater **deregulation** and thereby promoting market forces which encouraged subscription channels and 'pay TV', published a discussion document which called for the BBC to become much more efficient and cost-effective while remaining a public service broadcaster. New Labour has continued to support the public service ethos of the BBC but continues to insist on efficiency cuts and has recently refused to allow the organization to create a separate licence fund for the growth of **digital** services. Whether the BBC can continue to exist in its present form, with the growth of new media technology and the extension of even more competition, without compromising its PSB ethos, is difficult to predict. Nonetheless, the fact that the BBC throughout the world is synonymous with quality and integrity should stand it in good stead for the difficult years ahead.

behavioural studies. Looks at the behaviour of humans in various circumstances. Media education draws extensively from social science and the study of human behaviour within social contexts. In particular analysing behaviour patterns has become central to the study of the **effects** of media on audiences especially with regard to 'impressionable' children.

One of the most influential behaviourists is the psychologist B. F. Skinner. He carried out experiments by conditioning learning behaviour through reinforcement as a technique (like the Pavlov's Dog experiment) using basic animal experiments. These have since been applied within human education strategies. The subjects' 'needs' and 'desires' must be fully appreciated and acted upon if learning is to take place. Perception, and therefore behaviour, is often intuitive and ordered according to the environment inhabited.

Curzon, L. B. (1989) *Teaching in Further Education: An Outline of Principles and Practices*. Holt Education.

benchmarking. This is beginning to be applied, particularly in higher education to affirm students' levels of attainment at various stages in their degree progression. Such standardization is designed to ensure that there is greater equity within the basic curriculum provision between degrees across the UK sector. However, it is understood that the media provision at degree level will be difficult to fully harmonize due to the wide range of practical/ theoretical courses from journalism to video and multimedia to name a few. It is expected, however, that such benchmarking criteria will be put in place in the near future.

BFI (British Film Institute). A government supported organization dedicated to production, distribution, and the education of the general public and related educational organizations with regard to audiovisual media. It is made up of various interconnecting departments including the National Film Theatre, which is dedicated to exhibiting films as well as supporting a UK network of Art Cinema centres as well as an extensive library and resource centre, which is invaluable for research into film and television history in particular.

Sight and Sound monthly magazine on new films and film education generally is an invaluable source for film studies and of course the BFI publish a large catalogue of books on media education and film generally.

See the BFI report of the Film Education Working Group *Making Movies Matter* (1999), which affirms the educational challenge of the future as being 'that critical and creative moving image skills will be a key element of literacy in the 21st. century' (p. 2). The report goes on to call on the UK moving image industries to invest in education as a long-term strategy. See also Colin **MacCabe**, who has been a controversial influence on recent developments in the organization.

website: www.bfi.org.uk

bias. Usually considered as a predisposition towards one particular viewpoint. It is seen as negative with regard to the media not reporting the full truth of a situation or person. The acknowledgement and study of bias in media representations has became a founding tenet of the subject, which sought to expose manipulation and distortion throughout the media. The concept is usually applied to news reporting, which suggests that there is a 'one-sided' use of material that ends up misrepresenting the truth of the story. This in turn infers that there is in fact an objective and 'balanced view' which is consciously not used for devious reasons. News organizations, particularly **public service broadcasters**, strongly refute any bias allegations made against them.

Nevertheless the **Glasgow Media Group** sought to expose media bias in the representation of a range of disadvantaged groups in (PSB) news and current affairs. For example, they argued through empirical research and content analysis that TV reports of the miners' strike favoured the management position and the status quo rather than the workers' point of view. This process of analysing bias in the media has remained a staple aspect of media studies. See also **ideology** and **racism**.

bibliography. A list of books referred to in a scholarly work, or by a specific author, or on a specific subject. Several bibliographies of media education in the UK and elsewhere currently exist which are cited under **dictionaries** and elsewhere in this Guide. The **British Film Institute (BFI)** has produced for example an extensive list of books about film, compiled by Cherry-Ann Chandler and Jackie Madden in 1995 and which is categorized into the following sections:

adaptations

bibliographies

biographies

careers

documentary

encyclopaedias

film and society

film appreciation

film history

film music

filmographies

film theory

genre

glossaries

production

scriptwriting

website: www.bfi.org.uk

Bloom, Benjamin. The creator of a taxonomy of educational objectives, classified into a hierarchy, where the later categories subsume the ones that have gone before. Such taxonomies can be applied to see whether the teaching and learning process, and more particularly its assessment, will help to develop simple or more complex forms of learning. In 1956 he edited and published arguably his most famous work, a *Taxonomy of Educational Objectives*.

Bordwell, David. A central critical influence on film studies, particularly with regard to **narrative** and **cognitive** analysis. Together with colleague Krisin Thompson, he popularized the formalist investigation of classic Hollywood narratives applying the theories of Todorov and **Propp**. Their studies have remained the dominant orthodoxy for film study ever since. However, critics find their rigorous models somewhat overly pedantic. Recently Martin **Barker** who fully endorses their formalist methods of **textual analysis**, nevertheless criticizes their lack of appreciation of emotion and actual audience interpretation.

Barker, M. et al. (2000) *From Ants to Titanic: Reinventing Film Analysis*. Pluto Press.

Bordwell, D. (1985) *Narration in Fiction Film*. Methuen.

Bordwell, D. (1989) *Making Meaning: Rhetoric and Inference in the Interpretation of Cinema.* Harvard University Press.

Bordwell, D. and Thompson, K. (1993) *Film Art: An Introduction*. McGraw Hill.

Bordwell, D. and Thompson, K. (1994) *Film History: An Introduction*. McGraw Hill.

Bordwell, D. (1996) *The Cinema of Eisenstein*. Harvard University Press.

Bordwell, D. (1997) *On the History of Film Style*. Harvard University Press.

brainstorming. An activity which media teachers and others use to allow creative ideas and solutions to flow without being impeded by immediate criticism or comment. This process is used extensively in group media projects to get ideas flowing and eventually help decide how to carry out a given assignment. The strategy encourages the process of problem-solving and answering questions by promoting the generation of spontaneous ideas. Once a group or class has made a range of points, these are then collated and evaluated through discussion in a more structured way. Brainstorming is often used to solicit opinions and initiate group discussion on a media theme or concept, so that a range of ideas and attitudes can be applied to aid learning and develop problem-solving strategies.

Brecht, Bertolt. An influential playwright and writer who constructed an **avant-garde** method of performing using techniques of estrangement and non-identification which were also applied to film. He has been used by ideological critics to demonstrate ways in which media products can become radical and motivate audiences for change. See for example the famous *Screen* debate in the 1970s where Colin **MacCabe** used Brecht's theories to affirm the non-radical form of naturalist TV and Hollywood cinema (see Price 1993, pp. 320–4). Peter **Wollen** has also used his ideas to compare Hollywood and avant-garde film.

Price, S. (1993) *Media Studies*. Pitman Publishing.

British Educational Communications and Technology agency (BECTa). Formerly known as the National Council for Educational Technology (NCET) and sponsored jointly by the UK government and other organizations to improve the use of information and communications technology (ICT) within education. Its aim is to ensure that the government's drive to raise educational standards is supported by the use of technology. BECTa works closely with the Department for Education and Employment (DfEE) and local education authorities (LEAs) to enhance developments within schools and further education.

mail: BECTa, Milburn Hill Road, Science Park, Coventry, CV4 7JJ
tel: 024 7641 6994
email: becta@becta.org.uk
website: www.becta.org.uk

broadsheet. Usually a large-size newspaper which is said to be of high 'quality' such as the *Guardian* or *The Times* as opposed to the so-called 'bottom end' of the market **tabloid** newspapers like the *Sun*. Broadsheets tend to attract smaller but more affluent, business and academic audiences who want more detailed news reporting. Because of greater detail and breadth of coverage, critics often assume that they are less prone to bias and ideological manipulation than so-called inferior but more popular tabloids.

Buckingham, David. A key theorist on the evolution of media studies/ education in the UK. See **progressive education**. He has been highly influential in developing educational methodologies and strategies for exploring children's audiences in particular.

Buckingham has effectively laid out a rationale and overview justification for studying the media:

1 Media refracts rather than simply reflects or replicates the world.

2 The media contains a multiplicity of different forms shaped by different technologies, languages and capacities.

3 Selection, compression and elaboration occur at every point in the complex processes of editing and presenting messages.

4 Messages are determined by a wide range of different factors – economic, political, social, cultural, linguistic and technological – and not simply by producers' or editors' individual decisions, or by governments, advertisers or media moguls.

5 Audiences are not passive and predictable but active and variable in their responses to media.

(Buckingham 1991, p. 9)

Buckingham, D. (1987) *Public Secrets: EastEnders and its Audience*. BFI.

Buckingham, D. (1990) *Watching Media Learning* Falmer Press.

Buckingham, D. (1991) Cited in W. Lusted, *Media Studies Handbook*. Routledge.

Buckingham, D. (1993) *Children Talking TV: The Making of Television Literacy*. Falmer.

Buckingham, D. (1993) *Reading Audiences: Young People and the Media*. Manchester University Press.

Buckingham, D. (2000) *The Making of Citizens: Young People, News and Politics*. Routledge

Buckingham, D. (2000) *After the Death of Childhood: Growing Up in the Age of Electronic Media*. Polity Press.

C

Calcutt Committee. Set up in 1990 to study press intrusion into the personal lives of individuals. A **press complaints** commission followed as a result and in 1993 a further report was produced which called for a statutory code for journalists and a press complaints tribunal. The issue of invasion of privacy has become a major issues, particularly with regard to royalty, politicians and celebrities in Britain and elsewhere, who often feel that their rights to privacy are being eroded. Journalists argue that if they are to carry out their role of informing the general public and remaining a public **watchdog** and protecting the general public's interests in all areas of public life, then what is needed is a '**free press**' without imposed restrictions. This debate is ongoing.

Campaign for Press and Broadcasting Freedom (CPBF). A pressure group which is devoted to making the press more accountable and democratic. It has held a number of important conferences and seminars on various issues, especially racism, the reporting of war in the press and growing pressures on journalists to maintain their independent voice in the face of increasing commercial pressures. For example, in 1996 they held a very successful conference, *Media and Democracy: The Real Share Issue*, which looked at how new technology and other commercial pressures were adversely affecting the democratic function of **public service broadcasting** and the role of the press in general. Union leaders and academics like James Curran and Bob Franklin spoke passionately in support of such press freedoms.

In an early campaign against **Murdoch**'s growing non-unionized print empire in Wapping – which became a hate symbol for many of the Left in Thatcher's Britain – the union-backed CPBF published a media manifesto which demanded:

- The right to know
- The right to fair representation
- Access and accountability
- Workers' participation

- The right to make contact
- Freedom of the airwaves
- Facilities for all
- The right of reply

mail: 8 Cynthia Street, London, N1 9JF

Free Press: Journal for the Campaign for Press and Broadcasting Freedom, ed. G. Williams.

Canadian media. See **media literacy/education (Canada)**

canon. The most highly recommended texts in any given discipline. Historically, media education in the UK has been opposed to the **Leavisite** notion of a hierarchical canon of literature, for example, which equates with the 'best of' British literature, because it promoted an elitist form of education. Nevertheless, particularly with the upsurge of a 'back to basics' approach to education, even media studies has become consolidated, and many curricula strongly suggest a canon of texts which must be studied.

capitalism. An economic system based on the creation of private ownership and economic growth through the manipulation of risk capital and labour to produce more wealth. Individuals/corporations invest capital in the production, distribution and selling of goods in order to maximize their income. The allocation of resources and wealth is dependent on market forces. Capitalism has become a central model of political, economic and cultural production, which many media critics and **Marxist** theorists fight against. Almost all Western media industries are driven and controlled by powerful individuals who are driven by the 'bottom-line', profit motive.

See **advertising**, which is the most directly related **ideological** media area of study as compared with the ideals of **public service broadcasting (PSB)**.

Harvey, D. (1982) *The Limits to Capital*. Blackwell.

Saunders, P. (1995) *Capitalism: A Social Audit*. Open University Press.

career. Paid work and employment as part of a progressive pattern rather than a series of unrelated jobs. A career refers to one's advancement through a chosen field of employment. Media teachers particularly have become much sought after in the UK and elsewhere. Students looking for a career in a media organization need to become both flexible and adaptable, and this the breadth of many media syllabi helps to foster.

Skillset, the official government body, is a good place to find information on careers and training within many of the audiovisual media industries in the UK.

cartoon. A drawing in a newspaper or magazine, which can be humorous in nature. The **comics** print industry is very popular, with children from a young age buying weekly comics such as the *Beano, Dandy, Jackie*, etc. But with the phenomenal growth of video games and pocket computer gaming machines, the humble comic and cartoon has become somewhat less successful with new generations of consumers and students.

Feminists in particular often use comics to explore gender issues, and cultural critics like Martin **Barker** have exposed **moral panic** debates using comics as his focus. See also **animation** and **Disney**. Some claim that alternative comics like *Crumb* have even helped to critique the dominant representations of mainstream comics.

McRobbie, A. (1994) *Postmodernism and Popular Culture*. Routledge.

catharsis. Taken from the Greek, meaning 'purging', the term was used by the philosopher Aristotle to represent the effect received by audiences of tragedy in drama of all types. He perceived that the function of great drama was the release of pent-up emotions in the audience which helps to 'cleanse and purify' the mind. While particularly applied to live theatre, mass mediated drama can also produce similar effects on **audiences**.

CD-Rom (Compact Disk Read Only Memory). A computer disk introduced by Phillips in 1986 which is capable of storing around 650 megabytes of data and is similar in appearance to an audio disk. The data on a CD-Rom may be in text form, or as sounds, graphics and/or programs, thus making it extremely valuable for use in all forms of education. When combined with a computer which has the capability to deliver sound and graphics this is known as a multimedia system (see **information and communications technology (ICT)**). The form has had a tremendous influence within education and the information technology (IT) area generally. Most new PCs have CD-Rom drives and students and teachers can use CDs as another highly flexible format.

However, with the phenomenal upsurge of the internet and **web**-based technology, many new information sources are defecting to this more universal and more easily accessed form. Yet the quality of the CD format for manipulating photographs, for example, has not been surpassed (Wise, p. 52).

Mayer, P. A. (1999) *Computer Media and Communication: A Reader*. Oxford University Press.

Wise, R. (2000) *Multimedia: A Critical Introduction*. Routledge.

censorship. The repression of free expression of ideas and representations. All films for example have to be presented to a Board of Censors who decide if any sections need to be cut altogether. However, more recently they tend to focus on deciding classification levels, ranging from universal (for all ages) to 18 certificates. Most analysis of censorship remains preoccupied with the representation of sexual and violent activity within media products, particularly film and videos for both ethical and moral reasons.

There are at least two major types of censorship: political/ideological and moral/ethical, focusing particularly on representations of sex and violence. From the beginning of print media, politicians and governments have used and manipulated the so-called 'freedom of the press' to get their message across and/or to suppress critical debate for what was considered treasonable opposition to the 'defence of the realm' in the UK. Some historians suggest that this form of political censorship, while being less blatant and more sophisticated, has continued up to the present day. For example, Noam **Chomsky**, in his seminal *Manufacturing Consent*, focused on American press censorship in places like East Timor; or see the **Glasgow Media Group** regarding representations of strikes and other minorities in the UK.

censorship in the UK: film. The historical roots of cinema presentation in circus acts and peepshows promoted an urge to censor. The passing of the Cinematography Act of 1909 gave local authorities the power to grant or veto licences to peepshow arcades and the newly built cinemas. Then in 1912 the British Board of Film Classification (BBFC) was formed, funded from the fees paid by producers seeking a 'certificate' for their films. The chief censor's decision was final and there were no grounds for appeal, as the legislation was first formed. George Redford was the first chief censor. When it opened its doors in Soho, the organization had no fixed codes but two rules:

1 No materialization of Christ.

2 No nudity.

It only had two classifications:

U for general exhibition

A for advisory, but not compulsory restriction for those under 16.

The First World War in particular led to many films being heavily cut or banned outright; primarily for political reasons, such as Eisenstein's *Battleship Potemkin* (1925), which was banned for its 'communist' expression until 1956. *The Cabinet of Doctor Caligari* (1919) was also banned for fear of upsetting viewers who may have had relatives in insane asylums!

In 1932, the coming of films like *Dracula* (1931) and *Frankenstein* (1932) led to the introduction of the H certificate for horror films. However, Tod Browning's *Freaks* (1932) was banned until 1963, when it was given an X certificate, first introduced in 1951, which made such films restricted for children under 16.

1958 John Trevelyan becomes head of BBFC.

1959 Obscene Publications Act is passed, allowing for the showing of partial nudity.

1970 Mary Whitehouse and others form 'Festival of Light' and actively campaign for more stringent censorship to combat the nation's 'declining morals'. The X certificate is raised from 16 to 18.

By the end of the century there was a more relaxed and less hysterical attitude to the functions of classification and censorship.

Examples of controversial films:

A Clockwork Orange (1971) taken out of circulation by director Stanley Kubrick and not re-shown in cinemas until after his death in 2000.

Straw Dogs, Last Tango in Paris, The Exorcist (1973) not allowed onto video until 1999.

Rambo 3 (1988) and the Hungerford massacre soon afterwards in the UK (the film was alleged to have influenced Michael Ryan to shoot a number of people at random in the small English town).

Child's Play 3 and the horrific killing of the infant James Bulger in Liverpool. (Again, the popular press sought a scapegoat for the horrific crime and claimed to have found it in the way the killing took place in the film. However, no firm evidence was supplied for this direct link.)

More recent concerns around David Cronenberg's *Crash* (1996), which featured violence and sex focusing on car crashes and victims, has meant that its video release was delayed. It is somewhat incongruous to recently observe the video selling at bargain prices in retail chain stores.

It is considered by more recent censors that video is more difficult to police than cinematic release, since certification can more easily be controlled. Because of the immediacy and rewind properties of video, it was felt particularly by James Ferman, who was head of BBFC from 1975, that censorship rules needed to be more stringent with the video format.

Matthews, T. D. (1994) *Censored.* Chatto and Windus.

Channel 4. A British television channel which was set up in 1982 to cater for minority interests and help to produce more innovative programming. The channel was designed to be a publisher-type organization which bought in and commissioned most of its programming from independent television companies and was controlled by the ITV network. It attracts about 10 per cent of the audience share, and in 1983 the channel became commercially independent of the ITV.

The current chief executive, Michael Jackson, states that the aim of the channel is: 'to be the channel of new ideas and new talent . . . and make television that matters' (see Spring 2000 factsheet). Most commentators, while accepting the central and innovative role of Channel 4 in commissioning independent film and promoting minority interest programming, see it as having moved more and more into the mainstream to maximize its audience. Nonetheless, the channel has certainly broken the otherwise cosy cartel which existed between the BBC and ITV up to then.

chequebook journalism. Usually associated with **tabloid** newspapers who offer large sums of money for scandal stories like 'kiss and tell', which editors hope will sell more of their papers. The phenomenon has led to a huge growth in so-called **paparazzi** photographers, who have scant regard for rules of privacy in their quest to capture some 'compromising photograph' of various celebrities or politicians. The apparently insatiable desire and prurience of 'tabloid readers' for such images has been a major focus for discussion within **censorship** debates in the media, particularly with the death of the ex-Royal Diana in 1997, having been chased by paparazzi photographers.

chiaroscuro. A technical term to describe the lighting often used in *film noir*. The term, derived from painting, focuses on the arrangement of dramatic light and shade in a shot and is often used to explore the 'darker' aspects of film protagonists. Many classic *noir* films, such as *Double Indemnity* (1944), *Farewell My Lovely* (1944), *Crossfire* (1947) and others can be used to illustrate this style of black-and-white lighting.

child-centred education. Places the child, rather than the teacher or the subject, at the heart of the educational process. Often supported by psychologists, and those who have been involved in the education of very young children, the child-centred tradition has played a strong role in the development of primary school education throughout the Western world in particular.

This form of education is rooted in the interests, abilities and needs of the individual child which are believed to be closely served by it. Contact with the outside world is highly valued as a positive, subjective experience. In many ways the *process* of education is seen as more important than the product. The influence of child-centred approaches on media education has encouraged children to explore their feelings and experiences of the world.

Buckingham, D. (1996) *Moving Images: Understanding Children's Emotional Responses to TV.* Manchester University Press.

Dewey, J. (1902) *The Child and the Curriculum.* Phoenix Books.

Rousseau, J.J. (1972) *Emile.* Dent.

Chomsky, Noam. An American **linguist** who became preoccupied with the 'deep structure' of language. He suggested that the human organism is programmed to speak and humans are designed to create meaning.

He has also become very preoccupied with how media, particularly American media, manipulates meaning for **ideological** reasons. Such media empires have too much power, he argues. See also **cultural imperialism**.

Chomsky, N. (1969) *Aspects of the Theory of Syntax.* MIT Press.

Chomsky, N. (1972) *Language and the Mind.* Harcourt, Brace Jovanovich.

Chomsky, N. (1989) *Necessary Illusions.* South End Press.

Cinéma Vérité. A **documentary** movement started in France in the early 1960s which claimed that its style of documentary captured the 'true social reality' of life. Aided by the development of lightweight cameras, filmmakers could go out into the street for the first time, without being shackled by weighty equipment and lights which were very obtrusive.

MacDonald, K. and Cousins, M. (eds) (1996) *Imagining Reality: The Faber Book of the Documentary.* Faber.

Nichols, B. (1994) *Blurred Boundaries: Questions of Meaning in Contemporary Culture.* University of Indiana Press.

cinematography. The aesthetic use of **lighting** and cameras to create narrative films. However, few cinematographers are remembered compared to directors and stars, which is often unfair since the whole look of a film is determined by these creative personalities. From Greg Toland's evocative *film noir* camerawork in *Citizen Kane* (which is eulogized by the film critic Pauline Kael) and many other generic pieces, to the often greater preoccupation with the aesthetic look in art cinema or the **avant-garde**, cinematography has remained very important in the make-up of film.

circulation. The size of the readership of a magazine, newspaper or journal. Such figures are used to determine rates charged for advertising together with the audience profile of the text's circulation. All magazines and papers are continually concentrating on circulation figures, since such figures determine the profitability and future of the paper. Circulation becomes more problematic, however, with so-called 'free-sheets'; these are distributed free to their intended audience, and income is raised solely from advertising based on the number of copies distributed.

Roy Greenslade of the *Guardian* is the specialist media correspondent who traces the rise and fall of major dailies and is worth looking at by students as part of their research into newspapers. The *Sun* still leads the **tabloid** race for readers in the UK, with around 4 million readers, whereas the **broadsheets** find it difficult to reach half a million readers at the best of times. But then it must be remembered that niche targeting is becoming most important in media advertising. The *Guardian*, for example, can still command large fees for its job/appointment pages and other advertisements which is out of all proportion to its circulation, because it captures the appropriate target audience in higher class and income brackets.

For example, the 1999 circulation figures of **women's magazines** in the UK were

Magazine	Sales
Cosmopolitan	470,000
Marie Claire	450,000
Company	250,000
Vogue	202,000
Elle	210,000

Cited in *Guardian Media Guide.*

Men's magazines on the other hand were the publishing phenomenon of the 1990s. For example, *Loaded*'s sales grew in 1996 by 172 per cent, and a year later its sales revenue was quoted at £2 million a month with its advertising revenue £500,000 a month, which is £30 million a year. Other success stories include *The Face*, *GQ* and *FHM*. Information on circulation figures in the UK can be found in BRAD, a directory of UK advertising media (see www.brad.co.uk).

citizenship. The legal relationship between an individual and the country in which he or she resides; a condition which confers rights and responsibilities on the individual. Citizenship studies gives pupils the knowledge, skills and understanding to play an effective role in society, at local, national and international levels. It helps them to become informed, thoughtful and responsible citizens who are aware of their duties and rights. It promotes their spiritual, moral, social and cultural development, making them more self-confident and responsible both in and beyond the classroom. It encourages pupils to play a helpful part in the life of their schools, neighbourhoods, communities and the wider world. It also teaches them about our economy and democratic institutions and values. It encourages respect for different national, religious and ethnic identities and develops pupils' ability to reflect on issues and take part in discussions.

In educational terms citizenship became a new 'buzz' word under New Labour at the end of the 1990s. This government regards the development of citizenship studies as an important element within children's education. This development would also encourage the study of the mass media, which can be considered as part of the aims of teaching citizenship.

DfEE (1999) *The National Curriculum: Handbook for Secondary Teachers in England*. HMSO.

QCA (1998) *Education for Citizenship and the Teaching of Democracy in Schools: Final Report of the Advisory Group on Citizenship*. QCA.

QCA (1999) *The Review of the National Curriculum in England: The Consultation Materials*. QCA.

class system. A key barometer within **ideological** and **audience** analysis. Together with **age, race** and **gender** divisions, class is used to describe crude divisions within society, between the 'working classes' (or the proletariat as **Marx** described them), and the middle/upper class (bourgeoisie). Marxist theory puts great emphasis on divisions between the controlling owners of capital as opposed to those who only have their labour to offer. Such divisions continue to focus on attitudes, values and beliefs as a means of exploring inherent tensions and contradictions within media texts which reflect the society from which they emanate.

classic narrative cinema. The dominant story-telling structure which particularly dominated Hollywood filmmaking. The term is most popularized by critics like David **Bordwell**, Colin **MacCabe** and others to describe the dominant narrative structure inherent in Hollywood cinema, at least up to the 1960s. See **narrative/narratology** and the study of how stories are told. Such critics argue that similar narrative codes and conventions are used across all genres over this extended period. **Ideological** critics emphasize how such narrative codes give little flexibility to critique the dominant ideology of **capitalism**. In particular critics focus on the neat ideological use of **closure** in almost all Hollywood films, where all loose ends are tied up, allowing no lingering questions or unresolved puzzles for the audience which might promote an interrogation of the world view presented in the film.

Aesthetically, the use of a dominant naturalistic form of presentation, using strict rules of **continuity editing**, ensures audiences do not recognize the constructed nature of the text. Also **naturalistic** forms of acting encourage identification with heroes and ensure that audiences are pleasurably engaged at all times, and in particular that the film's artifice is never questioned.

See also the **avant-garde** as an alternative form of narrative construction.

Cook, P. (ed.) (1985) *The Cinema Book*. BFI.

clip art. Commercially prepared artwork which does not require copyright permission and is available on **internet** and **CD-Roms**.

closure. A term to describe the closing down of meaning and the tying up of loose ends at the end of a classic Hollywood film, when the narrative is resolved. It remains a key term within narrative theory. **Ideological** critics assert that Hollywood films and **classic narratives** in particular always strive to avoid any loose ends, which results in the ideological 'status quo' being reasserted and no radical change being promoted or even considered for the audience. An assumption is often made that narrative resolution remains the most important and memorable aspect of a story.

CNN (Cable News Network). A 24-hour cable news organization which was initiated by the media tycoon Ted Turner. By 1991 the channel was received in 58 million American households and by satellite in 140 countries (Price 1997, p. 47). The channel became particularly successful in broadcasting the Gulf War live, and the BBC and other world channels have followed suit by producing similar 24-hour news channels.

Price, S. (1997) *The Complete A–Z Media and Communication Handbook*. Hodder and Stoughton.

code. A system of meanings common to members of a culture or subculture. It consists both of signs and of rules or conventions that determine or limit how and in what context these signs are used and how they can combine to form complex messages. Often they are implicit within the generic formula of the text. For example a chequered tablecloth in a **western** usually signals a poor but honest homestead.

Roland **Barthes** created five subheadings/codes.

(a) Hermeneutic or enigmatic codes – which set up, formulate and finally resolve major film puzzles.

(b) Proairetic or action codes – the sequences which can be observed to take forward the narrative and could be described as action events.

(c) Cultural codes – the body of knowledge a culture is presumed to know, e.g. the role of good/bad in a given society.

(d) Semic code – the code which organizes the construction of character in a text through e.g. clothes, movement, even place.

(e) Symbolic code – the fundamental meaning structures upon which the text is based.

Brooker, P. (1999) *A Concise Glossary of Cultural Theory*. Arnold.

cognition. Knowing or perceiving, which includes the processes of reasoning, problem-solving and understanding. Cognition is usually held to be distinct from subjective emotion.

cognitive development. The intellectual acquisition of information and concepts through sensory perception, memory and observation. It also refers to the growth in a child's ability to understand concepts, relationships and patterns of ideas. For example Piaget, the influential educationalist and child psychologist, concludes that there is a staged growth in a child's development, such as the development of an ability for reasoning and problem-solving.

Cognitive domain is the area of learning involved with the intellectual acquisition of information, concepts and principles. Bloom (1956) created taxonomies of cognitive objectives linked to the cognitive domain, which relate to a hierarchy of thinking skills:

- knowledge
- comprehension
- application
- analysis
- synthesis
- evaluation

Here each 'level' subsumes the next, with higher levels only being achievable once the lower ones are acquired. This implies that there are certain higher-order thinking skills that should be aimed for in both teaching and learning.

Bloom, B. (ed.) (1956) *Taxonomy of Educational Objectives: Handbook 1: Cognitive Domain.* Longman.

Chomsky, N. (1968) *Language and Mind.* Harcourt Brace Jovanovich.

cognitive film analysis. Cognitive theory expresses the belief that both thought and information-processing involve choices being made by individuals as determined by certain goals. This contrasts with **behaviourist** theory, which emphasizes the role of environmental stimuli in creating an individual's responses, which may render thought processes of secondary importance.

Cognitive film analysis is most closely associated with David **Bordwell**, who examines the process of narration as a system of cues for audiences to engage with. Without having predetermined, framing mechanisms for understanding and appreciating film – be they ideological or psychological – Bordwell affirms how the sensory experience of the text can be more clearly explored as a 'bottom-up' experience rather than a 'top-down' abstract theoretical application.

Anderson, J. (1996) *The Reality of Illusion: An Ecological Approach to Cognitive Film Theory.* Southern Illinois University Press.

Bordwell, D. (1989) 'A Case for Cognitivism', *IRIS* 9 (Spring).

Bordwell, D. and Carroll, N. (eds) (1996) *Post-Theory: Reconstruction Film Studies.* University of Wisconsin Press.

Bruner, B. (1960) *Process of Education*. Random House.

Cohen, G. (1983) *The Psychology of Cognition*. Academic Press.

www.mailbase.ac.uk/lists/film-philosophy/files.

Cold War and McCarthyism. The Cold War was the long stand-off which began shortly after the Second World War with Russia and America in an arms race. The superpowers' resolve was tested through their opposing political and economic ideologies – **communism** versus **capitalism**. The 'war', which thankfully never became 'hot' (except for skirmishes like the Cuban crisis), ended with the fall of the Berlin Wall (1989) and the subsequent break-up of the Soviet Union.

Joe McCarthy was a powerful American governor who believed that communists were infecting and infiltrating American culture and society generally. He sought to expose this communist infiltration in America in the 1950s, particularly within culture industries like **Hollywood**. (The description of 'reds under the beds' is often used in describing the paranoia of the period.) As a result many **left-wing** filmmakers and media workers were blacklisted by the commission set up to investigate allegations through the House Un-American Activities Committee (HUAC). Several **right-wing** filmmakers like Walt **Disney** supported HUAC activities and named possible communists.

The investigation raised the issue of the power of the mass media to manipulate the public and questioned what constituted 'communist' stimuli in film and other cultural products. This was the ultimate conspiracy theory which incidentally became reflected and refracted through the new teenage B movie science fiction preoccupation. Many critics later affirmed that such movies which dealt with fears of invasion were allegorical reminders of the contentious communist witch-hunts being carried out by McCarthy in the 1950s.

In particular films like *Invasion of the Body Snatchers* have been analysed in this way, with the invaders who take over the bodies of Americans and become indistinguishable but 'non-human', with no emotion, remaining a symbol of communist invasion. Ironically it took the power of the media and a popular TV reporter, Ed Murrow, to help bring down such show trials and expose McCarthy for what he was.

Biskind, P. (1983) *Seeing is Believing: How Hollywood Taught us to Stop Worrying and Love the Fifties*. Pluto Press.

Jancovich, M. (1996) *Rational Fears: American Horror in the 1950s*. University of Manchester Press.

comedy. A category of performance which is designed to make its audience laugh or at least become amused. As a theoretical study, this wide-ranging and highly popular **genre** remains very difficult to analyse, with many difficult if engaging academic studies of the area. Of course what makes **audiences** laugh is very dependent on individual social/historical and cultural contexts, and even then such categorization often remains highly subjective. However, comedy remains possibly the most prevalent genre in both TV and film, and to a lesser extent on radio.

Bergson, H. (1956) *Comedy*. Anchor Press.

Cavell, S. (1981) *Pursuits of Happiness: The Hollywood Comedy of Remarriage*. Cambridge University Press.

Durgnat, R. (1970) *The Crazy Mirror: Hollywood Comedy and the American Image*. Dell.

Freud, S. (1963) *Jokes and Their Relation to the Unconscious*, trans. James Strachey. Norton.

Gombrich, E. H. and Kris, E. (1940) *Caricature*. Penguin.

Marcuse, H. (1955) *Eros and Civilization*. Beacon Press.

Mast, G. (1979) *The Comic Mind: Comedy and the Movies*. University of Chicago Press.

Neale, S. and Krutnik, F. (1990) *Popular Film and Television Comedy*. Routledge.

Sikov, E. (1994) *Laughing Hysterically: American Screen Comedy of the 1950s*. Routledge.

comics. Originally a series of short and mainly humorous drawings or **cartoons** which appeared in newspapers. There has even been a long tradition of political cartoons going back to 1796. Before video games in particular, comics were the staple popular cultural medium for children of all ages. In America the superhero comic like *Superman, Spiderman* and the *Incredible Hulk* became very popular and fed into film culture as more and more super comic-book heroes have been filmed for the big screen. More recently, specialized and niche market comics have become very popular. *Viz* sells over one million copies to an adult audience. In Japan in particular (the home of *manga*, which has become popular in the West and also spawned film adaptations) the comic remains extremely popular for all ages and types of subject matter. Even academic and scientific books are written in a comic form. Comic studies continue to be focused on **representation** and **ideology**. Nevertheless the study of comics has become possibly less popular in media education, with the video game explosion.

Barker, M. (1989) *Comics, Ideology, Power and the Critics*. Manchester University Press.

McRobbie, A. and MacCabe, C. (1981) *Feminism for Girls*. Routledge and Kegan Paul.

Price, S. (1993) *Media Studies*. Longman.

commercial. A film, television or radio **advertisement** that is presented during 'commercial breaks' to promote some product or service. Advertising remains of course central to the success of all commercial media industries.

commodification. Occurs when human qualities or attributes become equated with the commercial business of goods which can be bought and sold in the marketplace. The term is frequently used within **Marxist/feminist** discourse to emphasize the way female **representation**, particularly within **advertisements**, could be translated into the **capitalist** system of buying and selling. For example the image of a girl represented as 'beautiful and sexy' alongside or inside a new car suggests a direct connection even equivalence between the product and her beautiful/sexy image. While it is often assumed that in these more **politically correct** (**PC**) times, such representations are less frequent, many contend that they have become more subtle and less blatant than they were in the past.

Related to this notion is the concept of objectification, which is used in a similar way, suggesting that female representations in particular are dehumanized and de-individualized and reduced to (sexual) objects. More recently such representational analysis has been applied to males as well as females. Also studies of **Madonna**, for example, illustrate how female agents often conspire in their own commodification yet are also able to subvert such objectification by taking control of their image construction.

communication. Includes the mass media and involves all forms of meaning exchanged between humans. Communications A Level for example focuses on various categories, including:

- **Intrapersonal**, which involves communication with the self. However, most critics assert that communication cannot occur until at least two individuals communicate.

- **Interpersonal**, when at least two people are communicating, which can include '**non-verbal communication**' or NVC.

- **Mass communication**, which involves standardized production and mediation of products aimed at a mass audience.

- **Extrapersonal**, involving communication between machines such as computers.

Argyle, M. (1978) *The Psychology of Interpersonal Behaviour.* Penguin.

Argyle, M. (1988) *Bodily Communication.* Methuen.

Dimbley, R. and Burton, G. (1990) *Teaching Communication.* Routledge.

Goffman, E. (1969) *The Presentation of Self in Everyday Life.* Penguin.

O'Sullivan, T. *et al.* (1987) *Key Concepts in Communication.* Methuen.

communication models. Used to illustrate in various ways how complex communications processes can be understood and exemplified. They are used extensively in **communications A Level** courses and are particularly relevant for appreciating the complexity of the interaction between mass media and audiences.

A selection of the most basic and popular models used follows:

- *The Lasswell Formula* (1948) is the most convenient and effective way to describe the communications process and is particularly effective when looking at political **propaganda**. (See Figure 1.)

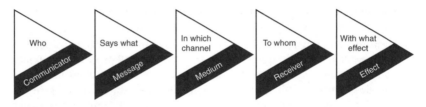

Figure 1   After Lasswell (1948): a model of a communication act.

- *Shannon and Weaver's Model* suggests communication is a 'one way process' and reflects the mathematical/engineering focus of telephony to which it was applied. (See Figure 2.)

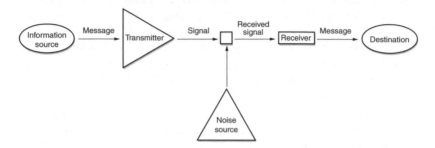

Figure 2   After Shannon and Weaver: a model of the communication process.

- *Newcomb's ABX Model* is a triangular model which when amended to include encoding/decoding remains one of the most student-friendly models for explaining meaning within texts. Producer – (encoding) – Text – (decoding) – Audience. (See Figure 3.)

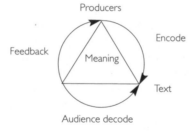

Figure 3   After Newcomb: a model for explaining meaning within texts.

Of course there are a huge number of variations of these and many other models which can be helpful in providing an overview of media communication throughout the study of media in general.

McQuail, D. and Windahl, S. (1993) *Communication Models*. Longman.

communism. A theory based on communal, rather than private, ownership and wealth generation. It advocates a society where all property is publicly owned and where people work, and are paid, according to their needs and abilities. **Marx** envisaged that eventually the state would lose its significance under a mature communist regime. However, this did not occur in communist countries in the twentieth century, where by contrast the state eventually grew to control all aspects of society. But with the end of the

Cold War, the fall of the Berlin Wall and the break-up of the Soviet empire after 1989, and the move by Russia towards embracing Western capitalism, many critics suggest that the communist experiment is all but dead! Nonetheless its influence on **ideological** and media theory remains potent.

Harvey, D. (1973) *Social Justice and the City*. Arnold.

Marx, K. (1967) *Capital* (3 vols). International Publishers Edition.

commutation test. Applied when one element in a complex process is altered to see how this affects the system as a whole. The test is used extensively in performance and star studies to explore the relative strengths and originality of the performances of stars, and their specific attributes and skills. For example, would the overall meaning of a text/performance change if another actor was substituted in their place? How would this change the meaning of the image/performance? Imagining such a scenario makes it easier to compare the relative effectiveness of both actors and evaluate the unique individual contribution of each performer.

competence. The **ability** to perform a specific task, or skill, to a given standard. For example in BTEC courses and vocational courses generally, students must acquire basic competency in using computer, radio, TV, video and photography equipment before they can be allowed to develop projects in a less supervised environment.

computer aided design (CAD). Describes a computer system/software which allows its user to creatively develop 3-dimensional drawings as well as other types of designs which can be applied for example within engineering/ architecture as well as creative media uses.

computer literacy. More commonly described as **information and communications technology (ICT)**, it is a general term for an ability to use and understand the language and grammar of computers. Whereas in the recent past, computer programs involved complex program sequences which had to be learned, now with more user-friendly drop-down menus and toolbars, together with help functions, it is much easier to teach yourself how to use various programmes. More and more, it is assumed that students must learn how to wordprocess and design their work, especially as they progress up the educational ladder. Also, it is essential that students are able to access the **internet**, which can provide all students with an invaluable source of information and material for their study.

Students also learn to access CD-Roms and a variety of other computer packages, so that they are able to function effectively within this growing interdisciplinary area. If students wish to find work in **multimedia** in particular, they will have to become proficient with graphic packages like *Photoshop* and authoring packages like *Premier*, *Director* and *Dreamweaver* and be able to create websites and digitally manipulate still, as well as audiovisual imagery.

concept mapping. Involves the creation of a diagram which is used to understand the basis of a concept. A concept (or spider) diagram is used to display important ideas within a theme or unit of work and may be devised by pupils to reveal what they know and whether misunderstandings exist. Concept mapping can be created through **brainstorming** and can be used at any point within a teaching programme.

connotation. Derived from **Barthes' semiotic** study of how the meaning of an image goes beyond the literal, common-sense, **denotative** interpretation to include social, cultural and historical associations. For example, a girl wearing a mini-skirt in the 1960s might connote freedom and sexual liberation. Developing students' ability to move beyond their subjective, even relativistic, appreciation of sign systems is of major importance in the learning process. Understanding connotative meanings is often the first major step in this process of exploring the varying levels of meaning within complex sign systems like mass-mediated texts.

conspiracy theory. Implies some secret reason or justification for events which happen in the real/fictional world. Such theories became very popular for instance after the assassination of President Kennedy in America. They have remained a potent organizing principle – for example within a wide range of Hollywood thrillers as well as TV series such as the cult *X Files*. In many ways they provide a forum for media texts to question dominant orthodoxies and **ideologies** within a given society.

constructivism. A theory, based on the work of **Vygotsky**, which states that learning is a process of building upon what is already known, or 'constructing' **knowledge** based on previously acquired information.

The constructivist approach to learning therefore involves pupils' engaging in experimentation and making mistakes, which in turn leads to a process of redefining and extending their knowledge and understanding. The active role of the learner is stressed in building up their understanding. This usually results in an interactive style of teaching and learning, with the teacher adopting the role of facilitator. Such discovery methods of learning often involve a process known as scaffolding, where a teacher initially supports and structures a child's learning experiences until they are capable of working independently. Media theorists such as David **Buckingham** have been particularly influenced by Vygotsky with regard to developing educational strategies for media education.

contact sheet. A sheet of photographic paper on which is printed a whole role of film, with the photographs reproduced in the same size as the negatives. Such sheets are used to get an impression of the best negatives to print up and enlarge for exhibition purposes.

content analysis. Can simply involve a counting exercise. For example, how often does 'x' occur in a media product or over a range of media in a given period of time. This standard research technique is often used to quantify volume or exposure in a given medium over a given period of time. For instance, counting up the number of stories relating to the subject under analysis in various newspapers over a given period. Accurate, factual information can be gained using this process.

However, critics of the method suggest that it gives an illusion of scientific rigour which reinforces the old adage about statistics being able to prove whatever you want. Nevertheless, it provides a very good initial strategy at least to develop the outline of a workable hypothesis. But ideally it should be used alongside other qualitative forms of analysis, such as extended interviews, and be carried out with a clear methodological appreciation of its aims and objectives as well as its limitations.

See for example the **Glasgow Media Group**, who have been extensively involved in carrying out content analysis research to detect **bias** and evidence of **ideological** manipulation in the British media.

context. Everything a critic focuses on around a **text**, be it social, political, historical or cultural influences which relate to the product that is being examined. It is used extensively when considering the wider meaning of media products. Media texts cannot be produced within a vacuum but are determined by various related influences and events. For example, an advertisement made in the UK in the 1960s, which represented 'swinging' London, is different from one made in America in the 1960s with its different social and political associations. Different again would be a 1990s advertisement which seeks to pastiche or send-up the 'swinging sixties'. The meanings of such adverts are dependent on several often interrelating contextual factors, like the ones mentioned above, which help to frame the meaning of any given textual analysis. Consequently media analysis should also involve extensive historical and contextual study if the full range of meanings of given texts are to be appreciated.

contextualize. To attempt to put a text into its historical, social or political **context**. The meaning of a term or sign is partly dependent on the context both in which it appears (or is produced) and is seen or read. The context would include everything which makes a text meaningful above and beyond the actual signs used in the performance of the text, such as sociocultural factors together with the historical time and geographical place of the performance. For example, the same Shakespeare play performed in Shakespeare's England would be different to the one seen in London in 2000, or the same play adapted into a Hollywood film. This implies that no text can be fully understood outside of its context. In particular, a historical appreciation is essential for a fuller understanding of the range of meanings within a given text. For example, Hollywood musicals made during the 1930s Depression have obvious contextual justifications around the need for escapism. It is suggested that audiences demand greater levels of escapism during times of economic depression.

A classic film like *Casablanca* (1942), on the other hand, addresses American tensions over entering the Second World War. Whether America should enter the war or remain isolationist is echoed in the moral struggle of

Rick (Humphrey Bogart), who has to decide whether to help the rebel French leader, as against the easier, more selfish option. His 'correct' decision is reflected in America's joining the war effort.

Ray, R. (1985) *A Certain Tendency of the Hollywood Cinema: 1930-1980.* Princeton University Press.

continued professional development (CPD). Any courses that are provided to enhance the knowledge, understanding and skills of teachers. For example, the present British government is backing a new initiative in higher education which encourages staff to join the Institute for Learning and Teaching (ILT), which is a UK-wide organization aimed at promoting good teaching practice within the sector.

continuity editing. Corresponds with the classic Hollywood convention of putting film together in a manner that makes it appear both logical and natural, and maintains the illusion of a **realistic** representation of actuality. Continuity editing ensures a smooth transition from shot to shot, avoiding for example '**jump-cuts**' which break the illusion of natural spatial representation or by crossing the 180-degree line which makes objects/characters appear to switch positions from one shot to another. Also it must be remembered that fiction films are often not shot in sequence, consequently it is important to maintain continuity of costume, for example, if the illusion of realism is to be maintained. See **classic narrative** for more detail.

continuous assessment. The assessment of work produced throughout a course of study, which may provide ongoing formative information on educational performance, as well as contributing to a summative profile of marks or grades. Various media A Level courses endorse this approach as do GNVQ and BTEC most particularly.

convention. The agreed practice or rule developed over time with any broad generic category of media production. Within media industries there are established conventions and working patterns which have evolved and often feed into established **genres** of production which ensure standardized production methods. A basic example would be with regard to music radio, where a DJ introduces the piece of music as a lead-in. Conventions are often used alongside **codes** to understand and articulate all generic output in the media, particularly with regard to film studies.

convergence. A topical catch-all concept which expresses the way various media have become more and more interconnected with each other. This is also happening at an institutional and economic level, with media companies taking over related media activities. Where **horizontal integration** involves links between similar institutions in the same business, vertical integration involves linking with organizations who are at another level in the cycle of production/or media services, for example a film company which controls a cinema chain to distribute its films. Within the global media business world, cross-media institutions like NTL, BT and Microsoft have come together to form a giant consortium, alongside other massive 'alliances' between global players, including TimeWarner, AOL and EMI.

New forms of media like the **internet**, it is argued, help to break down divisions between conventional newspaper and broadcasting journalists and publishing while at the same time helping to promote new forms of writing and communication, like **hypertext** and discussion groups. The University of Luton's international journal *Convergence* is dedicated to exploring this and other related issues.

Convergence: The Journal of Research into New Media Technologies.

www.luton.ac.uk/convergence

copyright. The protection of source material, which is produced by an individual or group, from illegal copying or piracy. The legal criteria are highly complex for all types of media products, including print-based, photography, audiovisual, etc. It is highly advisable for students who wish to work in the industry that they study the general rules.

Baker, R. (1997) *Media Law: A User's Guide for Film and Programme Makers*. Routledge.

Cassell, D. (1997) *The Photographer and the Law*. Routledge.

Courtney, N. R. (1995) *The Law of Journalism*. Butterworth.

core concept. See **key concept**.

core curriculum. Introduced by the UK School Examination and Assessment Council (SEAC) for Advanced and Advanced Subsidiary Levels (A and AS Levels) in the early 1990s as a means of creating a more uniform standard of subject syllabus coverage between examination boards. In general terms the core is analogous to the common trunk of a tree of knowledge, with the branches optional and depending on various factors. Each board had to design its subject syllabus around a nationally agreed 'core' of subject knowledge, skills, techniques, abilities and understanding. With the new **benchmark** proposals for higher education it is also likely that an agreed core will be proposed for all media degrees in the UK in the near future.

core subject. One of the primary subjects to be studied; in most countries media education has not yet achieved this high status. In the UK the Education Reform Act (1988) introduced a subject-based National Curriculum which defined curriculum subjects as either 'core' or 'foundation'. As the term suggests, core subjects (English, maths, science) form the heart of the curriculum. Of course, designated core subjects attract more curricular time, assessment status and funding than foundation or other subjects.

Subsequent revisions of the National Curriculum following the **Dearing Report** (1994) further complicated these arrangements and added an optional strand alongside core and foundational levels.

costume. What actors wear when they are performing in a play or in an audiovisual production. The study of costume is often used as part of a **semiotic** and **representational** analysis of character and overall performance.

Bruzzi, S. (1997) *Undressing Cinema: Clothing and Identity in the Movies*. Routledge.

counter-culture. Usually associated with 1960s youth rebellion and a reaction to the conformity of the 1950s, but more generally the term is used to denote opposition to the dominant culture. The 'hippie' counter-culturalists of the 1960s rejected **capitalism** and consumerism as well as distrusting the US political system which supported the Vietnam War. The movement was made up of a new generation of students, **feminist** activists and pacifists who believed in striving for a better society for all. The cult and extremely successful road movie *Easy Rider* (1969) is often cited to illustrate the movement with its philosophical endorsement of **alienation**, together with a radical endorsement of a 'sex, drugs and rock and roll' lifestyle. The reasons why the movement collapsed has taxed many cultural and historical critics.

Gitlin, T. (1993) *The Sixties: Years of Hope, Days of Rage*. Bantham Press.

coursework. Completed student work which is often used for **assessment** purposes, during a course of study. Coursework can take a variety of forms, such as, in media, simulated production exercises, or an extensive 'professional' report.

crime TV. Fictional texts which usually involve the representation of criminals and the police. Study of such texts has been popular to illustrate **ideological** manipulation, focusing in particular on the 'thin blue line', as it is called, of the 'law and order' thesis. The police, often in their symbolic blue outfits, serve to protect the law-abiding public from the chaos of criminal anarchy. Such texts act as a barometer of ethical norms within a given society and often reflect the dominant consensus of society over the period viewed.

Extensive studies in Britain in particular began with the seminal affirmation of the police as surrogate 'social workers' maintaining the social glue of society and embodied in *Dixon of Dock Green*, which ran from the 1950s to the growing splintering of this consensus through the 1970s. This famous series is compared with *The Sweeney*, which reflected 1970s (American) ambivalence towards fixed ethical positions regarding law and order. The London cops in this series are represented as hard-edged and often as morally bankrupt as the criminals they are fighting, thereby exposing the changing equilibrium of societal tensions. This public moral ambiguity is echoed through the representation of family breakdowns and individual cops being exposed as immoral, even sadistic, which was a long way from the righteous goodness of Dixon. Ideologically, media and social critics argue that the police (re)present the 'thin blue line' between civilization and anarchy, serving to protect society from the polluting effects of crime and disorder. This ambiguity of representation has continued with a recent series, *Cops* (1999).

Hall, S. *et al.* (1978) *Policing the Crisis: Mugging, The State and Law and Order*. Macmillan.

Hall, S. (ed.) (1997) *Representation: Cultural Representations and Signifying Practices*. Sage.

Sparks, R. (1992) *Television and the Drama of Crime: Moral Tales and the Place of Crime in Public Life.* Open University Press.

criterion-referencing. A principle or standard against which something is judged and assessment is measured in terms of specified criteria, levels or standards of mastery. Criterion-referenced assessment systems 'fix' the standard of performance by stating criteria against which pupils will be assessed.

critical language studies (CLS). Focuses on the power behind **discourse** as it reflects ideological positions. The dominant discourse it is suggested involves a process of 'naturalization' and application of so-called common-sense notions to make the ideology truly effective. **Foucault**, in particular, cogently affirms the centrality of discourse analysis.

critical theory. Originally conceived as a form of intellectual resistance to the political and social developments within Europe and developed through the work of Habermas, **Foucault** and others. In America in particular the term has become a euphemism for **Marxism**. Critical theory has previously been widely supported by sociologists and political theorists both within and beyond the field of education. In essence it provides a form of analysis of social, political and economic life where one gains a fuller appreciation of the ideological forces that govern one's existence. Education, as exposed by **Althusser** and other Marxist critics, is viewed as a further control mechanism of the state which ensures social regulation.

Critics, however, suggest that critical theory is overly crude and does not focus on the actual intricacies of individual texts, and remains preoccupied with dominant **metanarratives** by looking for generalizable overall patterns which often do not add much to overall meanings and understandings of specific texts. Hence post-structuralists like Derrida developed a questioning position on such theory. Nonetheless, as a working and educative model which allows students to appreciate the big picture and engage with high-level analysis, the method is still highly valued and used at all levels of study.

cropping. Cutting out parts of a photograph, which concentrates attention on what the editor wants the audience to focus on. Exercises in manipulating photographs, together with changing the by-lines or **anchoring** texts to be positioned with the image, helps to illustrate how meanings can be manipulated and distorted.

cross-curricular. Describes a subject which crosses over several discrete curricular subjects. Media education and 'literacy' generally is often regarded as a cross-curricular subject or theme. It is taught as an aspect of a number of different subjects, rather than as a discrete subject in its own right. The National Curriculum Council (NCC) in the UK established five cross-curricular themes, each of which was considered equally important:

- *economic and industrial understanding (EIU)*: financial decision-making, economic roles (e.g. producers, consumers and citizens), government economic policy, and the impact of economic activity on the environment;

- *careers education and guidance*: self, roles, career, transition, work;
- *health education*: use and misuse of various substances, sex education, family life education, safety, nutrition, personal hygiene, health-related exercise, environmental and psychological aspects;
- *education for citizenship*: participative citizenship, information on which to base the development of skills, values and attitudes towards citizenship, local, regional, national and international community relationships including the European dimension, democracy, human rights, law, employment, public services and leisure;
- *environmental education*: responsible attitudes towards the environment, knowledge and understanding of the processes by which environments are shaped, the vulnerability of different environments, and opportunities for protecting and managing the environment.

Media educators regard many aspects of the cross-curricular themes as embedding a range of issues and **core concepts** from within media education generally. In particular **citizenship** achieved prominence in the revised National Curriculum (DfEE 1999) when it became a part of the statutory curriculum at Key Stages 3 and 4 (from September 2002) for the first time.

DfEE (1999) *The National Curriculum: Handbook for Secondary Teachers in England.* HMSO.

cultural competence. The level of ability audiences have to engage with and appreciate a range of media products. The theory was advanced by the French critic Pierre Bourdieu, who also suggested the school system created a form of 'cultural reproduction', with class attitudes and values being reproduced within the schooling system. Consequently, at one extreme it could be argued that mass audiences cannot appreciate 'high culture' such as theatre because they have not learned how to enjoy it. This notion related to **Althusser**'s conceptualization of **ideological state apparatus**.

A hierarchical evocation of a range of cultural competencies can also be appreciated, for example, within high culture, like opera or theatre, where audiences are positioned as requiring greater 'knowledge' to appreciate such texts compared with soap operas. Yet at another level the melo-dramatic and heightened emotional acting in opera can in some ways be regarded as equivalent to the often exaggerated and stylized performance in **soap**-operas.

cultural imperialism. When one country – often America – is regarded as dominating the rest of the world's media/culture industries by 'swamping' them with their 'own culture'. This phenomenon is usually debated from the context of native indigenous cultures, like Britain and Ireland being swamped by another, especially through film and television exports. Media products are America's greatest economic exports, producing a larger return than the gross national product (GNP) of many sizeable countries, and America has fought to maintain her **global** dominance in the recent GATT negotiations. The study of cultural imperialism constitutes a way of reading media culture, primarily in economic and institutional terms rather than in purely aesthetic and creative ones. The economic and institutional power of media conglomerates can never be forgotten, since most media products are produced within a global competitive business framework.

Tomlinson, J. (1991) *Cultural Imperialism.* Routledge.

cultural literacy. A core of knowledge about people, places, events, language, traditions and concepts which exists within a particular culture. Many media educationalists suggest that contemporary education fails to provide pupils with a full sense of their cultural heritage because of its lack of cultural reference points within the curriculum. An extension of media into the curriculum could greatly aid in this development.

cultural studies (American). In American studies, interdisciplinary study became a means for practitioners to challenge a particular hierarchy, but it did not offer an alternative to the elitism of the academy. Consequently many critics suggest that interdisciplinarity lost its effectiveness and legitimacy. Cultural studies also embraces interdisciplinarity and hopefully has learned from the mistakes of American studies.

cultural studies (UK). In Britain cultural studies has been one of the major influences on the development of media education generally. As evidenced from the shortlist of recommended titles below, the area has attracted a wide range of critical analysis and has been a major growth area within publishing. Appreciating how the mass media create and reflect national and sub-group culture remains a continuing preoccupation with the subject. From Richard Hoggart, Raymond **Williams** and E. P. Thompson's evocation of working-class culture and identity, a major strand in cultural studies has been appreciating and valuing all aspects of cultural diversity. In particular the Birmingham group led by **Hall** and others has been instrumental in kick-starting cultural studies as a separate discipline. From teenage girls and comics (Angela McRobbie), to working-class youth (Walkerdine and Willis), and youth/pop culture (Hebdige, *et al.*) – to name a few – many cultural critics/historians have been writing extensively on the growing diversity of expression within so-called **postmodernist** culture.

Nevertheless, there remains major criticism of the area of study. In particular, it is felt that such academic discourse has become over-generalized, often lacking in critical academic rigour, while remaining purely celebratory of the pleasures of 'bottom-up' popular culture. For **Althusserian/Frankfurt School Marxists** in particular, the unconditional glorification of popular cultural expression remains at odds with their belief in 'top-down' dominant ideological control of culture.

Carey, W. (1989) *Communication as Culture: Essays on Media and Society.* Routledge.

Cultural Studies journal published by Routledge (especially special issue vol. 12 no. 4 Oct. 1998).

Curran, J. and Gurevitch, M. (eds) (1991) *Mass Media and Society.* Arnold.

Curran, J., Morley, D. and Walkerdine, V. (eds) (1996) *Cultural Studies and Communication.* Arnold.

Davies, I. (1997) *Cultural Studies and Beyond*. Routledge.

Dyer, R. (1992) *Only Entertainment*. Routledge.

Featherstone, M. (1991) *Consumer Culture and Postmodernism*. Sage.

Fiske, J. (1989) *Reading the Popular*. Unwin Hyman.

Hall, S. (ed.) (1997) *Representations: Cultural Representations and Signifying Practices*. Sage.

Hall, S. and Dugay, P. (eds) (1998) *Questions of Cultural Identity*. Sage.

Hebdige, D. (1988) *Hiding the Light*. Routledge.

Hoggart, R. (1992) *The Uses of Literacy*. Penguin.

Inglis, F. (1993) *Cultural Studies*. Blackwell.

Kellner, D. (1995) *Media Culture: Cultural Studies, Identity and Politics between the Modern and the Postmodern*. Routledge.

McRobbie, A. (1991) *Feminism and Youth Culture*. Macmillan.

Punter, D. (ed.) (1986) *Introduction to Contemporary Cultural Studies*. Longman.

Story, J. (ed.) (1996) *What is Cultural Studies: A Reader*. Arnold.

Strinati, D. (1995) *An Introduction to Theories of Popular Culture*. Routledge.

Thompson, E. P. (1963) *The Making of the English Working Class*. Golancz.

Turner, G. (1991) *British Cultural Studies: An Introduction*. Unwin Hyman.

Williams, R. (1958) *Culture and Society*. Columbia University Press.

culture. A large strand in media education which involves the collective beliefs, traditions, symbols, ideas and values which influence the behaviour and social structures of a particular group. Media texts make up a large part of a nation's cultural artefacts. Culture helps to define a society and may be transferred from one generation to the next, undergoing changes in the process. Cultural theorists discuss the divisions between high and low culture. Where high culture was considered of value and worth maintaining and supporting, popular (low) culture is often dismissed as worthless and disposable. Critics like **Fiske** and many others seek to 'value' the wide range of pleasures which mass audiences acquire from such texts while striving to legitimize their academic study.

curriculum. Aspects of the content of a subject to be taught, or the total programme of teaching within an educational establishment (the 'official curriculum'). The school curriculum is not merely a collection of subjects, but the wider education actually offered within the school. In essence, the curriculum is a structured series of intended learning outcomes, with statements provided on aims, objectives, learning activities and methods of evaluation and assessment.

Media studies curriculum development has been particularly influenced by a **core concepts** approach which avoids some of the dangers of being overly prescriptive and allowing teachers and practitioners to use contemporary texts and resources which best fit the educational agenda, students' interests and their **cultural competencies**.

Lawton, D. (1983) *Curriculum Studies and Educational Planning*. Hodder and Stoughton.

curriculum development. Creates a focus on a particular area of the curriculum, often subject-based, with the aim of improving the teaching and learning undertaken. Usually this involves the creation of new teaching materials and schemes of work, but may equally involve teachers re-appraising the aims and objectives of their pedagogy. With the continuous development of mass media this remains a necessary process and ensures the subject discipline remains fresh and relevant to students' needs as well as addressing media's ever-changing technologies and standards.

cyberspace. A term invented by the science fiction writer William Gibson in his novel *Neuromancer* (1984), it describes the hallucination of video/computer games where the player appears to enter another fictional world. The term has become commonly used to describe the growth of new media from the **internet** to all forms of virtual reality computer programmes. (See for example films like *The Matrix* (1999) or *EXistenz* (1999).)

Dery, M. (1996) *Escape Velocity: Cyberculture at the End of the Century.* Hodder and Stoughton.

Loader, B. (ed.) (1997) *The Governance of Cyberspace.* Routledge.

cyborgs. The hybrid creatures who are part-human and part-machine. They have been particularly prevalent in science fiction since *Metropolis* back in the 1920s, but have come to even greater popularity with the recent hi-tech examples of *Blade Runner* and the *Terminator* series. Feminist theorists like Donna Haraway and others have made important representational claims for such metaphorical characters which help to overcome the otherwise crude polarization between so-called passive females and active male gender politics. Cyborgs can step out of such regressive opposition and even posit new 'post-human' ways of seeing reality and appreciating what it means to be human.

Haraway, D. (1991) *Simians, Cyborgs, and Women: the Reinvention of Nature.* Free Association Books.

D

data. Observations collected as the basis for statistical analysis, inference or reference. In its original form such data is often referred to as 'raw data' signifying that it has not yet been ordered, sorted, summarized or grouped in any way. Data is often collected for media projects to justify the development of new products, for example.

data protection. Legal measures designed to control access to stored information in computers. **Journalists** most especially must become fully conversant with the range of constraints with regard to information retrieval if they are to remain inside the law.

Crone, T. (1995) *Law and the Media.* Butterworth.

Greenwood, W. and Welsh, T. (1999) *MacNae's Essential Law for Journalists.* Butterworth.

Dearing Report (National Curriculum and its Assessment). This report (1994) focused on the UK's National Curriculum and its assessment and resulted from an investigation into the scope for slimming down the National Curriculum following the expression of widespread concern about its complexity, over-prescription and domination by subject content. Following his well-received report on the future of the National Curriculum, Dearing was again commissioned by the Secretary of State for Education to review the framework of age 16–19 qualifications in England and Wales. His review was published as a final review in 1996 and emphasized the equivalence between academic and vocational education which has promoted the General National Vocational Qualification (GNVQ), as well as the reduction in the number of syllabi. Dearing also recommended the introduction of modular courses which have been widely used within media education.

Dearing, R. (1996) *Review of 16–19 Qualifications: Final Report.* SCAA.

decision-making. The use of various strategies or techniques to achieve a goal, or to evaluate the potential benefits and drawbacks of different solutions to a given problem. The decision-making process is usually influenced by the available access to information and the ability to interpret, evaluate and analyse such information. Media projects often develop decision-making skills in students, particularly within group projects.

decisive moment. In photography, the ideal instant when all elements of a scene come together and make the 'perfect' picture. The term was used extensively by the French photographer Henri Cartier-Bresson, who said that his images were taken as a result of such split-second decisions. Capturing such dramatically real situations became the touchstone of images made by numerous photo-journalists, particularly from the Magnum agency which he helped to set up. Often photographers would wait long periods for some movement or intervention to dramatize the foreground/background of the final captured image.

decoding. The process of interpreting coded meanings and messages. All media messages are coded in various ways and one of the primary functions of media analysis is to find tools for decoding meaning(s).

See for example the various models of the media, particularly the triangular model which links audiences, producers and text. This is probably the most important and influential model for an understanding of the mass media. In very simplistic terms media critics and debates can be categorized by the way they concentrate on particular aspects of this communication triangle. In the 1970s there was a predominance of ideologically based readings of media texts which focused particularly on the institutional factors that predetermined producers' encoding of meaning in media texts. **Textual analysis** was therefore predetermined by socio-historical and political debates.

More recently, the pendulum has swung back towards a more audience-centred approach to analysis, which serves to validate **active readings** by viewers who are not necessarily dominated by top-down ideological manipulative frameworks.

deconstruction. The breaking down of structures of meaning that have become 'normalized' and 'naturalized' through extensive use. The influential theorist Jacques Derrida, for example, became strongly associated with the method and criticized **structuralism** in particular for creating the illusion of a core of meanings which provided security and control. Derrida and other post-structuralists rejected this and sought to 'deconstruct' various discourses and create new ways of reading. Similarly, for example, the avant-garde play-wright **Brecht** speaks of laying bare society's 'causal network' in relation to sign systems in cinema and other media. Media studies has been built on this critical discourse, aiming to reveal the often deep but contradictory structures embedded in the mediated text.

Brooker, P. (1999) *A Concise Glossary of Cultural Theory.* Arnold.

demystification. A primary critical approach that proposes to reveal practices or processes that are normally hidden or effaced within the apparently natural but sophisticated media apparatus. The educational aim seeks to break down various barriers to appreciating and understanding the media in general. The term is often associated with **Masterman**'s study of the media in particular, but usually as a simplistic critique of his methodology.

There is a danger of falling into the trap of '**false consciousness**' – perceiving demystification as a *raison d'être* of media studies which seeks to unlock the hidden secrets of the text. This begs the question, how do teachers/critics know they have the secret truth, unlike mass audiences? Masterman and others are often unfairly criticized for their so-called utopian wish to promote students' confidence in engaging with hi-tech media equipment and critiquing elitist knowledge and **cultural competencies**. Media education, it was argued, should initially involve the demystification of the processes and apparatus of media industries, which would then allow 'true learning' to take place. Other educationalists assert that this is a pedagogical illusion.

denotation. According to **Barthes**, the first order of signification which expresses the most obvious and common-sense meaning of an image, for example. See also **connotation** and **semiotics**.

depth of field. What is in focus between the foreground and background in a photograph or on film. See **F-stop** for more detail.

deregulation. A recent major political and economic development, particularly within the UK, with the ending of strict controls by government on public service broadcasters like the **BBC**, for example. The BBC was conceived, like any other public utility, as being owned and controlled for the general public at large. The TV medium, back in the time of Reith in the 1920s, was considered as too important to be let into private company hands which would simply be controlled by the 'profit principle'. However, more recently it was felt that creating 'internal market' competition afforded greater openness and cost-effectiveness both for the media products made and for the consumers. In any case the consumer, rather than an elite monopolistic corporation, should be allowed to decide what was 'good television'. However, critics of the move towards deregulation and commercialization assert that the overall quality and the 'public service ethos' would become eroded through such lack of intrinsic quality controls.

Other technical influences, particularly the **digital** revolution, will greatly affect the proposed deregulated future of TV in the UK and elsewhere. Commercial TV companies appear to be embracing the digital future because of greater band-width possibilities which would allow even more niche, 'narrow-casting', producing TV scheduling with greater numbers of channels to suit all commercial interests. For example, channels for gardeners and for weather enthusiasts, as well as the more conventional, sports, films, comedy and porn channels. This, however, appears to be at odds with the ethos of **public service broadcasting** (PSB), which demands 'broadcasting' rather than 'narrow-casting' as exemplified above. PSB conventionally means creating a diet of programmes which will maximize audiences (and maintain a cultural homogeneity – a form of national/regional identity) while at the samc time appeal to a full range of minority interests. But with the rise of digital TV and the probability of proliferation of channels, there is a serious danger of an erosion of group/national identity. Digital TV costs a lot of money, so to remain competitive, public service broadcasters have to be highly cost-effective to compete with more commercial and bigger organizations like those funded by Murdoch. Nonetheless deregulation appears to have become the dominant orthodoxy as we move into a new century.

Steemers, J. (1998) *Changing Channels: The Prospects for Television in a Digital World.* University of Luton Press.

determinism. The belief that human behaviour is guided by observable and measurable causes which are predetermined by factors beyond individual power. **Marxist** theory in particular has developed ideas regarding economic and **technological determinism** that affect media production and censorship in particular. Attempting to uncover the various factors which determine change is a continuing pursuit of all strands of historical analysis and has been heavily influenced by Marxists, who privileged economic and ideological determinism as of primary importance.

For example, economic determinism in the film industry would suggest that financial factors are the primary reason in deciding what films get made. This is linked to their implied profitability. On the other hand technological determinism suggests that change and evolution in the media is more driven by innovation and new technology than any other factors; so the films that are made are determined by the technology available at that time.

developing media in education. The historical growth of media degree courses in particular is related to the diversification of A Level syllabi in media, communications and film studies together with the development of BTEC and more recently GNVQ courses. A large proportion of these courses deal directly with the mass media. The BTEC in media and communications develops extensive 'vocational/practical' skills alongside a basic grounding in theoretical analysis which connects with more 'practical'-based degree programmes and HNDs. The GNVQ in media and communications was originally designed to bridge the gap between the theoretical rigour of an A Level syllabus and the more practically designed BTEC courses.

For example, many syllabi focus on the following general areas:

1 Mass media and the modern world (social, cultural and political debates)

2 Mass media (institutions and histories)

3 Mass media (forms and analysis)

4 Mass media (comparisons, change and futures)

These second-level courses concentrate on a critically informed understanding of the history of mass media together with developing competencies in the use of technical equipment which are related to the syllabus as a whole. Difficulties encountered by most syllabi include the perennial one of linking theory and practice and how to tease out a hierarchy of 'factual knowledge' to deliver. Getting the balance between a theoretical underpinning of '**key concepts**' alongside the more immediately rewarding practical application of media production, remains a difficult pedagogical issue within media education.

development education centres (DECs). Small independent organizations working in partnership with teachers to bring a global dimension to the development of the school **curriculum**. Each DEC has a policy of teacher involvement in all aspects of its work and management.

dictionaries. Reference books which usually contain the words of a language arranged in alphabetical order. A glossary like this Guide is a partial dictionary designed for a specific purpose. Media glossaries/dictionaries which have influenced this book include:

Brooker, P. (1999) *A Concise Glossary of Cultural Theory*. Arnold.

Hayward, S. (1996) *Key Concepts in Cinema Studies*. Routledge.

O'Sullivan, T., Hartley, J., Saunders, D., Montgomery, M. and Fiske, J. (1994) *Key Concepts in Communication and Cultural Studies*. Routledge.

Price, S. (1997) *The Complete A–Z Media and Communications Handbook*. Hodder and Stoughton.

Watson, J. and Hill, A. (1991) *A Dictionary of Communication and Media Studies*. Arnold.

Williams, R. (1976) *Keywords: A Vocabulary of Culture and Society*. Fontana.

didactic teaching. Sometimes considered to be an old-fashioned, teacher-centred form of educational instruction where the teacher often engages in whole-class teaching. Recent emphasis has been given by the Department for Education and Employment (DfEE) to the perceived benefits of didactic teaching, for example with respect to numeracy and literacy hours. In common with many forms of education, didactic teaching can be carried out well or badly, leading to either enhanced learning or stagnation.

diegesis. From the Greek word for **narration**, but used regularly in film theory since the 1950s to designate what a film denotes, the narrative itself, but also the fictional space and time dimensions implied in and by the narrative, namely the whole fictional world represented by the film.

An example of non-diegetic sound would include hearing the orchestral music on the sound track. If the orchestra is later actually seen on film playing in the scene, then the music becomes diegetic music/sound.

differentiation. The targeting of teaching and learning materials and pedagogy for different abilities of children. In the broadest sense it can involve applying different educational goals, curriculum structures, subject content, assessment and teaching and learning approaches to different individuals and groups of children. In assessment terms, differentiation refers to the presentation of opportunities for pupils of all abilities to perform appropriately to show what they know, understand and can do. Media studies in particular, because of its diverse subject area and range of assessment tools available, can address this difficult area quite successfully.

digital. As a technical medium of communication has to a large extent overtaken an analogue system and is mathematically reflected by 0s and 1s. Digital transmission of information and signals is faster, takes up less space and is less prone to corruption than analogue transmission. For example, in the **telephony** industry the analogue voice is transferred into digital signals before being reformatted back into analogue signals at the receiving end of the transmission process. With the tremendous growth in mobile phones, internet and text transmission generally, telephony would not be able to cope with this increase in traffic without the use of digital technology. The benefits of digital technology are also being applied to radio and television and are heavily promoted for economic reasons. With CDs and mini-disks now dominating the music industry, compared to old-fashioned records, the push is also on to promote DVD and digital TV in Britain and elsewhere.

Steemers, J. (ed.) (1998) *Changing Channels: The Prospects for Television in a Digital World.* University of Luton Press.

BskyB website: www.sky.com

digital photography. Allows all the benefits of digital technology without needing 'old-fashioned' and much slower chemical developing and printing. This is highly beneficial within the news industry in particular, which demands instant images. Such images can be fed directly to the transmission centre where in turn the digital images can be manipulated before being finally broadcast.

With digital cameras there is no need for such a laborious process since the 'images' can be directly fed into a computer to produce off-prints of high quality colour almost immediately. The benefits of speed are very important for news-rooms and media organizations generally, who can have images fed through almost immediately rather than having to wait for the much slower chemical process to take place. Even more critically from a media context, the hi-tech process is much more malleable, even manipulable. Colours can be changed, size manipulated and, more dangerously, new elements can be added on to the image at will and almost at the touch of a button. So the old and always problematic adage that 'the camera never lies', becomes even more suspect and open to question.

There have been some very contentious cases of news editors abusing the truth of news stories they are presenting by using 'manipulated' or 'doctored' images that present a more dramatic and exciting image for the general public. However, once such images are exposed for what they are, it causes major moral dilemmas within the media industry and particularly questions the **public service** ethos and ethical values of the media in question. **Photojournalists** in particular remain at the centre of such ethical debates. Should they remain detached or become involved if witnessing some horrific incident? What strategies and intentions are acceptable when filming in for example war/famine zones? Is any form of manipulation acceptable and how is such manipulation defined, particularly since they must decide what/how and when to photograph?

Barthes, R. (1984) *Camera Lucida*. Flamingo.

Grunberg, A. (1990) *A Crisis of the Real*. Aperture.

Lister, M. (1995) *The Photographic Image in Digital Culture*. Routledge.

Mitchell, W. J. (1992) *The Reconfigured Eye: Visual Truth in the Post-Photographic Era*. MIT Press.

Ritchin, F. (1990) *In Our Own Image: The Coming Revolution in Photography*. Aperture.

Sontag, S. (1977) *On Photography*. Penguin.

Squiers, C. (1990) *Critical Image*. Bay Press.

Wells, L. (1996) *Photography: A Critical Introduction*. Routledge.

direct address. See **documentary**.

discourse. A fashionable and often over-used term which is difficult to pin down since all forms of communication, particularly languages, involve some form of interactive connection. **Linguistic** theories of discourse are used to analyse popular media texts and how they produce meaning.

Michel **Foucault** has been particularly influential in developing discourse analysis. He asserted that 'dominant discourses' are reinforced by existing systems of law, education and of course the media which again echoes **Althusser**'s theories on **ideological state apparatuses**. Media texts all involve various audiovisual discourses. Colin **MacCabe**, for example, suggests that there is a 'hierarchy of discourses' embedded in Hollywood films just like in classic nineteenth-century novels.

discovery-learning. Occurs where students work out the basic principles of thinking and learning for themselves. This form of learning has clear links to pupil-centred and active-learning approaches adopted in progressive forms of education. Media education, particularly through practical application using media technology of all types, applied discovery-learning methodologies to develop student thinking and learning processes.

discrimination. Unfavourable treatment of groups or individuals based on **prejudice**. In the context of **education** this may mean that the rights of a particular group or individual are infringed, or that someone is favoured over another. Extreme forms of discrimination lead to racism, which has become a growing study particularly with regard to representation and how to encourage 'positive' rather than negative **stereotypes** within media texts.

Disney. One of the largest filmmaking studios, synonymous with making 'classic' children's films/**animation** as well as numerous entertainment pleasure parks in America and even Paris. The studio's extensive output can be divided into two distinct periods: the 'fantasy' of the early period and the 'idealization' of the later, which stand in direct contrast to each other. Experts suggest with the Depression of 1932, there was a definite change in Disney stories, with tales becoming highly moral and everything having direct consequences.

In particular the Disney aesthetic is criticized by many **Marxist** critics as creating an infantile view of life and nature, particularly through the use of **anthropomorphism** – where animals act like humans. Some even go so far as to suggest that films like *Lion King* (1994) have an inherent **fascism** built into the storyline. The extreme popularity of Disney makes many **cultural** critics worry about its effects without always accepting, much less appreciating, the utopic pleasures Disney provides for its global audiences.

Bell, E., Haas, L. and Sells, L. (eds) (1995) *From Mouse to Mermaid: The Politics of Film, Gender, and Culture.* Indiana University Press.

Dorfman, A. (1983) *The Empire's Old Clothes.* Pluto Press.

Schickel, R. (1968) *The Disney Version.* Weidenfeld and Nicolson.

Warner, M. (1994) *'Six Myths of Our Time: Managing Monsters'. The Reith Lectures.* Vintage.

documentary. Generally considered a non-fictional representation of reality. The form has a long history which, according to Bill Nichols, can be traced roughly through four categories:

- **Direct address** follows the classic British tradition emulated by John Grierson, which is typified as 'voice of God' style of documentary-making, where the polemical purpose of the text is fully developed while remaining both didactic and authoritative.

- *Cinéma vérité* was helped by new lightweight technology developed in the 1960s, when filmmakers could more easily go out into the streets without having to carry around heavy equipment and set up studio lights and cameras. This produced an immediacy and a direct impression of capturing raw, unmediated real events. Many exponents regarded this form of filmmaking as transparent, letting the viewer reach their own conclusions without a voice-over to **anchor** and tie down meaning. But critics of this form speak of its surface realism and lack of historical context or multi-layered perspective.

- **Interview** typically involves a character speaking directly to the viewer via a 'professional' interviewer and remains a dominant strategy for documentary up to the present day.

- **Self-reflexive** applies all of the above techniques, but at the same time draws attention to its constructive and manipulative methods by consciously mixing and matching various techniques together.

Aitkin, I. (1990) *Film and Reform: John Grierson and the Documentary Film Movement.* Routledge.

Kilburn, R. and Izod, J. (1997) *An Introduction to Television Documentary: Confronting Reality.* Manchester University Press.

Nichols, B. (1994) *Blurred Boundaries: Representing Reality – Issues and Concepts in Documentary.* Indiana University Press.

Winston, B. (1995) *Claiming the Real: The Documentary Film Revisited.* BFI.

docu-soaps. A relatively recent phenomenon. They owe their success to a skilful blending of the dramatic and audience-pleasing conventions of a soap-opera, and more 'serious' realistic documentary conventions. The first docu-soap in the UK, or as it was then called 'reality TV', was made 25 years ago. *The Family*, which was conceived by Paul Watson, followed the lives of a real family for a whole year.

Many critics suggest its phenomenal growth was due to its relative cheapness and easy formula. At its height in the late 1990s there was a wide range of variations in production or on air across the terrestrial channels in Britain. To find an organization (hotel, ship, vet's practice, etc.), and 'follow' the lives of characters who do their everyday job, was the apparent simplistic formula and structure. Higher ratings went to the package which produced the greatest surfeit of tension and most volatile likeable/dislikeable characters: in particular *Hotel*, *Driving School*, *Vets in Practice*. However, more recently the format appears to be losing its appeal, especially on **BBC**, where they have become most prolific. This is aided by an over-saturation of the form and continuing criticism of their low **cultural** value as compared to 'serious' **documentary** production, which remains at odds with the **public service broadcasting** (PSB) ethos.

dominant ideology. Usually applied as a shorthand for Western **capitalism**, together with the dominance of **patriarchy**. See **ideology** for more details.

www.theory.org
www.aber.ac.uk

dumbing down. The way entertainment providers seek to maximize audiences by appealing to the lowest common denominator. Instead of a wide variety of media products which appeal to as many niche audiences as possible, particularly the quality end of the market, such a phenomenon suggests that nothing too difficult or unconventional and challenging gets produced. Few risks are taken, with schedulers relying on the safety of endless repeats and commercially driven topics specifically involving sex and violence.

The term is used as a shorthand to suggest that the culture industries are pandering to cheap exploitation and formulaic production processes. As part of this debate, **public service broadcasters** are most severely criticized, since they are not supposed to be controlled by commercial pressures to produce large audiences, a strategy which is not always predicated on 'quality' and 'originality'. Often they are criticized for churning out **soaps** and more recently **docu-soaps** as exemplary of this dumbing-down process.

Mosley, I. (ed.) (1999) *Dumbing Down: Culture, Politics and the Mass Communication.* Bowling Green Press.

E

economic imperative. A term used in media education to highlight the central importance of economic pressures on the development of media. See also **technological determinism, horizontal/vertical integration** and **Marxism** in particular, which highlights this phenomenon.

education. A complex term which is often applied generically to the diverse processes and activities associated with learning. Education implies improvement, nurture and development and should be defensible as a worthwhile activity; it therefore differs from instruction and training, which may not involve making the learner a 'better person'. Some definitions of education also highlight its role in the acquisition, conservation and renewal of worthwhile culture. Media educators in particular have evolved from within what many consider an idealistic or even utopian notion of empowerment for all children with regard to their relationship with the media environment which permeates all our lives. (See Introduction and **Why study the media?**)

Education (Schools) Act (1992). Required UK schools and local education authorities to publish league tables of their examination performance and introduced the principle of school inspections. A later Education Act (1997) established the Qualifications and Curriculum Authority (QCA) by merging the National Council for Vocational Qualifications (NCVQ) with the School Curriculum and Assessment Authority (SCAA).

effects theory. See **TV and effects theory**.

Eisenstein, Sergei. One of the most influential theorists and practical filmmakers of all time. Aside from his many notable films, he also continues to influence film and media practice. He created a form of editing using various types of **montage**, which involves linking images together to create new radical meanings. For example films like *Strike* (1924) dramatized Russian workers rising up against their oppressors. His technique can be illustrated by the example of cutting from images of a stone statue to a crowd and back again to show the statue of the lion magically transform with two legs rising-up after being supine in the earlier shot. The scene is then edited with a crowd running towards the camera, which helped create, for Eisenstein, the visual signifier of a crowd rising-up and rebelling. Another equally famous sequence which is continuously analysed to teach the grammar of cinema is the steps sequence in *Battleship Potemkin* (1925) – natives fleeing from the regimented marching army descending the steps. Tension and drama are packed into this highly choreographed sequence.

Eisenstein has become a required study particularly for the **avant-garde**, for his radical experiments on the political use of the film medium. Yet there is some dispute concerning his later, more operatic film productions like *Ivan the Terrible* (1944–6). Recent biographies like David **Bordwell**'s assert that the magic of such a text, which he also eulogizes, is in many ways equivalent to the otherwise bourgeois aesthetic of romantic Hollywood.

Bordwell, D. (1996) *The Cinema of Eisenstein.* Harvard University Press.

For an introduction to Eisenstein, see Mark Joyce's essay on Russian cinema in the 1920s, in Nelmes, J. (ed.) (1996) *An Introduction to Film Studies.* Routledge.

electronic media. Includes all mass media transmitted through wires and other forms of signals. Even publishing is becoming more and more electronic, especially on the internet. Other more recent technological innovations like CD-Roms, teletext, databases and video disks have also extended the scope of electronic media.

electronic news gathering (ENG). Uses lightweight digital video cameras rather than film cameras to feed live pictures directly back to studios. Such a method has made news programmes more capable of broadcasting live from anywhere in the world. As long as there is the possibility of a satellite link-up, TV programmes can be transmitted from anywhere.

ellipsis. In film studies, some part of a sequence that audiences might expect to see being left out, thereby condensing or altering an action in some way, in time or space. Of course, all editing manipulates time and space, but **continuity editing** makes such manipulation appear smooth and avoids any sudden **jump-cut** which could be described as an unannounced ellipsis in time or space.

empiricism. Proves something through experience or experimentation. Philosophers have applied the term extensively in their attempts to understand the world. For media practitioners the notion is central particularly for practical research which involves trying to find out 'objective' evidence rather than simply relying on generalizations and hypotheses about how the mass media might affect the general public, for example. Scientific experimentation and rigour is not always possible when analysing human behaviour regarding the media. For example, an empirical experiment which seeks to prove a media **effects theory** that children are more aggressive after consuming 'violent' cartoons, begs many questions. What is meant by 'violent', and how do you measure it – both before and after the introduction of the stimulus? Even more philosophical questions and assumptions connected with the **nature/nurture** debate, for instance, should also be taken into consideration before findings can be validated.

Nonetheless, I would suggest much media theory remains 'woolly' and full of over-generalizations which could possibly be refined or even discounted by appropriate empirical research. Consequently, primary research is often necessary to underpin educational learning and to help question and problematize a range of given assumptions.

empower. The notion of empowering has been used by media analysts such as **feminists** to explore how media texts and representations in particular serve to encourage female audiences to take strength and encouragement from such representations. For example *Thelma and Louise* (1991) is sometimes read as a film which represents the strength of women within a male genre fighting an unflinching **patriarchal** system. Critics, however, have difficulty with the **closure** of the movie, which has divided audiences. How can consciously choosing suicide as an escape from the clutches of the police be regarded as empowering? Some critics even go so far as to imagine the reaction if it was two men rather than women holding hands, as they drove towards the cliff face! Consequently this notion is highly contested yet frequently called upon within film and media analysis.

encoding. Giving expression to a communication message in a coherent language, which can then be decoded by audiences. For example, to construct a film, a script is usually visualized with the help of actors as well as the application of various technical, generic or even symbolic devices. It is then finally decoded by mass audiences, who view the finished product. In a very famous essay entitled 'Encoding/Decoding', Stuart **Hall** explores how messages are encoded within texts and decoded by audiences.

Hall, S. (1980) *Culture, Media, Language.* Hutchinson.

Price, S. (1993) *Media Studies.* Longman.

encryption. The creation of codes, usually to protect computer information so that any user needs the correct 'key' before they can access the information. However, especially with regard to the **internet**, there is a growing underground culture of hackers who seek to dismantle any form of secrecy and even get their kicks out of breaking codes. Consequently code-making has to be designed and reconstituted through even more complex procedures.

environmentalism. The philosophical and practical protection of all the flora and fauna of our planet so that life can be sustained. Such an issue has become very influential across all media formats. The political and intellectual movement which sought to protect our planet came into existence initially in the West as a result of 'fear of the bomb' alongside other radiation and pollution fears which particularly came to light within the counter-cultural 1960s.

Rachael Carson's *Silent Spring* is often cited as the first piece of research which showed a link between the use of a well-known pesticide, DDT, and human infection. Recognizing the precarious interrelationship between species on the planet, particularly the role of humans in upsetting the ecological harmony of nature, helped to create the radical new idea of a holistic approach to nature and life which has helped spawn the modern environment movement.

Like many popular concepts it has grown to mean often contradictory ideas. In crude terms, ecology can be divided up into two broad categories: 'light' ecological expression, which suggests a gentle reworking of priorities to ensure the planet is protected; and the more extreme and radical 'deep' ecological expression which demands total transformation of ideological values and philosophies.

What has this to do with media studies? Because of the tremendous interest in environmental issues, many young people in particular appear to be more interested in protecting the planet rather than conventional **political** activity. An example is the *Blue Peter* phenomenon on children's BBC and its continuing fascination with ecological issues. Many now consider that representations of environmental issues have become the most important touchstone of ideological/political expression for audiences in the West. How the mass media are used to articulate and mobilize public opinion is central to politics and reflection study.

Environmentalism has become a forum to address and articulate a huge raft of world issues which are becoming more and more contentious as the planet becomes more and more mediated by TV cameras. For example, the global 'Live Aid' phenomenon, spearheaded by the Irish pop singer Bob Geldof back in the 1980s, gave popular music culture a voice in the global economy – even if cynically regarded as a soft liberal expression of Western guilt-alleviation towards poverty in the Third World. At least such environmental and economic issues became foregrounded with the aid of the world's powerful media and were seen as a global problem not just an African one. In spite of the often patronizing representation of poverty, more recent charity events have helped to develop less stereotypical images of such peoples and have even begun to articulate what Ulrich Beck calls the 'Risk society', which exposes how otherwise localized problems affect all human life on this planet.

The environmental disasters dramatized particularly in a number of 'pre-millennial-tension' films often involve global destruction, such as in *Deep Impact* (1999), where the threat to humans does not respect national borders. Marshall **McLuhan**'s often-dismissed notion of the 'global village', which he believed would be created as a consequence of the mass media – where nowhere on the planet would be out of sight – has in fact become a reality.

Hollywood cinema has also used the environmental movement as a 'feel-good' narrative device which nonetheless expresses many important issues. Sometimes Hollywood film even pushes the boundaries of ecological expression by constructing utopic/dystopic environments, allowing a greater appreciation and representation of the holistic nature of all biotic ecologies as conventionally expressed in films like *Emerald Forest* (1985).

Beck, U. et al. (1997) *The Reinvention of Politics: Rethinking Modernity in the Global Social Order.* Polity Press.

Chapman, G., Kumar, K., Fraser, C. and Gaber, I. (1997) *Environmentalism and the Mass Media: The North-South Divide.* Routledge.

Dobson, A. (1990) *Green Political Thought.* Routledge.

Glotfelty, C. and Fromm, H. (1996) *The Ecocriticism Reader: Landmarks in Literary Ecology.* University of Georgia Press.

equilibrium/disequilibrium. Equilibrium is a state of balance within some structure and is used in narrative film theory through Todorov's analysis of a **narrative** structure, which is applied by **Bordwell** to explain how narratives 'work'. In Hollywood film, such narratives begin with an exposition of order (equilibrium) – setting out the scene, explaining where/when the film is set and who the main characters are. After this brief exposition of character and place a 'disruption' (or disequilibrium) occurs, when something happens to break the normal equilibrium. For example, someone gets killed, a relationship is broken up or some other disruption is caused which has to be resolved. Finally after a series of mini-crises and resolutions, by the **closure** of the film there is a return to a state of equilibrium again, though often of a different kind from the start of the narrative.

essay. A formal means of testing knowledge and comprehension which is used extensively at all levels of education. Added difficulties within media essays include the breadth of discourses and approaches which can be taken and the dangers of degenerating into relativism and common-sense assertions which ignore the range of discursive debates which should be addressed or at least recognized if higher grades are demanded. As in all humanities subjects, attitudes, values, beliefs and positions taken in essays need to be anchored in research and substantive evidence of reading and engagement with texts using the various theories and conceptual methodologies applied within the curriculum. While such material should not be slavishly applied, ignoring such debates can lead to poorer grades.

But finished essays must read well and flow naturally, with a solid structure which addresses the question asked, and provide relevant and cogent examples. So many essays students produce could be improved by more careful drafting, making examples more explicit and relevant, and linking ideas together more smoothly. Students should think of themselves like Spock in *Star Trek* when writing an essay and remain ordered and most importantly coldly logical. You cannot jump around the place, which is so easy with such a wide, all-encompassing subject like media, where it is relatively easy to evoke ideas and opinions.

At a formal level so many students continue to tell the story of the film they are analysing rather than detailing *how* and *why* the narrative functions as it does, which is more often relevant than the more basic *what* happens. Like all skills, essay writing demands practice and a logical process to ensure students become better at what remains highly important in this so-called (post)literate culture. One of the best study guides, by Andrew Northedge, suggests a seven-stage approach:

1 Thinking about the essay title

2 Gathering together material for the essay (the most time-consuming part)

3 Getting some ideas on paper

4 Organizing the material

5 Writing a first draft

6 Reviewing your work in the light of the essay title

7 Writing the final draft (I suggest a few drafts helps!)

Northedge, A. (1992) *The Good Study Guide*. Open University Press.

estrangement. When audiences are not encouraged to identify with the protagonists in the drama. The term was popularized by **Brecht** in the theatre to ensure actors did not become simply identified with by the audience, which he believed led to an inability to appreciate the intellectual message of a text. Hollywood and mainstream audiences, he argued, 'wallowed' in and became hypnotized by the actor's performance and could not see through their surface presentation. This form of identification and total immersion in character was promoted by **Stanislavsky** and the **'method' school of acting** that developed his ideas in New York. The aim was to get actors to totally empathize and almost become the character they were playing. This method came to dominate Hollywood.

By contrast, Brecht sought to get actors to 'stand outside' the personae in which they were acting and attempt to get audiences to almost 'see through them' or at least come to appreciate how they were manipulating them. To do this Brecht used acting techniques like getting his performers to suddenly and without warning wink at the audience for example, thus breaking the spell of their performance and allowing audiences to become 'estranged' and thereby appreciate the game that was being played. Such acting techniques were used most particularly within **avant-garde** film, which sought to counter the dominance of Hollywood and wished to highlight the political and critical function of film as a communications medium.

ethics. See **media ethics**.

ethnography. Study of the way of life of a people or culture which comes from **anthropology** and often involves some form of direct observation. Ethnographic studies of media audiences have become very popular, with researchers attempting to discover more specific details concerning audience behaviour and attitudes, for example. They usually involve in-depth analysis and observation and are often used to complement more quantitative, empirical research into audiences.

Morley, D. (1992) *Television Audiences and Cultural Studies*. Routledge.

Willis, P. (1990) *Common Culture*. Open University Press.

evaluation. An assessment of the value and quality of education, or of an individual's educational experience and attainment. The effectiveness of the teaching and learning process is often central to educational evaluation, although if too closely linked to assessment it may be considered too narrow to give a realistic judgement. Evidence for evaluation can come from a variety of sources and may involve complex qualitative measures of educational experience such as interviews of teachers and pupils. Evaluation can occur with respect to the curriculum, a lesson taught or student attainment.

The companion Guide, *The Continuum Guide to Geography Education*, provides a comprehensive model for evaluation in education:

1. Aims	Were the aims of your lesson wholly or partly achieved?
	Did you manage to cover the media content of the lesson?
	Could pupils understand and use the media knowledge and skills you introduced?
	What do you think the pupils learnt?
2. Methods	Did you have success with the various methods used?
	-question and answer technique
	-visuals, OHP, video
	-pair work, group work
	-games, role plays, simulations
	-teacher-led sessions
	-etc.
3. Management	Was the start and finish of the lesson orderly?
	Was the change of activities orderly?
	Were pupils organized into effective learning (groups)?
	Were your instructions clear?
	Did you cope with interruptions?
	Did you create a positive learning atmosphere?
	Was prior preparation of resources sufficient?
4. Control/discipline	Type and use of reward/praise (smile, look, encouragement)
	Type and use of censure (look, talk, action)
	Tone and approach adopted towards class and individuals

Stuart Price also suggests the following questions should be asked in a self-assessment evaluation:

- Was the project chosen relevant to a particular audience?
- Was the project enquiry focused through the use of a problematic or hypothesis?
- Had all relevant sources of information been identified and edited?
- Were the most suitable methods of textual research used?

- Were the most useful forms of audience research selected?
- Were all alternative decisions and courses of action analysed?
- Was the social and ideological context of the communications process understood?
- Was the project tested on an audience?
- Was a synopsis provided for the guidance of the reader?

(Price 1997, p. 85)

Butt, G. (2000) *The Continuum Guide to Geography Education*. Continuum.

Price, S. (1997) *The Complete A–Z Media and Communication Handbook*. Hodder and Stoughton.

examination. A test of student attainment including knowledge, understanding and skills, usually by means of written and/or oral questions. An external examination is conducted by a body established to assess student attainment and award certification but which has not been involved in their teaching.

New and innovative types of examination are being used in media education which include computerised exams particularly with the development of GNVQ media. But there has always been some resistance to formalized exams with critics claiming students would simply regurgitate notes. Because the subject is often predicated on a core concepts approach that encourages debate and discourse, many practitioners resisted the use of what were regarded as 'closed' and ultimately reductive forms of assessment.

Nonetheless, to gain legitimacy, computerized exams, especially with GNVQ, became extensively used, which often required students to choose the correct answer out of a small choice of options. New and improved methods of computerized examination are being developed in the UK by consortia including Luton University.

exemplar. Provides an example of something, possibly within an overall structure of key ideas and concepts represented in a scheme of work, specification or curriculum.

experiential learning. The process of learning through direct, concrete experiences rather than through more traditional, formal means of transmission of knowledge by teacher and text. The strategy of learning has remained a founding principle in media education, which continues to get students to experience an audiovisual text first-hand and apply their own **cultural competencies** towards responding creatively and with guidance from the teacher to the text.

exposé. When something out of the ordinary is brought into the public domain by some media form; for example, a news item which exposes sensitive or secret information. The resultant story must fit in with the **news values** of the media organization in question. Investigative journalists are often looking for a so-called 'scoop' which will make the news and hopefully make them famous.

expressive language. A form used in writing and speech which is personal and exploratory. Sometimes referred to as 'thinking aloud', expressive language tends to reveal what the writer (or speaker) feels or believes, uninhibited by the more structured and formal patterns of language often seen in the transactional mode. Media students constructing presentation reports for controversial debates often use this style of writing.

extra-personal communication. See **communication**.

F

F-stop. The size of the lens opening in a camera. The number on the lens indicates how far the aperture is open, and thus how much light can pass through the lens onto the unexposed film. Remember, the bigger the number, the smaller the amount of light getting in, because of the reduced size of the opening.

F1   F1.4   F2   F2.8   F4   F5.6   F8   F11   F16   F22
(the largest opening)   (the smallest opening)

Each stop difference doubles or halves the amount of light let through the lens. For example F5.6 lets in twice the amount of light of F8 and half that of F4.

Also, there is a correlation between **depth of field** and F-stop; the bigger the number, the greater the depth of field. Photographers and cinematographers have always to be aware of the relationship between film-stock used (which has a particular light sensitivity), the lighting available, the shutter speed (length of time the film is exposed to light) and the F-stop. While all this appears overly complex, many cameras automatically determine the appropriate levels to expose the film correctly. But students need to be able to manipulate such variables if they are to become 'creative' and 'innovative', and therefore it is often more appropriate to use manual cameras for these reasons.

For basic details of technical terms regarding film/photography, look at 'A Glossary of Film Terms' on Rosebud: A digital resource for film studies – www.inform.umd.edu/rosebud/glossary/index.

fairytales. Stories told to children over the centuries which resurface and pervade popular culture and are retold for a modern audience. For example, *Pretty Woman* (1990) is a reworking of the Cinderella story; *Star Wars* (1977), like many other blockbusters, recycles old heroic legends, myths and fairytales which become relevant for new audiences within popular culture. Cultural critics suggest that such tales told to children are often ways to impart moral and social norms to a new generation. For example the 'Little

Red Riding Hood' story warns little girls in particular against talking to strange men and not to 'stray from the path'.

A Russian writer, Vladimir **Propp**, produced an analysis of 100 Russian folktales which he discovered had a consistent number of elements, and applied these to extrapolate a **narrative** theory.

Warner, M. (1994) 'Six Myths of our Time: Managing Monsters' – The Reith Lectures. Vintage.

false consciousness. A highly contentious **ideological** term which is often used as a term of derision against groups who cannot see through the ideological manipulation used upon them. At an extreme level it is asserted that the inarticulate under-class is most at risk of being manipulated by the mass media. Some critics go so far as to suggest that this was the primary *raison d'être* for the evolution of media studies – to '**demystify**' the power of the media. However, it is more appropriate to argue that the subject now takes a broad overview which seeks to uncover general manipulation of all types against all media subjects.

That the general public and students in particular must be taught to resist the power of the media, became the subtextual agenda of early media educationalists, who sought to guard against the danger of 'false consciousness'. Only the academic investigator could perceive the truth, with the 'victims' remaining the inarticulate under-classes! (Of course this is a crass, even objectionable over-simplification of the debate, but it certainly dramatizes many of the inherent complaints within ideological analysis.)

See **Masterman** and a range of **ideological** debates for a greater appreciation of this much-abused term.

fantasy. Based on imaginative re-creation, it can be contrasted with **realism** and 'realistic' representation, which remains a central core concept for studying media. For instance many critics, including Trauffaut and much later V. R. Perkins in his seminal study *Film is Film* (1972), suggest that since its beginnings, film has always been pulled in two opposing directions: realism and fantasy. The rules of realistic representation were begun by the filmmaker Lumière and his 'Train Entering a Station' film (which reputedly was so 'realistic' for its audience that they hid under their seats as the projected train came towards the front of the screen!). This preoccupation with **documentary** realism has continued to the present time in film and television in particular. The fantasy direction began with the magic of Méliès and his 'Journey to the Moon'; **surrealism**, for example, and the proliferation of science fiction fantasy have remained indebted to this strand of cinema.

Perkins, V. F. (1972) Film is Film: Understanding and Judging Movies. Penguin.

fascism. An extreme **right-wing** form of political activity which promotes a very powerful leader and suppresses democratic rights and freedoms, as with Mussolini in Italy and Hitler in Germany. The dangers of such an ideology were instrumental in the development of the **social responsibility model** of the media which helped define **public service broadcasting** (PSB). See in particular the discussion of the rise of fascism in **German propaganda**.

feminism. Literature which recognizes the misrepresentation of females both in actual public life and within media representations, and uses their writings to articulate and respond to such **ideological** effects. Feminism became very popular with the rise of the counter-cultural movement in the 1960s, when women's issues were considered an important civil rights issue in the same way as **race** was regarded. Within education, feminist discourse has become a major force for analysis for all aspects of communication media.

Feminist theory has in fact been central to the evolution of media education across various strands of investigation. In particular, ideological analysis of media products and the preoccupation with power inequalities and politics naturally focused on gender issues and how the media reflect social, cultural and historical realities. The study of **representation** in particular is often predicated along gender lines.

Laura Mulvey's (1975) seminal essay 'Visual Pleasure and Narrative Cinema' is probably the most cited reference within media analysis. Her construction of the notion of the 'male gaze' to articulate the voyeuristic nature of Hollywood cinema, which she subsequently amended to accommodate 'female pleasure', remains potent in media/film analysis.

Some key texts which reflect feminist debate, cited in date order:

Dyer, R. and Geraghty, C. et al. (1981) *Coronation St.* BFI.

Hobson, D. (1982) *Cross Roads: The Drama of a Soap Opera.* Methuen.

Kuhn, A. (1982) *Women's Pictures: Feminism and the Cinema.* Pandora.

Modleski, T. (1984) *Loving with a Vengeance.* Methuen.

Radway, J. (1984) *Reading the Romance: Woman, Patriarchy and Popular Literature.* Verso.

Ang, I. (1985) *Watching Dallas: Soap Opera and the Melodramatic Imagination.* Methuen.

Brunsdon, C. (ed.) (1986) *Films for Women.* BFI.

Buckingham, D. (1987) *Public Secrets: EastEnders and its Audience.* BFI.

Gledhill, C. (ed.) (1987) *Home Is Where the Heart Is: Studies in Melodrama and the Women's Film.* BFI.

Pribram, E.D. (1988) *Female Spectators.* Verso.

Seiter, E. et al. (1989) *Remote Control: Television, Audiences and Cultural Power.* Routledge.

Geraghty, C. (1991) *Women and Soap Opera.* Polity Press.

film A Level syllabus. Has had a long association with the Welsh **awarding body**. Film studies has been accepted into the academic mainstream more readily because of its apparent coherence and academic rigour, and many theories and methodologies associated with its study have also permeated media studies. Since the beginning of so-called art cinema, film appreciation clubs began to spring up across the UK and elsewhere which privileged the development of discriminative viewing as opposed to what was considered the populist Hollywood product. But with the propagation of 'auteur theory' in the 1950s it became acceptable to appreciate 'factory-produced' Hollywood films by directors like Hitchcock, Welles and Ford, together with more conventional non-American art filmmakers.

film noir. Describes films made in the 1940s and 1950s which used low-lighting techniques and tended to be thrillers and detectives reflecting the 'dark side' of American society. The **lighting** style was aided by German émigrés who had worked on 'expressionist' films which used lighting highly creatively unlike more conventional Hollywood 'three-point-lighting'. Lots of shadows also meant that films could be shot cheaply, which in many ways added to the effect. Critics have endlessly debated whether it is a **genre** or an overarching style of filmmaking. The form became popular again in the 1990s within colour variations and was dubbed 'neo-noir'.

Grant, K.G. (ed.) (1997) *Film Genre Reader 2.* University of Austin Texas.

fine grain. Fine-grain analysis promotes a deep textual approach to writing about film and the arts generally which is in danger of elevating the quality of writing and analysis to an elitist level of value. This analytical technique echoes the Leavisite debate which sought to construct a canon of important texts which prioritize 'value' and 'quality' and could be used to inoculate students against the pernicious influences of 'cheap' popular culture. Critics like V. R. Perkins and others promote the reappraisal of the function of textual analysis above and beyond ideological and psychological mapping of texts. In a recent film conference on 'Style and Meaning' at Reading University (1999), it became apparent that many film theorists wish to reassert this form of textual analysis.

Perkins, V. R. (1972) *Film is Film: Understanding and Judging Movies.* Penguin.

Fiske, John. One of the most widely read theorists of **popular culture**. He argues in *Understanding Popular Culture* (1989) how it is the culture of the subordinated and disempowered which always bears within it signs of power relations and the forces of domination and subordination. Equally, however, popular culture also shows signs of resisting or evading these forces. Fiske remains optimistic with regard to the power of audiences to subvert dominant culture and suggests that despite nearly two centuries of capitalism, subordinated cultures continue to exist and refuse finally to be incorporated into the dominant ideology.

Fiske asserts that if critics totally accept an all-powerful ideological model, then mass culture is imposed upon a powerless and passive people by a culture industry whose interests are in direct opposition to audiences. Fiske takes a middle ground, promoting popular culture as a site of struggle (endorsing Gramsci's notion of **hegemony**) and finding optimism in the vigour and vitality of audiences. Popular culture, according to Fiske, is not just about consumption but remains an active process of generating and circulating meanings and pleasures within a social system. Culture remains a living, active process and cannot be imposed from without or above. Few critics would disagree, however, that the primary motivation of popular culture involves creating marketable pleasure for audiences. This remains the bedrock assumption of a Marxist critique of the media. Nevertheless, as a cultural theorist, Fiske particularly focuses on the pleasure of producing one's own meaning of social experience and the pleasure of avoiding the social discipline of an ideological controlling power apparatus.

Fiske extensively cites various popular icons for analysis, including Levi jeans as a fashion icon. He has also championed **Madonna** the singer (not the religious icon), who became extremely popular within cultural analysis, with degree programmes being created devoted to her multimedia representation.

Fiske, J. and Hartley, J. (1978) *Reading Television.* Methuen.

Fiske, J. (1982) *Introduction to Communications Studies.* Methuen.

Fiske, J. et al. (1987) *Myths of Oz: Reading Australian Popular Culture.* Allen and Unwin.

Fiske, J. (1987) *Television Culture.* Routledge.

Fiske, J. (1989) *Understanding Popular Culture.* Unwin Hyman.

Fiske, J. (1989) *Reading the Popular.* Unwin Hyman.

Fiske, J. (1993) *Power Plays, Power Works.* Verso.

Fiske, J. (1994) *Media Matters.* University of Minnesota Press.

fitness for purpose. A measure of the fitness of **assessment** for the purpose to which it is put. The choice of the form of assessment strategy adopted to collect evidence of attainment must fit the purpose for which it is used.

focus groups. Tightly selected representative groups of people who typify an audience/group of consumers and who are analysed to discover changing attitudes, beliefs or values, etc. They have become very popular recently with political parties like New Labour in the UK. They were first used over 50 years ago by Robert Merton to find out detailed information, using audience research on targeted groups of individuals chosen because of their representative importance. At present they are much favoured by film companies and **advertising** agencies to determine the most appropriate media stimulus to use in advertising campaigns, for example. Social scientists of course use a range of research methods to observe the **effects** of the media, but focus groups can help to overcome the division between qualitative and quantitative research by effectively combining the two methods.

Morrison, D. E. (1998) *The Search for a Method: Focus Groups and the Development of Mass Communication Research.* University of Luton Press.

formative assessment. Involves providing feedback from assessment that can be used for educational purposes. Formative assessment is part of daily teaching and learning and aims to further the educational progress of students by providing helpful information about what they know, understand and can do. Consequently it is diagnostic while using both formal and informal assessment methods.

Foucault, Michel (1926–84). A French **post-structuralist** who has been very influential in a range of disciplines, including criminology, mental illness, history and language. His influence on media studies comes most directly from his work on power/**ideology** and **discourse** theory. His major studies include *Madness and Civilisation*; *The Order of Things* and *Discipline and Punish*.

In *Madness and Civilisation*, his first major work, he uses the language of structuralism to understand mental illness and its deep structures of meaning within culture. Later in *The Order of Things* he analyses three discrete historical eras: 'the Renaissance (which saw words as things), the Classical age (which saw words as representations of things) and the Modern (which saw words as autonomous, self referring entities with no external relations whatsoever)' (Parker and Sim 1997, p. 84). In *Discipline and Punish*, which owes a lot to Nietzschean philosophy, Foucault explores how all penal reform involves the discovery of new techniques for regulating forms of punishment. At the same time there are continuous developments in surveillance techniques to control public actions alongside internal controls which continue to normalize behaviour.

Parker, N. and Sim, S. (eds) (1997) *The A/Z Guide to Modern Social and Political Theorists*. Prentice Hall.

fourth estate. A term derived from the French republic, which regarded the media as an essential antidote to the primary estates or power structures controlling society. The fourth estate has come to suggest the role of the press/mass media as a counter power-bloc to ensure the other estates are not misusing their power. The notion underpins the idealism of **public service broadcasting**. For example, journalists in the **BBC** or on ITV regard themselves as representing the ordinary person in the street when they question politicians who sometimes evade telling the whole truth. This combative form of interviewing – perfected by the late Sir Robin Day of the BBC – is driven by a belief system which regards the media as having a central role in protecting the rights of the general public and exposing unscrupulous people in positions of power. Investigative journalism in particular is central to this function of the press.

Curran, J. and Seaton, J. (1997) *Power without Responsibility*. Routledge.

Frankfurt School. Founded in 1923 in Germany for social research. The school's leading thinkers included **Marxists** like Marcuse, Fromm, Adorno and Horkheimer, who had to leave Germany with the rise of Hitler and moved to America. They produced what has come to be known as '**critical theory**', which emphasized the **ideological** power of capitalism aided by the growth of the 'culture' industries. In many ways, therefore, they can be regarded as the first contemporary media theorists, who consolidated Marxist theories regarding the media. Such critics often remained highly pessimistic regarding the power of the media to manipulate audiences, obviously influenced by the pernicious propaganda power of Nazis over the media in Germany. However, they went on to regard the so-called 'free' American media as even more potentially dangerous. Their writings have remained highly influential on all aspects of media and **cultural studies**.

free press model. Defines how the media should function within a society as a most valuable agency for protecting democratic rights and responsibilities and therefore should not have legal and other governmental constraints put upon it. One of the most powerful examples of a 'free press' is America, which has the notion of freedom inscribed in its written constitution and demands freedom of expression and the outlawing of most forms of censorship.

The debate focuses on what is in the 'public interest' and what is not. For example, if a politician is having an affair yet espouses 'family values', are the media ethically correct in printing reports of such affairs? Or if the son of a government minister is found smoking illegal drugs, should such a story be used? All media news editors have major ethical dilemmas like this to decide on a regular basis. Many critics in the UK particularly consider that complaints regarding privacy are not dealt with effectively in spite of various government reports. In countries like America, which is legally controlled by a written constitution that guarantees the right of free speech, journalists apparently have greater rights of public expression. This can be exemplified in the infamous case when two *Washington Post* journalists uncovered evidence that helped to bring down President Nixon, and which became known as the **Watergate scandal**. This crisis is explored in the film *All the President's Men* (1976). Before the publication of contentious stories, newspapers and other media always have to weigh up the possibility of a libel suit which might be lost and the prospect of hefty compensations, compared with the kudos of publishing a story and hopefully increased circulation.

Snoddy, R. (1993) *The Good, the Bad and the Unacceptable*. Faber and Faber.

Freire, Paulo. An influential teacher and an advocate for the third world who focused on the necessity of any pedagogy to be based on lived experience. Consequently teaching strategies using his ideas seek to apply and call upon students' pleasures and experiences which have become a dominant underpinning approach to media education. Through the validation of students' personal experience, strategies can be developed which actively address models of consumption and focus on engagement with media texts at all levels.

functionalism. A sociological approach to the study of communication which has been highly influential in America particularly – through writers like Emile Durkheim and Talcott Parsons. They suggested that various sections in society serve clear purposes within society as a whole. In many ways communications within society are determined and defined in terms of their effectiveness and efficiency.

functions of the media. Many media theorists seek to defend the overall aims of the media apparatus which include:

1 Surveillance of the world to report ongoing events

2 Interpretation of the meaning of events

3 Socialization of individuals into their cultural settings

4 Deliberate manipulation of the political process.

As a result the primary media questions which need to be asked include the following:

- Who is **addressing** who and why?
- What **narratives** are told?
- How are **representations** of class, gender, race and age employed and often normalized within the text?

O'Sullivan, T. *et al.* (1994) *Studying the Media: An Introduction.* Edward Arnold.

Price, S. (1993) *Media Studies.* Longman.

G

game show. A popular 'light entertainment' television or radio show which usually involves a gamesmaster(s) asking questions and/or getting contestants to carry out some activity which is rewarded if done correctly. Such shows range from the very competitive *Who Wants to Be a Millionaire* to the parodic **postmodern** send-up by the comedy duo Reeves and Mortimer, *Shooting Stars*, which makes fun of the conventions of a game show and even its celebrity guests. Because of its popularity within broadcast media and often its relative cheapness to produce, such a sub-genre has often been dismissed by cultural critics. However, its ideological and entertainment value and popularity has encouraged more academic study particularly by students who often choose this format for practical assignments.

Fiske, J. (1987) *Television Culture*. Routledge.

Goodwin, A. and Whannel, G. (1990) *Understanding Television*. Routledge.

gate-keeping. A term used in media studies to explain control mechanisms which are used within media organizations which often restrict what is brought into the public arena. For instance, the role of a news editor involves deciding what stories are finally used. A small percentage of stories can be 'spiked' (old newsroom convention: stories which were not used were placed on a spike). Journalists, however, quickly learn the boundaries of what is acceptable, and it is claimed that there is a strong possibility of 'self-censorship' by such journalists to avoid having their stories spiked. Other gate-keepers include proprietors who try to protect their commercial and political interests by manipulating their editors and other staff. In fact at each stage in the process of production of a media text, there are important gate-keepers who can help to manipulate the original source material. Nonetheless, such gate-keepers are often necessary, both as a quality-control mechanism and to ensure the finished mediated product meets legal and other requirements demanded of the organization and the industry.

gender. Focuses on the socially and culturally defined differences between men and women – whereas sex is the biologically determined difference. Early **feminist** research focused on the ways girls were socialized through media representations into endorsing often passive stereotypes of behaviour and agency. More recent research traces how excessive forms of masculinity as displayed by strong action heroes often serves to question masculine roles within Western culture. Gender identity politics, in particular, has become a growth industry and a major case study project within media studies. Textual analysis also focuses on the 'gendered' appeal of media products and how **audiences** of men and women decode texts differently. While soaps and melodramas are crudely regarded as 'passive', female-addressed texts, action movies and even the news are considered 'active', male-addressed texts.

genre. A French term which means a type or category. Genre study and analysis remains a primary means of categorizing subsections of media output which thereby helps the media industry, audiences and of course students of media to perceive differences between the various codes and conventions within different genres. As in any discipline, the ability to break down subgroups into categories is essential for their study and interpretation. This is most essential in mass media with so much product spread across the various media areas. For example, with television there are genres like soaps, news, sports, etc.

A primary debate within genre analysis focuses on whether it is either a formulaic straightjacket which therefore restricts creativity particularly for the makers of media products, or alternatively if such **codes** and **conventions** are a necessary system of categorization, a template/blueprint/palette of expression which allows communication and meaning to be exchanged between mass audiences and individual texts. It is suggested for instance that producers/directors need such a template to frame the unwieldy creative production process and audiences need the knowledge of such conventions to find pleasure and thereby fulfil their expectations. In simplistic terms a horror film would not communicate its generic message if all sides in the communications process did not realize that the primary aim of the exercise was to scare the audience.

Critical approaches to genre analysis can be adapted within a teaching context to include:

- historical evolution of a genre through comparison, description, etc.;
- relation of a text to a genre;
- how genres relate to other genres, especially through conventions, styles, etc.;
- regional variations, for example UK versus US soaps or comedies;
- aspects of heroes/heroines/villains in various genres;
- what different genres reflect about society and culture, for example how different genres appeal to a range of classes and gender, etc.;
- impact of mythic and folklorist content on texts and genres;
- rise and decline of a genre, for example why did the western die?;

- how do audiences use genres, and how do different genres provide different gratifications for differing audiences?;

- how the star system and other film theories, particularly **narrative** and **auteur**, relate to genre.

Grant, B. K. (ed.) (1997) *Film Genre Reader I I*. University of Texas Press.

German propaganda. Allowed Nazism to achieve and maintain power in the 1930s and 1940s. This was the most potent example of the power of the mass media to manipulate people that was seen in the twentieth century. Many historians and media theorists suggest that the horrors of Nazism and the rise of Hitler in Germany were in many ways aided by the growth and propagandistic use of the mass media. Such roots of modern-day propaganda have been extensively analysed in the media.

As a case study, Hitler and his powerful party dominated and controlled the media to make sure there was no dissent or opposition. Joseph Goebbels was appointed the first minister of propaganda for the mass media. Unlike Hitler, Goebbels encouraged a more subtle form of propaganda, claiming that it was more effective when not noticed by its audience. Consequently, he looked to the methods used in Hollywood, which he considered the most effective strategy for inducing propagandistic influence, and applied this to the German propaganda machine. Hitler preferred a less subtle and more didactic form of propaganda as espoused in *The Jue Suss* which made direct connections between the representations of rats and Jews scurrying around in the ghettos of Europe. Leni Reifenstahl became a very controversial and influential documentary filmmaker under Hitler. She produced 'documentaries' on Hitler's Nuremberg rally, *Triumph of the Will* (1933), as well as on the 1936 Olympics, which have remained the most potent propagandistic films ever made.

Of course all sides were engaged in propaganda wars which were considered more and more important to maintain morale and sustain a fighting spirit both for the troops on the ground and for civilians at home. Some critics go so far as to assert that all media, particularly **advertising** and political broadcasts, are essentially propagandistic by seeking to change and affect audience attitudes and beliefs. Few would disagree, however, that war, and particularly the German example, provide the most extreme with regard to manipulation of the mass media.

Kracauer, S. (1947) *From Caligari to Hitler: A Psychological History of the German Film*. Princeton University Press.

Nelmes, J. (ed.) (1999) *An Introduction to Film Studies*. Routledge.

Glasgow Media Group. Includes a number of writers and researchers attached to the University of Glasgow who take an institutional and ideological approach towards examining how media organizations present a biased interpretation in their coverage. For example, they argue that major new stories like the British miners' strike were manipulated by news management, particularly through formal devices used in their presentation on the media.

Their application of scientific, empirical research techniques is much needed within a discipline which is often given to unsubstantiated abstract theorization. Content analysis studies make up an important part of their work over the years.

But critics have cited several problems with this methodology, particularly with regard to:

(a) the choice of sample (which is often considered by its critics as unrepresentative),

(b) categorizing stories,

(c) methodology and evaluation.

It is extremely difficult to find a single research method which has the 'fine tuning' necessary to reveal the overall deeper ideological messages of the mass media. Questions which seem 'natural' or 'common sense' are important because these are the murky waters in which ideology is so often concealed.

The group produced very influential readers like *Bad News* (1976), *More Bad News* (1980) and *Really Bad News* (1982), which focus on content analysis of press and broadcasting news in particular to illustrate an inherent **biased** perspective, especially towards the workers. Their studies most certainly highlight a biased representation within the mediation of the 1970s miners' strike in the UK, which helped to bring the issue of manipulation of the news into the open and encouraged **public service** providers to be more vigilant towards obvious misrepresentation and other forms of textual bias.

globalization. A process of increasing liberalization of world trade and investment, although the term is most frequently used to refer to the effects of this process together with enhanced communications worldwide. These processes often result in increasing the gap between rich and poor, reducing job security in the developed world, and exacerbating the economic problems of less developed countries. Globalization, which is symptomatic of an increase in multinational corporate ownership, has of course economic, cultural and technological as well as social and political dimensions.

Related notions like **cultural imperialism** propose that dominant economic and cultural providers such as America are capable of exploiting through the globalization of popular culture using all their media products and services.

Allbrow, B. (1996) *The Global Age: State and Society beyond Morality.* Cambridge University Press.
Smart, B. (ed.) (1999) *Resisting McDonaldisation.* Sage.

GNVQ (General National Vocational Qualification). First introduced in the UK in 1992 through the National Council for Vocational Qualifications (NCVQ), it aims to provide vocational skills and knowledge for students who wish to progress into employment or university. It covers three levels (Foundation, Intermediate and Advanced) and can be awarded as pass, merit or distinction.

Farthing, M. *et al.* (1996) *GNVQ Media Communication and Production* (Intermediate and Advanced). Longman.

grammar of film/TV. As in a language, this involves the rules for putting programmes together. The ultimate goal of academics particularly at the early stage of the discipline was to discover a comprehensive 'grammar' which would explain and define the rules of audiovisual media, in the same way as grammar defines the rules of how written language is constructed in newspapers and books. Great strides were made towards producing visual literacy tools, especially **semiotics**, to help in this process. Theorists like Christian Metz at least at first believed that all audiovisual media could be consolidated within a coherent grammar.

While the codification of the grammar of visual construction of meaning has come a long way, most critics now appear to accept that because of its complexity and range of often competing languages, the audiovisual media cannot always be appreciated within one coherent system of rules.

For example, *camera techniques* can be codified around specific types:

Long shot (LS); establishing shot; medium shot (MS); close-up (CU).

Point of view of shot (POV); wide angle; telephoto; etc.

Zoom; pan; tilt; crab; tracking.

Editing

Cut, (match, jump, motivated); shot length.

(ASL) average shot length.

Fade, dissolve, mix, wipe, superimposition, split screen.

Manipulating time

Long takes, simultaneous scenes, slow motion, accelerated motion, freeze frame, flashback, flashforward.

Sound

Diegetic versus non-diegetic sound. Added and extended sound.

Sound bridge – adding to continuity through sound, by running sound (narration, dialogue or music) from one shot across a cut to another shot to make the action seem uninterrupted.

Dubbed dialogue – post-recording the voice track in the studio.

Wildtrack – sound which was self-evidently recorded separately from the visuals with which it is shown.

Commentary – voice-over. Spoken off-screen over the shots shown.

Lighting

Soft and harsh.

Backlighting – can create a halo effect on hair, thus semiotically signalling a sense of innocence.

Classic Hollywood: historically used three-point lighting – helps to maintain the illusion of naturalism and can be compared to *film noir* with its stylized and creative use of shadows and low lighting.

Graphics

Putting titles and credits on the film.

For further details see the very useful website www.aber.ac.uk

group work. Usually established to try to foster collaborative learning. The process often involves students working together on a task or question to gain the benefits from co-operation, discussion, clarification, negotiation, sharing and constructing knowledge.

H

Hall, Stuart. A very important and influential writer on the development of media and cultural studies. He helped expose how the media manipulated representations of blacks and other **racial** minorities in Britain through the creation of moral panics particularly with regard to the law and order thesis. His essay 'Encoding and Decoding' (1980) proposed three levels of reading or decoding a mediated text, which included the

dominant (the most ideologically acceptable which also equated with a majority audience);

negotiated (where meaning neither resided wholly in the reader or in the text but somewhere in-between); and

oppositional (where audiences sought to extract a reading which appears counter to what was intended within the text).

Throughout his long career he has written extensively on **ideology**, particularly regarding **representations** of race and class. He has also written on the rise of **Thatcherism** as a new phenomenon within culture, alongside the growth of **postmodernism**.

Hall, S. *et al.* (1980) *Policing the Crisis: Mugging, the State and Law and Order.* Macmillan.

Morley, D. and Chen, K. H. (eds) (1996) *Stuart Hall: Critical Dialogues in Cultural Studies.* Routledge.

Hawthorne effect. Discovered as a result of a business research project which famously exposed the problem, with participants in experiments conforming to expectations rather than acting 'normally' and 'individually'. Subjects in the experiment wanted to please the research project organizers by responding as they believed was expected rather than producing an authentic response as required. Results were therefore compromised by the 'pleasing' attitudes of the experimental group.

This cautionary tale helps to highlight how media research must remain aware of the danger of merely reinforcing preconceived ideas and attitudes within a so-called scientific experiment. Most research projects for example seek to prove/disprove some hypothesis, and this is particularly true for

effects studies on audiences, whose results could easily be skewed by such research. How to avoid this dilemma is more difficult to address and depends on the 'professionalism' and sophistication of the methods used. Being aware of its possibility is a first step towards not allowing it to influence the findings of a research project.

hegemony. A very popular term derived from Gramsci's ideological analysis of society and culture which focuses on the ability of one class to articulate the interests of social groups other than their own. Consent is achieved according to Gramsci by 'the prestige' which 'the dominant group enjoys because of its position and function in the world of production' (cited in Price 1997, p. 104). The phenomenon represents a state of tension in society. Meanings and symbols that legitimate dominant interest groups alongside the practices that structure the general public's daily experience, became diluted and reabsorbed, according to media critics like Stuart **Hall** and others. Within academic media discourse, Gramsci's theory became very popular in serving to legitimize **audience** and **cultural studies** while at the same time having the potential to counteract the more reductive and pessimistic ideological orthodoxies of Louis **Althusser** in particular, who did not recognize a progressive ideological role for the mass media.

Price, S. (1997) *The Complete A–Z Media and Communications Handbook.* Hodder and Stoughton.

hermeneutics. A form of analysis which tries to interpret both the structural meaning of a text and its reference or context. To fully appreciate any media text a huge range of 'knowledges' are required which demands extensive analysis.

Blackburn, S. (1996) *Oxford Dictionary of Philosophy.* Oxford University Press.

hidden agenda. A term often used to focus on what appears to be kept secret within some aspect of the media. In more general terms media theorists speak of the 'subtext' of the communications act or the **iceberg principle**. Ideological critics of course suggest that the controlling principle behind this agenda is that all media help to maintain the status quo of the dominant ideology.

high-order questions. Posed to ensure that students use thinking and reasoning abilities that involve high-order skills such as analysis, synthesis and **evaluation**. Often such questions are open in structure and extend beyond the need for simple recall and comprehension. For example, on a degree programme, questions used at level 1 have a different order of complexity than the more higher-order questions used to test students at level 3. Higher-level questions demand a greater level of evaluation of media concepts rather than simply knowing and understanding them as required at lower levels.

history of newspapers in Britain. Social historians have traced the evolution of the democratic process as it became mapped onto the history of the press. Since Caxton's press was first introduced into the UK in the fourteenth century, the press has allowed the dissemination of information and communication which, as audiences became more literate, helped to promote democratic government. However, politicians were quick to realize the potency of printed news and sought to curb publishers' power by taxing the printed word. This resulted in a long struggle over the 'freedom of the press' from government interference, which has continued to this day.

Boyce, G. et al. (eds) (1978) Newspaper History: From the 17th Century to the Present Day. Constable.

Curran, J. and Seaton, J. (1997) Power without Responsibility. Routledge.

Hartley, J. (1996) Popular Reality: Journalism, Modernity, Popular Culture. Arnold.

McNair, B. (1994) News and Journalism in UK. Routledge.

Seymour-Ure, C. (1991) The Press and Broadcasting in Britain since 1945. Blackwell.

horizontal/vertical integration. Terms used for the way a business can grow and acquire similar/related businesses through mergers and takeovers. Particularly with the rapid growth of multinational takeovers it is important to be aware of who owns what and how media industries are linked and cross-owned. For example, the owner of multiplex cinemas who purchase other cinema chains would exemplify horizontal integration by increasing market share of the cinema business. However, as has happened in Hollywood, when studios who make films also purchase distribution companies as well as cinemas to show their films to the general public, then they are creating a vertically integrated system of ownership. They can control the production process as well as ensuring that there are cinemas available to distribute their product to the general public. In America this strategy was found to be against monopolies and mergers regulations and thereby eventually ruled illegal. (Bill Gates and his giant Microsoft computer corporation for example has recently lost his case with regard to protective monopolistic practices.)

In more recent times, the film industry as well as other media industries have reformed into giant multinational corporations with connections in many other industries, particularly the lucrative new media technologies. It is often very difficult to determine who owns what, since the picture changes so quickly. Nonetheless, in spite of such research and teaching resources difficulties, appreciating the connections between ownership and control is of central importance for an understanding of media industries.

Maltby, R. and Craven, I. (1995) Hollywood Cinema. Blackwell.

hot-spot. (Or **hypertext**), used in **web pages** to allow the user to quickly transfer into another site or link-up somewhere else in the same site without laboriously having to key in the web address.

house style. The standard conventions used by a media organization to produce texts, such as layout, writing style and the selection of items to include. In particular, with regard to newspapers/journals, editors insist that certain words and phrases are used in certain cases. Journals often have unique house styles for referencing and citing other books. If you want to submit an article to a magazine you need to know these conventions if you want your work published.

For example, the academic house style for *Convergence: The Journal of Research into New Media Technologies* includes the following instructions to authors:

> Papers submitted to *Convergence* should be typed in double line spacing with minimum 1 inch margins and pages numbered consecutively throughout the entire manuscript. Two hard copies (with dark legible print) printed on one side only of A4 or nearest equivalent size paper and where possible one disk copy (Macintosh Word5 compatible) of all papers should be sent to the editors. All authors should also attach on a separate sheet the following information: name, institution and address for correspondence, telephone, fax and e-mail address, a 150-word abstract, keywords and a 50-word biography of each author.
>
> *Titles in the text*
>
> - Enclose in quotation marks titles of articles, essays, short stories, short poems, songs, chapters and sections of books and unpublished works such as dissertations.
> - Italicise titles of published works, films, television programmes, journals, multimedia products, plays, long poems, pamphlets, operas, classical works and the like. On their first reference in the text, film titles should be followed by director, country and year of release; television programmes should be identified by the channel on which they are/were broadcast and dates of transmission; CD-Roms, computer and video games by the manufacturer (company or author).
>
> *Quoted material*
>
> - Quotations of less than 40-50 words should run on within the text and should be indicated 'like this'.
> - Longer quotations should be separated from the text by a line break, indented and not enclosed in quotation marks.
>
>   . . .
>
> Copyright of articles published in *Convergence* rests with the publisher John Libbey Media at the University of Luton Press.

hypertext. (Hot-spots) allows the user accessing a **web page** to jump into a 'third dimension' – another website address – without leaving the existing one or alternatively another part of the same document. This allows for greater access and interactivity within surfing, for example, when you are looking for specific information.

hypodermic needle model. Remains the most suggestive and pessimistic model for media **effects** on **audiences**. The model assumes audiences are vulnerable and isolated and passive victims who can be literally injected with the direct influences of the mass media. This model is adapted particularly by the populist **tabloid** press as a means of apportioning direct blame to the mass media for many of the social ills and **moral panics** in society.

However, if one accepts this model of media effects, so-called pro-social messages can also be directly inculcated in mass audiences. This was the strategy behind the making of *Sesame Street*, for example, developed by **public service broadcasting** (PSB) in America, which targeted poor disaffected pre-school children and aimed to promote a culture of learning through play. *Blue Peter*, the long-running children's programme on BBC, adopts similar strategies.

Price, S. (1993) *Media Studies*. Longman.

Winn, M. (1977) *The Plug in Drug*. Penguin.

hypothesis. A proposition put forward as a proposal which requires testing or discussion. Many media research projects and assessments begin with some hypothesis, question or problem which can be researched within predetermined frameworks. A difficult example might be a very open study examining how minority representations reflect a range of cultural issues and ethnic differences. Students might seek to question the representative differences from an ideological perspective between majority/minority ethnic groups through a comparative study of UK and American crime series in the 1990s.

I

iceberg principle. A metaphor which suggests how the majority of an object remains hidden from view. Media analysis often suggests that most of the meaning of a media text remains buried beneath the surface and has to be excavated by media tools, particularly through various forms of **ideological** analysis.

icon/iconography. An icon is a primary semiotic sign system first applied to religions like Christianity, where for example the crucifix remains a powerful icon which represents suffering, 'sacrifice', as well as religious faith. Similarly the virgin Madonna, the mother of Christ, embodies purity and religious faith. Iconography is used extensively through the stylistic and formal analysis of painting and has been imported into **semiotics** and media/film analysis as a result. Film critics for example speak of the dominant imagery of white/black hats in the more dated **westerns** to denote good/bad characters as well as the use of a chequered tablecloth as part of a primary iconographic shorthand for a poor but honest homestead.

identification. How members of the audience in a film/theatre/TV and so on strongly connect with the actions/motives/feelings/predicament of the character(s) on the screen. Hollywood cinema, it is argued, encourages such identification through its **narrative** structure and style of acting. The latter is highly influenced by the **method school**, initiated by the theatrical writer Stanislavsky, and compares with the more 'distancing' style of acting promoted by avant-garde theorists and practitioners like **Brecht**.

ideological state apparatus. See **Althusser** and **ideology**.

ideology. The most-used notion and conceptual framework for appreciating the study of media, which addresses issues of power and manipulation in society. Karl **Marx** most succinctly proposed that 'the ideas of the ruling class are in every epoch the ruling ideas'. All ideologies therefore are specific to a particular culture and a particular moment in history. Cultural products, Marxists argue, always mask the reality of power inequality in society. This notion helped to consolidate the **dominant ideology** thesis, which in Western society is associated with **capitalism**. It must be remembered that Marx himself did not write much about the mass media, which did not exist in his time except for newspapers. However, critics ever since have applied his ideas and often describe themselves as followers of Marx, i.e. Marxists.

In particular Marxist critics suggest that mass media 'normalizes', 'naturalizes' and 'legitimizes' what is considered the dominant ideology of capitalism so that it appears not unnatural to promote competition and thereby inequality. All media are analysed to determine how they reflect and even promote such ideological positions.

For important theorists like Habermas and Baudrillard, ideology is less a matter of **'false consciousness'** or of the irrational content of deluded minds, than of the formal structures of communication. Yet if everything is ideological, there remains a danger of degenerating into a non-contextualized relativism, making it impossible to create a hierarchy of power structures/forces within society. The question must be asked, how can you distinguish or discriminate important from unimportant information and therefore be able to prioritize arguments regarding a range of 'ideologies'. With the pervasive influence of **postmodernist** relativism, many students question the relevance of understanding such an 'outmoded' structure of ideas. However, even if one was to accept such a pessimistic deduction, it is impossible to understand and appreciate postmodernism without first engaging with the range of debates embedded within Marxist theory, which has regenerated itself in so many ways and remains a bedrock structure for engaging with the mass media apparatus.

Price, S. (1993) *Media Studies*. Longman.

IMAX. An extremely wide-screen film process in which a 65mm (rather than conventional 35mm) film stock is run horizontally through the camera and projected onto 70mm for film projection. The screen is often up to 21m high. More IMAX cinemas are being produced as audiences demand greater spectacle within their film viewing. The format is particularly effective for nature programmes which dramatize the sublime aspect of nature, and sports like mountain climbing or underwater diving.

in-camera editing. Involves the shooting of material on film or on video in the order in which it is to be viewed; this means less post-production editing is required. However, in general, most films are rarely shot in sequence, since it is more expensive to set up scenes again and again than to film all scenes from the one set at the same time – even if they are out of sequence.

Independent Television Commission (ITC). The successor to the Independent Broadcasting Authority, which was set up after the 1990 Broadcasting Act. It is responsible for the licensing and regulation of all commercial TV in Britain, including that provided by cable and satellite.

In a dramatic recent review of television prohibitions, it is proposed that of the 29 prohibitions reviewed, 16 are recommended for deletion. These include allowing personalities such as newsreaders to appear in

advertisements as well as allowing various types of religious advertising which has hitherto been banned.

The ITC is a good point of contact for students looking for information on television projects they are researching. The organization provides valuable leaflets on various areas of the organization's remit, including:

- Watching over commercial television
- Programme regulation on commercial television
- Digital television in the UK
- Satellite, cable and local delivery in the UK
- Advertising and sponsorship on commercial television

mail: 33 Foley St, London W I P 7LB
email: publicaffairs@itc.org.uk
website: www.itc.org.uk.

index. A direct link between the sign and what it represents. See **Peirce** and **semiotics** generally.

information and communications technology (ICT). See **computer literacy**.

infotainment. A common term used to explain a broadcast programme which mixes light entertainment and information. The growth of breakfast and morning TV provide good examples of this hybrid **genre**.

in-house. A term applied when production facilities are used to create media products within the company or organization, rather than having to buy them from outside organizations. For example, the **BBC** might speak of making a programme inside their own organization and using their unique **house style** rather than buying in a programme from a freelance, independent company, or working on a joint venture with another organization to produce a new series.

Intentionalist Fallacy. Suggests that it does not matter what the maker of a mediated text meant, since this is not the key determinant in the meaning of the finished text. It is proposed that a text has a life of its own independent of its creator. Nonetheless, theories such as **auteur theory** are built around the romantic notion of the unique creative film director signing their individuality through their film art.

interactive. Denotes how new media in particular can be regarded as more of a two-way communication, with audiences and consumers able to 'talk back' to their Game-boys, Digital TV, Video games, **web pages**, etc. and become active participants rather than merely 'passive' consumers of pleasure. Such interactivity is often cited as a major achievement and benefit of **new technology** which is even being endorsed within education. By providing increased learning opportunities through interactive engagement, the **internet** for example is becoming highly valued as an educational tool. Critics, however, warn that such utopian notions of interactivity are far from realized, with games and other new media continuing to manipulate audiences instead of allowing 'real' freedom or control.

Convergence journal, edited by Knight, J., Steemers, J. and Weedon, A. University of Luton Press.

internet. An international computer network that links together computers used in the home, in businesses, in educational institutions and in governments. It is an information and communications system which is accessible to computer and phone owners with a modem, giving them access to a wide range of information. The main part of the internet is known as the World Wide Web or just **web** (www). The benefits of such a system are many fold, including the ability to search a vast amount of data as well as instant and interactive communication.

Also, with the development of what is called 'hyperlinking', by clicking on a highlighted word, the user is directly switched to another database, perhaps on the other side of the world. The ease with which web pages can be placed on the internet means that the information contained is both lively and topical. One of the positive features of the internet is its decentralized structure, which encourages less control and even, some argue, the potentiality of encouraging democratic access to information.

On a communal level, the internet has also encouraged users to come closer together through increased communication. With the development of 'chat-rooms' and internet cafés, for example, users can communicate almost instantaneously and cheaply, which in many ways is similar to telephony. Within media education there are also numerous chat-sites and **web pages** which are both informative and sociable for students and teachers alike. Probably the biggest growth in business over the last decade has been through 'e-commerce', which allows companies and services to advertise and trade using the global reach and ease of the internet.

Kennedy, A. (1998) The Rough Guide to the Internet and World Wide Web. Cox and Wyman.

Wise, R. (2000) Multimedia: A Critical Introduction. Routledge.

interpellating the audience. An **ideological** notion which can be described as 'hailing the audience' as individuals, as part of a community which helps to confer a social identity. This phenomenon is often illustrated through the study of **advertisements**, where they speak directly to their target audience. If you want to enjoy and adopt the material status which the product or service provides, advertisements suggest you must buy the product. For example, car advertisements often confirm the relationship between appropriating the sought-after automobile and its related higher status in society, while ensuring that the consumer remains satisfied with their fantasy 'beautiful wife' and lovely kids, etc. Ideological critics suggest that all media texts speak to their audience in similar ways and while not always directly trying to sell them products, the mass media tend to promote and validate moral/ethical and lifestyle norms for audiences.

Dyer, G. (1982) Advertising as Communication. Methuen.

Price, S. (1993) Media Studies. Longman.

interpersonal communication. The ability to communicate with other humans. Media education has always sought to develop group skills, particularly through practical projects which depend a great deal on the success of group dynamics. All aspects of vocational training put specific emphasis on developing these very necessary skills for the workplace. The BTEC ethos in particular seeks to develop students' group and interpersonal skills through explicit assessment criteria.

Argyle, M. (1978) *The Psychology of Interpersonal Behaviour.* Penguin.

intertextuality. How a text borrows, copies, makes reference to or is influenced by some other text. It is impossible to fully analyse a text in isolation without appreciating the influences on the mediated text, either direct or otherwise. For example a film performance cannot be fully appreciated without awareness of the other roles the actor has played previously, as well as interviews given by the star while being consciously placed in the public domain, or gossip about their personal life. Similarly, the film produced is generically linked with other films of the same or related **genres** which help to provide extra meaning and pleasure. Such pleasure is added to by advertising trailers, reviews, even soundtracks, etc. (for example over 20 million copies of the *Titanic* soundtrack was sold worldwide on the back of the recent successful film version) which provide added intertextual knowledge for understanding and appreciating the film.

Berger, A. A. (1991) *Media Research Techniques.* Sage.

Hall, S. (ed.) (1997) *Representation: Cultural Representation and Signifying Practices.* Open University Press.

Ray, R. (1985) *A Certain Tendency of the Hollywood Cinema 1930–1980.* Princeton University Press.

Strinati, D. (1995) *An Introduction to Theories of Popular Culture.* Routledge.

interviews. At their most elemental, involve an interviewer discussing with an interviewee in an attempt to abstract some information. Within media broadcasts and in the press they are extensively used to discover and affirm various levels of information for the media's audience. Studying the skills of carrying out successful interviews has become an important aspect of media analysis. Also within media research, interviews have become a very popular tool for obtaining primary data for any study being carried out. With the exception of **focus groups**, they are often conducted on a one-to-one basis with each participant asked the same questions in the same order. Answers can be written down or recorded for analysis. The art of carrying out successful research interviews together with the more presentational media interviews has become a key skill which is developed in many media courses.

Journalists and presenters in particular have to be proficient at carrying out successful professional interviews by applying various guidelines yet at the same time having the ability to ad-lib changes to the script through reading body language alongside any other cues which can be observed. An interview style of **documentary** has become very popular within television.

Price, S. (1996) *Communications Studies.* Addison Wesley Longman.

intra-personal communication. See **communication**.

Irish identity on film. There is a growing preoccupation with how national identity is reflected and affirmed through the media. The history of 'Irish cinema' suggests patterns that reflect what can be regarded as a 'fractured identity'. Many critics assert that a film culture can help structure, solidify and codify a sense of national identity. From the joyous if highly stereotypical evocation of the fighting-stage Irishman played by John Wayne and directed by the famous American Irish western director John Ford's *The Quiet Man* (1952); to the fatalistic and noirish romantic representation of an IRA activist in Belfast played by James Mason and directed by Carol Reed, *Odd Man Out* (1947); – such 'foreign' representations have become internalized through various reworkings of violent Irish myths by Irish directors, like Neil Jordan in *Angel*, *Crying Game* and *Michael Collins*.

Crude **structuralist** approaches can be used to divide the island of Ireland across two axes:

- The North/South divide and the fractured political identity embodied in nationalist as opposed to unionist attitudes towards the 'Troubles'.

- The East/West divide, with the west stereotypically representing pure primitive romanticism (as embodied in the writings of Joyce, Synge and Yeats in particular) compared to the urban centre in the east which reflected for many a cosmopolitan British sensibility. This phenomenon is effectively dramatised by *Into the West* (1992).

Academics have remained fascinated by the way the 'Troubles' have been mapped and reflected through films and TV programmes written and produced within the culture as well as those conceived and directed from outside of the island.

Cathcart, R. (1984) *The Most Contrary Region: The BBC in Northern Ireland 1924–1984*. Blackstaff Press.

Hill, J. and McLoone, M. (eds) (1996) *Big Picture, Small Screen: The Relations Between Film and Television*. John Libbey (University of Luton) Press.

Kiberd, D. (1995) *Inventing Ireland: The Literature of the Modern Nation*. Jonathan Cape.

McLoone, M. (ed.) (1991) *Culture Identity and Broadcasting in Ireland: Local Issues, Global Perspective*. BFI.

Pettitt, L. (2000) *Screening Ireland: Film and Television Representations*. Manchester University Press.

Rockett, K., Hill, J. and Gibbons, L. (1988) *Cinema and Ireland*. Routledge.

J

jargon. A term used to describe a specialized language applied to particular discipline areas. Media education is no different from other areas of study with its applied nomenclature or system of words/terms which need to be appreciated if students are to understand the language of media education. Such academic language has to be understood by students before they can read and understand many of the textbooks they have to study. Consequently a primary aim of this Guide is to help demystify such language and make terms more explicit and easily understandable. A danger, however, which must be avoided by students, is applying jargon words for effect and academic kudos, while often not fully appreciating the implications and complications of such concepts, as signalled in the Introduction.

jingoism. An extreme form of national pride in one's country. In particular it has manifested itself during wars or other international rivalry such as football matches. Often the media, particularly the **tabloid** press, is accused of inciting a jingoistic attitude in their readers when a major international conflict is forthcoming. See also **German propaganda**.

journal. A collection of **research** papers of scholarly articles bound together into a periodical which is published at frequent intervals. Often journals have a particular area of specialism and they are usually reserved in libraries for the purposes of research and scholarship. Students, particularly as they progress up the educational ladder, must regularly dip into a growing range of media-related journals if they are to become proficient with current research and develop their own research skills and new areas of study.

Media-related journals/magazines include:

Ads International

Audiovisual

Broadcast

Camera Obscura

Campaign

Communications Law

Convergence

Cultural Studies

Documentary Film Quarterly

English and Media Magazine

Film Comment

Film History

Free Press

Historical Journal of Film, Radio and Television

Hypermedia

Journal of Film and Video

Journalism Quarterly

Media Culture and Society

Millennium Film Journal

Multimedia

Quarterly Review of Film and Video

Screen

Screen Educational

Sight and Sound

Total Film

Wide Angle

(together with numerous web-based journals – see **web pages**).

journalism. Any form of non-fiction media writing, usually related to newspapers or broadcast news. The traditional view of journalism is, however, that news is not found but made and constructed by journalists to meet the needs of the media outlet they are working for. Issues particularly around **news values** affect what becomes printed in various publications. While there are of course many specialist journalist courses, the general study of the function of journalism has become part of the overall skills development within media education.

Barzun, J. (1986) *On Writing, Editing and Publishing.* University of Chicago Press.

Butcher, J. (1992) *The Cambridge Handbook of Copy-editing.* Cambridge University Press.

Chomsky, N. (1989) *Necessary Illusions: Thought Control in Democratic Societies.* Pluto Press.

Curran, J. and Seaton, J. (1997) *Power without Responsibility.* Routledge.

Keeble, R. (1994) *The Newspapers Handbook.* Routledge.

jump-cut. A film edit which breaks the illusion of continuity. Whereas **continuity editing** always hides the constructed nature of film production by maintaining temporal and spatial (time/space) continuity, jump-cuts actively break down these conventions. The technique was used extensively by

avant-garde filmmakers like Godard to break the illusion of continuity editing and **realism** in film. The technique has now become more common within mainstream film and television.

See www.inform.umd.edu/rosebud/glossary.

Jung, Carl. A follower of Freud who later rejected his master's fixation with sexuality as being the unique key to the subconscious. He asserted that the 'libido' or sex drive was a general life force and not only sexual as Freud insisted. Freud also regarded the unconscious as a sort of 'store cupboard' for the individual's repressed memories, whereas Jung saw the unconscious as also holding a bank of social or cultural ideas and images and what he called a universal 'species memory' which is shaped by the experience of mankind throughout history. **Anthropology** and the study of so-called primitive tribes has used this idea, and many representations of Native American Indians and Australian Aborigine peoples, for example, appear to engage with such ideas. From a media perspective Jung's concept of *archetypes* has been very influential on **representation**, **narratology** and **myth** and the understanding of human character types. Such character types include the following:

Persona – social mask the individual wears to face the world

Shadow – dark side – fears, etc. (e.g. *Star Wars*)

Animus – 'male' aspect of the female psyche (e.g. *Aliens*)

Anima – 'female' aspect of male psyche (e.g. *Thelma and Louise*)

Wise Old Man – combines images of hero/leader (e.g. *Little Big Man*)

Great Mother – counterpoint to the wise old man (e.g. *Mommie Dearest*)

Self – ideal state of individuality

juxtaposition. The use of contrasting ideas/structures, etc. which are often used to demonstrate the contrasts between such elements. The term is applied in all forms of writing to denote effective comparison.

K

key concepts in media education. (Which are also examined throughout the Guide) include:

representation (who is being represented and why, by whom, as well as fairness of representation);

media institutions (how a text is influenced by various institutions and in particular how ownership and other organizational controls affect texts, etc.);

media language (how to understand the media through its use of forms and analysis; for example using **semiotics** and other visual techniques – **narrative** and **genre** in particular);

values and ideology (how power is represented and manipulated through **agents** and events);

media audiences (who is the text addressed to; focusing on assumptions regarding audience, etc.);

media histories (how the media is part of a **contextual** history and can only be fully appreciated when such contextual and intertextual relations are fully explored).

key light. The main source of light in a studio setting. Within portrait and studio lighting generally there are often at least three light sources used. These are: the main or key light; a fill light, which overcomes many of the shadows cast by the main light; a 'hair light', which is positioned behind and at an angle to the subject and which literally creates a light around the hair of the sitter and ensures a greater depth of field in the otherwise two-dimensional image.

key skills. Currently defined as the generic skills required for lifelong learning and effective membership of an adaptable workforce. Originally developed by the National Council for Vocational Qualifications (NCVQ), key skills cover:

1 communication

2 application of number

3 information technology

4 working with others

5 improving own learning and performance

6 problem-solving.

In the revised National Curriculum (DfEE 1999) the six skill areas are described as being 'embedded' within the curriculum and promoted as helping learners to improve their learning and performance in education, work and life. Media education has adopted this model for many of its courses. For example, BTEC courses are designed to address all six of these key skills while concentrating in particular on developing students' group skills, which is often regarded as the most important ability in the workplace. Also the new revised **A Level** syllabi directly address these key skills.

DfEE (1999) *The National Curriculum: Handbook for Secondary Teachers.* HMSO.

key stage. One of the time divisions into which the UK National Curriculum requirements for children's education is split. The National Curriculum is divided into four key stages, which cover the age ranges from the start of compulsory education to age 7 (Key Stage 1), from 7 to 11 (Key Stage 2), from 11 to 13 (Key Stage 3) and from 13 to the end of compulsory schooling (Key Stage 4).

King, Rodney. Became famous as a media story in America and around the world when amateur footage of him being beaten up by the Los Angeles Police Department was shown on television. It resulted in a major investigation into **racism** in the American police and helped to spark off riots in Los Angeles – the worst since the 1960s, at the height of the civil-rights movement. The incident is often used to illustrate the power of the media to directly affect and incite its audiences.

knowledge. Can be broadly defined as the information, facts, intelligence or experience of something held by an individual. Debate continues about the division of educational attainment into its major components of knowledge, understanding and skills. Many educationalists have major concerns about the generation, or provision, of knowledge through a curriculum, and the form of the curriculum necessary to 'deliver' different types of knowledge most effectively. A fundamental division, for example, occurs between a curriculum that stresses the importance of 'knowing that' – linked to attainment of content; and one which promotes 'knowing how' – linked to the development of skills. Media education has in many ways become more predicated on 'knowing how' the media works, but of late has become preoccupied with the need for more prescribed content within various syllabi.

Kulshov effect. The emotional or intellectual meaning that is created by the juxtaposition of shots in editing (**montage**) rather than by the isolated content of a single image. The idea was developed particularly with regard to Russian cinema in the 1920s, when Kulshov taught in the state film school in Moscow. For example, the image of a 'dead child' was considered to evoke grief, whereas an 'attractive woman' might denote lust. His ideas should be appreciated together with the work of his pupil Sergei **Eisenstein** also.

See Mark Joyce's chapter on Russian cinema in the 1920s, in Nelmes, J. (ed.) (1996) *An Introduction to Film Studies*. Routledge.

L

league tables. Graphical representations of different types of educational performance data applied to schools, often used as a means of crudely assessing their standards. Following the creation of the UK's Parent's Charter in 1991, schools were legally required to issue parents with a statement of their child's educational progress as well as a level of attainment within National Curriculum subjects, sometimes defined by a Standard Assessment Task (SAT). This information has been amassed by academics, the government and a variety of official educational bodies into league tables of schools locally, regionally and nationally. Local education authorities (LEAs), awarding bodies and educational magazines and other publications have also begun to imitate this process by creating league tables of General Certificate of Secondary Education (GCSE) and Advanced and Advanced Subsidiary Level (A and AS Level) results. A variety of different league tables have now been devised using education-related data. These represent categories as diverse as truancy rates in schools, and inspection performances of initial teacher training (ITT) courses.

Assumptions about schools' or universities' performances are often made on the basis of such league tables. Many consider them to be unfair, particularly where factors such as the socio-economic profile of the school's catchment area are not considered. The 'value added' to the educational development of the child by the teachers is also not fully recognized within most tables.

University courses on media and communications in the UK were all assessed by the QCA in the last few years and a table of comparisons can be found at www.educationunlimited.co.uk/specialreports/universities2000.

Many universities were particularly unhappy with how the various statistics were used to rank and categorize individual courses. The maximum grade was based on: student/staff ratio; job prospects (which is always contentious – depending on how you define 'vocational employment' in particular); and grade entry requirements for students gaining entry into higher institutions (which raised the issue of access education and the notion of 'value added'). Mixed messages were given by various newspapers as they compiled their often confusing league tables.

learning style. The preferences in the way in which an individual learns, reflecting his or her previous educational experiences, personality and environment. Learning styles are very personal, may change with time or subject matter, and are defined by a complex mix of factors including cognitive, social, psychological and affective dimensions.

The study of media is often assumed to accommodate a variety of learning styles due to the diverse nature of its content and the range of skills to be gathered. The most effective learners seem to be able to apply a wide range of different learning styles, or more correctly learning strategies, which suit a range of subjects and issues.

Leavis, F. R. Leavis has been the *bête noire* of UK media education and research. Although writing much earlier in the twentieth century, he promoted an exclusive and elitist approach to the canon of literature which should be inculcated into students. Many radical critics in the 1970s reacted against the Leavisite approach to literature and popular culture generally. (See **popular arts** and **popular culture**.) However, within revisionist cultural histories his influence on literature and even media has become revised, with critics reasserting the need for some form of **canon** of key texts/concepts/methodologies within a more mature discipline.

Hoggart, R. (1957) *The Uses of Literacy*. Chatto and Windus.

Leavis, F. R. and Thompson, D. (1932) *Culture and Environment*. Chatto and Windus.

left wing. A political position which broadly supports a socialist/communist ideology. The term is used as a shorthand within media/cultural analysis to suggest a critique of dominant **capitalist** ideological positions as well as inferring an alignment with the political theories of **Marx** and his followers.

leitmotif. Used particularly in music and applied to film, it can be defined as a recurring phrase which creates meaning by its use. Like a shorthand way of expressing something, it is a way of making meaning obvious. For example, each of the main protagonists in a film may be signalled by a certain type of music to reflect their character; like in Serio Leone's classic *Once Upon a Time in the West* (1968). A similar strategy may be deployed through the use of lighting or colour.

Lévi-Strauss, Claude. An important **anthropologist** who developed a binary oppositions model for understanding culture, language and **myth**, which has become very influential in cultural and film studies. The **structuralist** analysis of a **western** focuses on primary divisions within society: nature versus culture.

library footage. Stored and catalogued images used to illustrate current stories and events. For example, 'stock' footage of the Houses of Parliament would be used to overlay a story about some current government debate. Media including the press and radio use library photographs and sound clips as a shorthand method of illustrating or locating various stories.

lighting. The study of how lighting is used in films, TV programmes and still photographs is central both from a practical perspective and for an aesthetic appreciation of the mass media. Different forms of lighting produce various often conflicting meanings; for example, with *film noir*, lighting became very effective through the use of shadows. Students learn how to 'paint with light', particularly in practical projects, as well as unpacking the various meanings which can be created using lighting and shade.

liminal/outsider. The notion of a liminal or outsider was first applied by the **anthropologist** Van Gennep, who wrote extensively on ritualistic forms of behaviour that helped to consolidate (primitive) communities. He also developed theories around rites of passage, which represented defined stages that humans progress through from childhood to old age. Related to this are transitional periods when the individual is left out of a given group but has not yet been incorporated into a new one. This is described as a liminal state. Many media **narratives** deal with such stages and characters.

Linked to this is the existential concept of 'outsider' which has become very important, especially within **cultural** and textual studies and more recently multicultural studies. For instance, Native American Indians had conventionally been represented as outsiders within the dominant white imperialism of American culture. Analysing agents and protagonists/ antagonists in cultural texts using this idea has become very popular, especially when reading 'against the grain' or in opposition to dominant cultural discourses.

linguistics. The study of language is also used extensively within media studies, particularly through **semiotics** and **communications** theory generally. Stuart Price divided linguistics into a number of related areas: historical studies; comparative linguistics; phonology; studies of grammar; psycholinguistics; and sociolinguistics (1997, p. 131).

Price, S. (1997) *The Complete A–Z Media and Communication Handbook.* Hodder and Stoughton.

literacy. An ability to read and write. The term has a particular meaning when applied to certain aspects of media education, especially visual literacy, which encompasses an ability to understand and analyse the complexity of audio and/or visual texts. Strategies of developing visual literacy include a close analysis of **still photography**, such as in advertisements and press photographs, to develop the skills to unpack often concealed or subliminal meanings from the images. **Semiotics** remains a key tool and strategy in this process.

M

MacCabe, Colin. His influence on media studies dates back to the 1970s and the journal *Screen*. MacCabe focused on the non-radical potential of the **classic narrative** form of Hollywood film, which he asserted remains closely related to the structure of the nineteenth-century novel. Both forms appear transparent, producing a level of 'objective truth' while avoiding drawing attention to their constructive fictional nature. Like the novel, he suggested, Hollywood film also has a 'hierarchy of discourses', with the voice-over of the protagonist dramatizing and controlling all other points of view and positions in the film. MacCabe concludes that Hollywood film, unlike the **avant-garde**, 'cannot deal with the real as contradictory' and therefore remains preoccupied with the illusion of a coherent style of naturalism. This makes Hollywood film appear to create a seamless reality, which is complemented by strict **continuity editing** and a naturalistic style of acting.

For MacCabe, Heath and other *Screen* theorists, the 'cinematic apparatus' is a concentrated version of **Althusser**'s, **ideological state apparatus**. Their critical position regarding Hollywood is in many ways a radicalized version of the **Frankfurt School**'s concern in earlier decades with the massifying properties of the culture industries. For such critics mass culture **interpellates** the masses as audiences of passive consumers.

In 1985 MacCabe was appointed head of production of the BFI, which was in many ways a move out of academic research. But in 1989 he also took over as head of research, which included publishing and education as well as production. However, after various conflicts, most notably the setting up of a new MA, he left the BFI and has moved back into university life.

MacCabe, C. (ed.) (1986) *High Theory/Low Culture*. Manchester University Press.

MacCabe, C. (1999) *The Eloquence of the Vulgar*. BFI.

Madonna. An American pop singer, film star and cultural icon, extensively written about by media theorists. Critics cite various reading positions of her music and film work which might include:

- feminist readings which negatively regard her **commodification** of the female form and the reinscribing of patriarchal values;

- girl fans who faithfully consolidate her persona as an agent of empowerment and liberation;
- others, usually male critics, who protest that she remains the object of voyeuristic pleasure.

But John **Fiske** in particular suggests that her gender politics lie not in her 'textuality', but in her 'functionality'. Her public persona constitutes an exemplary popular text because she is so full of contradictions. While her persona was a suitable icon for the 1980s and 1990s, more contemporary female icons are needed to reframe such engaging debates for students and academics.

Fiske, J. (1989) *Understanding Popular Culture.* Unwin Hyman.

Fiske, J. (1989) *Reading the Popular.* Unwin Hyman.

male gaze. See **voyeurism and pornography**.

mark scheme. Details how grades should be awarded for questions set within an examination, or for coursework, classwork or homework. The scheme itemizes the number of marks for each subsection of an answer and guides the examiners towards acceptable parameters for candidate answers.

market research. Enables organizations to describe and segment markets, to understand customers and to predict their likely responses to its marketing activities.

Central to a good marketing strategy is the development of sound market research. It is little use producing a comprehensive prototype for a new TV programme if there is no evidence of a market for such a product. Media companies – like all commercial companies – will not take risks without assessing the availability of potential markets. Consequently, vocationally driven media students in particular must become proficient in the use of scientific methods to collect information relevant to the marketing and selling of their media texts.

Researching a market would involve:

- systematically using an organized and clear method or system;
- gathering information on the market, etc.;
- recording and keeping clear and organized records of what is discovered;
- analysing and making sense of information found to draw out relevant trends and conclusions;
- finding out answers to questions and details of the marketplace;
- predicting the future, which is of course very difficult – but market research must give some guidelines for narrowing the probability of future trends with regard to consumers/audiences in particular.

A parallel activity of investigating **audience research** is applied extensively in many vocational media courses, for example to justify the provision of a new media product which is being constructed.

marketing. This is not simply **advertising**, nor is it PR/promotion, nor is it just selling, it is a collection of all these activities. According to many experts, it should be seen as a philosophy, a way of thinking, from the customer's perspective, about how the firm/media organization can meet the needs of customers. Peter Drucker, a business management guru, says that the aim of marketing is to make selling superfluous – matching what people want with what the seller supplies. Or matching the seller's strengths to market opportunities. Even more so than in other disciplines, students must acquire the skills of successful (self-)marketing if they are to thrive in the highly competitive world of the media. Producing innovative ideas and applying these to the making of technically competent media artefacts is often not enough if you cannot market these products and achieve a return on investment.

The goal of marketing, including media marketing, is to find consumers with unsatisfied need which can be fulfilled by the company's product or service. This requires the ability to explore, identify and interpret customers' behaviour, attitudes and preferences. It relies on a deep understanding of the company's customers and the society in which they live.

Hill, N. (1989) *Marketing for BTEC*. Business Education.

Marxism. An **ideological** doctrine based on the political, social and economic theories of the German philosopher Karl Marx (1818–83) and Frederick Engels (1820–95). Broadly speaking, Marx's ideas focused on how economic and social interaction are seen to be driven by the 'mode of production' and how class conflict will create an impetus for change in this mode of production resulting ultimately in a classless society. See various entries, including **ideology** together with key Marxist theorists from **Althusser**, to **Hall** to begin to appreciate how embedded Marxist ideas are within critical media education.

Maslow, Abraham. Famous for his 'hierarchy of needs', which is used extensively within advertising to appreciate the levels of needs of audiences/consumers. Different adverts appeal to different human needs. He suggested that all human needs are arranged in order, with fundamental ones such as food, shelter and sleep (physiological needs) having to be filled before higher-order needs are met, which include:

- safety needs;
- social needs (love and acceptance within a social group);
- esteem needs (often linked to feeling competent and to achievement);
- self-actualization (the highest need, which involves the fulfilment of one's full potential, often linked to expression of creativity).

(Price 1993, p. 127)

Price, S. (1993) *Media Studies*. Pitman.

Masterman, Len. Has been very influential in the development of media education/studies as a discrete study within the UK. His contribution is extensively cited throughout this guide within various debates, particularly the legitimacy of media studies as opposed to media education – as explored by David Buckingham *et al*. Nevertheless, in spite of various criticisms, Masterman's overpowering contribution to the growth of media studies both at a 'grass roots' level and at a more abstract, pedagogical level can never be underestimated. His seminal studies of the media have remained a primer for the subject since they were first published.

Masterman, L. (1980) *Teaching About Television*. Macmillan.

Masterman, L. (1984) *Television Mythologies: Stars, Shows and Signs*. Comedia.

Masterman, L. (1985) *Teaching the Media*. Routledge.

Masterman, L. (1985) *The Making of Television Literacy*. Falmer Press.

websites include: http://interact.uoregon.edu/MediaLit/FA/MLArticleFolder/e

www.aber.ac.uk/education/undergrad

McLuhan, Marshal. An important influence on media education whose ideas are coming back again into fashion after a long period of being considered crude and overgeneralized. He coined the phrase, 'the medium is the message', by which he meant that the communications environment humans create at any given period also serves to define the medium's function and role in that society. This notion has remained prevalent if often questioned within media studies.

His passion for a 'classroom without walls' included championing the central role of mass media, particularly film, in the Western educational system. This has helped validate the power of new media in particular. (Some writers assert that 'New Labour' in the UK and the Clinton, Democratic administration in the USA, have adapted his ideas by their apparent total conversion to the educational benefits of computer/internet technology, for example.) If we do not quickly master these new languages, it is suggested, they will serve only to weaken or corrupt previously achieved levels of verbal and pictorial analysis and culture.

McLuhan, M. (1967) *The Medium is the Message*. Allen Lane.

McLuhan, M. (1994) *Understanding Media*. MIT Press.

meaning. A primary goal of **textual analysis** in particular and understanding the mass media in general. However, media analysis like literary analysis has to face up to the difficult, if not the impossible task of defining a uniform and coherent meaning. Instead, various often contradictory meanings can be discovered within texts, often depending on the investigative tools used. For example, **semiotics** at its most basic looks at how texts can be read at a **denotative** surface level compared with the more subjective even ambiguous and culturally determined **connotative** level of reading. If a **psychoanalytic** model is applied, the unconscious analysis of character representation for example might throw up yet more and quite different deep-seated subconscious meanings. In particular, **postmodernist** theory problematizes the very notion of a uniform or coherent meaning.

One popular model to analyse meaning remains an **ideological** one, which would uncover various subtexts and meanings related to a range of contextual aspects from which the text is produced, and which usually serve to affirm the dominant ideology.

A most helpful **communication model** to map the process of determining and discovering meaning already cited is the triangular connection between *audience, text* and *producer*. The producer encodes meaning into the text and the audience decodes it. There is never any guarantee that the same meaning is decoded and it is fairer to say that meaning is positioned in the centre of the triangle between all three constituents but not controlled by any single one.

Important theorists like Stuart **Hall** have posited at least three related categories of meanings: *dominant, negotiated* and *oppositional*. While the dominant reading is agreed by most readers/consumers, an oppositional reading is driven by niche audiences and specific needs; for example, homosexual readings of Hollywood icons like Judy Garland, who appears at odds with the dominant heterosexual encoding of Hollywood texts. Meanwhile for negotiated readings, as the term suggests, meaning lies between the two extremes of dominant and oppositional readings.

Storey, J. (ed.) (1996) *What is Cultural Studies: A Reader.* Arnold.

media education versus media studies in Britain. This underpinning debate was first promoted by Len **Masterman** and others and focused on the desire to carve a pedagogical and curricular niche for media studies as a separate discipline and thereby provide it with legitimacy and firm foundations. However, many pedagogical critics suggested that media education could alternatively permeate other more established but related disciplines like English studies. Consequently, it was argued the curriculum could be broadened from within and thereby maintain traditional subjects like English and history, which are in many ways essential foundations for the study of the media. In particular, educationalists propose that the use of media texts to broaden the English canon would enable students to acquire a greater appreciation of the interconnections between texts, be they written or within an audiovisual format.

Masterman and others, however, fought for a distinct and separate discipline and continued to assert that the aim of teaching media studies was distinct from related disciplines, and encouraged the eliciting of a response from students which is non-evaluative, but should be 'felt and authentic'. Nevertheless, at the teaching chalk-face, many teachers use popular mass media as a means to teach related subjects like history, literature, even politics, etc., through a broad-based critical analysis approach. By tapping into students' popular cultural pleasures, critical and analytical skills were developed which could then be deployed across various other disciplines.

The justification for media studies as a distinct pedagogic discipline, according to **Masterman** and others, includes:

1 Focusing on an understanding of media systems and processes rather than laboriously accumulating data.

2 Encouraging practical activity as a means of exploring and reinforcing conceptual understanding.

3 Encouraging autonomous thinking rather than the reproduction by pupils of teachers' ideas.

Core debates developed in media education courses often address the following thematic questions which underpin the aims and objectives of all media curriculum programmes:

Who is communicating and why? (media agencies)

What type of text is it? (media categories)

How is it produced? (media technologies)

How do we know what it means? (media languages)

Who receives it and what sense do they make of it? (media audiences)

How does it present its subject? (media representation).

While many critics appear to agree that 'pleasure' should be the starting point for media education, Masterman affirms that such pleasure is produced 'for us not by us'. There is a danger, however, according to David **Buckingham**, of remaining preoccupied with defining *content* at the expense of understanding *process*. Attempting to carve out a discrete subject area around media studies, which is outside of the protective umbrella of English or some other more established discipline area, results in the major danger of inhabiting an educational ghetto.

Buckingham suggests that the move from the notion of a separate media studies discipline towards media 'education' is an ongoing process of making connections with other pedagogical areas. Media education in the UK has begun to permeate across the whole curriculum. However, with the tremendous growth in interest in the media, discrete media studies type courses have been developed at second- and third-level educational institutions. Compared to the often dogmatic ideological debates in education in the late 1960s–1970s, more recently there has been a broadly discernible shift from the concentration on a methodology for teachers and teaching to a renewed focus on the learner and how learners learn.

media ethics. Focus on moral questions concerning what is right and wrong, preoccupying much media analysis. All media organizations, for example, have to make decisions, particularly with regard to news and print, over what is 'ethically correct' with regard to invasion of privacy, versus what is in the 'public interest'. Various watchdog organizations have also been set up to police and critique media output. For example, the **Press Complaints** Committee.

Such debates are not easily resolved, however. To fully appreciate the implications of such debates, students often study so-called 'hypotheticals' which explore the complexities of the debate and usually include **role-play**, which produces lively debate and presentations. For example, if students wish to learn the art of becoming 'professional' journalists, editors or media practitioners generally they must appreciate the moral/ethical implications of their decisions. Vocationally, media workers, almost as much as the legal profession, must be fully conversant with a wide range of legal and ethical issues which pervade the industry. See also **Calcutt Committee**.

media literacy/education (Australia). Media literacy in Australia is probably the most developed in the world. In almost all states the subject is required to be studied at all levels as part of the English curriculum.

See *Teaching Viewing and Visual Texts: Secondary* (1995) which includes:

- information that explains the value and relevance of viewing activities to students' educational development;
- ready-to-use activities and units from which teachers can select those most appropriate for their classes, etc.

email: r.quin@cowan.edu.au (Robyn Quin)

media literacy/education (Canada). The following organizations support media literacy in Canada:

Alliance for Children and Television (ACT)

Canadian Association of Media Education Organizations (CAMEO)

Jesuit Communications Project (JCP)

MediaWatch

The question of why teach media literacy is addressed by a *Media Literacy Resource Guide* compiled by Barry Duncan *et al*. Some reasons given are:

- Media dominate our political and cultural lives.
- Almost all information beyond direct experience is mediated.
- Media provide powerful models for values and behaviour.
- Media influence us without our being aware.
- Media literacy can increase our enjoyment of the media.
- Media literacy can make a passive relationship active.

Such justifications echo almost directly **Masterman**'s polemics for the need for media studies together with **McLuhan**'s influential beliefs.

The **key concepts** of media literacy according to Duncan *et al*. include:

- All media are constructed.
- The media construct reality.
- Audiences negotiate meaning in media.
- Media have commercial implications.
- Media contain ideological and value messages.

• Media have social and political implications.
• Form and content are closely related in the media.
• Each medium has a unique aesthetic form.

Again, the approach to education is reminiscent of the UK and elsewhere: 'Media literacy should not be considered as an add-on to the already crowded curriculum. A truly interdisciplinary activity, media literacy should be conceived as a means of facilitating the integration of critical thinking skills' (Duncan *et al.* 1989).

A scaffold approach to media education is suggested.

1 Providing students with an overall picture of what will be expected of them.

2 Breaking up and sequencing the order in which various concepts, skills and applications of skills will be taught and assessed.

3 Checking for students' understanding of what is being taught and requiring students to complete parts of the project as they go along.

4 And finally the project – students' demonstration of their understanding and teacher and/or peer evaluation of their understanding.

Duncan, B. *et al.* (1989) *Media Literacy Resource Guide.* Ontario Ministry of Education.
Pungente, J. and O'Malley, M. (1999) *More than Meets the Eye: Watching Television Watching Us.* Centre of Media Literacy (only $5).
email: pungente@epas.utoronto.ca (John Pungente SJ)
website: www.media-awareness.ca/eng/med/bigpict/medapp.htm

media literacy/education (Ireland). While it is not officially on the curriculum, a growing number of schools are including some form of media education linked to English literature studies. The new syllabus cites several films, including *Dances with Wolves*, and more literary adaptations, as recommended texts which can also be used for study within the English literature curriculum. However, critics suggest that such lip-service to media literacy is not adequately resourced either through teacher training or through curricular development. While this may be true, it will take time and effort to get it right, but at least a start has been made by introducing a wider range of media texts into more conventional curricula. In particular, with the growth of a 'gap' year of study after completing the Leaving Certificate (which is almost equivalent to A Levels in the UK, except students study often twice the number of subjects), many students are encouraged to study the use of media. There has been a large growth in degree and other courses on journalism, film and new media technologies which is also feeding back into the curriculum.

In Ireland there is a very high rate of media consumption, and particularly print media – which is one of the highest pro rata within Europe. Nevertheless, unlike the relatively long tradition in the UK, there has as of yet not been a groundswell of support to place media literacy firmly into the mainstream of the Irish curriculum.

media literacy/education (UK). As cited elsewhere, the evolution of media education and specific media courses has resulted as a consequence of the growing awareness and demand for more forms of media literacy and education generally. The post-**Dearing** *National Curriculum English Order* (DfE 1995) asserted that pupils should be taught to:

- extract meaning beyond the literal;
- analyse and discuss alternative interpretations;
- consider how texts are changed when adapted to different media;
- evaluate how information is presented;
- recognize, analyse and evaluate the characteristics of different types of text in print and other media.

Subsequent research cited by Andrew Hart found that the status of media studies within Britain has been enhanced by its assessment position within the new 1998 GCSE syllabuses. Also, progression and continuity within media have been enhanced since 1992 with all departments introducing a media policy into their English schemes of work. This demand for a comprehensive media literacy has never been as powerful as it is at present. The *Film Education Working Group Report* (BFI 1999), which was set up by the government's Department of Culture, Media and Sport, has proposed a detailed model for mandatory media teaching and support. The new mandatory post-2000 National Curriculum framework for ages 5–16 includes, for the first time, a requirement for learning about moving-image texts within the teaching of English.

British Film Institute (1999) *Making Movies Matter.* BFI.

Bowker, J. (ed.) (1991) *Secondary Media Education: A Curriculum Statement.* BFI.

Buckingham, D. (1990) *Watching Media Learning.* Falmer.

Buckingham, D. (1993) *Children Talking Television.* Falmer.

Buckingham, D. (ed.) (1993) *Reading Audiences: Young People and the Media.* Manchester University Press.

Hart, A. (1995) *Developing Media in Education.* Hodder.

Hart, A. (2000) 'Teaching Media in the Classroom: Research and Practice', *Australian Screen Education* 22, pp. 64–70.

email: copies of the report from aph1@soton.ac.uk
website: www.soton.ac.uk

media literacy/education (USA). Attempts to make media literacy uniform across the US states have been at best patchy. Some states like California, Hawaii and New Mexico at least embraced the discipline on paper, often to affirm a multicultural diversity and in the fight against **racism**. Notable organizations include San Francisco's Strategies for Media Literacy or the Los Angeles Centre for Media Literacy. The Clinton administration appears to be promoting media, especially new technology and other forms of literacy, but primarily, as with New Labour in the UK, for instrumental vocational reasons more than purely altruistic and empowerment motivations.

Melissa Phillips, a director of media literacy workshops for teachers in New York, asserts however in a recent article, that media education in the USA is a 'vague and unorganized effort'. With no central control by government, new technology in particular is regarded as the primary means for making students literate. Nevertheless there are pockets of hope, but in general media educationalists often look to the UK for examples of good practice. See the Phillips article, in *The English and Media Magazine* 40 (Summer 1999), pp. 35–8.

AMERICAN MEDIA LITERACY

The website www.medialit.org cites seven great debates in the media literacy movement, which include:

1 Does media literacy protect kids?

   (That is, by transforming a deeply flawed culture where the media act like a virus, or is such literacy merely an antidote for a culture which continues to 'amuse ourselves to death' (using Neil **Postman**'s famous phrase)?)

2 Does media literacy require media students to develop production activities?

   (Is it only by creating as well as interrogating media texts second-hand that students can begin to appreciate the complexity and literacy of media texts?)

3 Should media literacy have a popular culture bias?

   (By connecting with the actual popular texts students consume, it becomes easier to motivate students to study them more critically.)

4 Should media literacy have a stronger ideological agenda?

   (Particularly within an American context, with so many cultural and even conflicting political agendas, there is a strong conformist trend within education to de-politicize all forms of literacy. This remains at odds with the roots of the discipline area, particularly in the UK, which is predicated on an ideological critique of dominant culture.)

5 Can media literacy ever reach large numbers of students in American schools?

   (Like all predetermined curricula, it is difficult to provide the resources and time to integrate media literacy into the formal curriculum without having to reduce other related disciplines such as literature and history.)

6 Should media literacy initiatives be supported financially by media corporations?

   (While UK education has always railed against any form of direct sponsorship or financial support, more and more this is becoming a financial necessity in America and elsewhere. For example, even in the UK, film education is financed by the film industry, and this has become highly beneficial for teachers looking for easily accessed resources to use in the curriculum.)

7 Is media literacy best used as simply a means to an end?

(To improve the quality of TV and journalism, by getting young audiences to acquire discriminatory skills and thereby help to promote a more fruitful relationship between national media and how audiences consume such texts.)

(Cited at www.medialit.org/)

email: cml@medialit.org (Elizabeth Thoman at the Centre for Media Literacy in LA)

melodramas. Fictional dramas, based on a theatrical tradition which often exaggerates the use of emotional acting and storylines. They have become a central investigation particularly by feminist critics in their attempts to **recuperate** the genre for a feminist agenda and make links with the very popular and related soap genre. Often such researchers have focused on films directed by Douglas Sirk made in the 1950s, which were conventionally denigrated as weepies and dramatized emotional problems involving interpersonal relationships. Up to then, critics read such films as affirming the **patriarchal** values of Western society. Hollywood **classic narratives**, it is argued, reproduce bourgeois **ideology** because they implicate the spectator within a single point of view into a coherent, hierarchical ordered representation of the world. Social contradictions such as **class** and **gender** are concealed and ultimately resolved through mechanisms of displacement, and narrative **closure** – with all complications finally resolved. But 1970s feminist critics like Gledhill, Feuer and Byars began to question this conventional **Marxist** reading and promoted a new critical technique of **excess** – where the acting and/or *mise-en-scène* draws attention to itself rather than blending into the classic narrative format. Such melodramatic narratives, instead of merely reinforcing patriarchal values with their tagged-on, conformist closures, actually helped to recuperate and promote progressive feminist values which helped to **empower** females.

The excess cited in melodrama corresponds with the use of 'over-acting', for example, and the conscious and over-dramatic use of colour/music which occurs over and above the narrative requirements of the text. This form of excess often helped to dramatize the chief protagonist's state of physiological imbalance and her need for self-actualization. Such imbalance was not always resolved within the conventional 'tagged-on' classic narrative closure, which forced the female protagonists back into the patriarchal norms of family and submission. Critics postulated that prototypical melodramatic texts could be read in this radical and critical way, allowing female protagonists to become 'progressive' and 'positive' representations of females. However, little historical/contemporary audience research was available to substantiate this radical (and difficult) reading. This project of recuperating the often dismissed female-addressed genre of melodrama was effectively used to legitimate the growing dominance of **soap** opera culture in the 1970s, whose roots could be traced back to 1950s melodramatic films.

Gledhill, C. (ed.) (1991) *Stardom: Industry of Desire*. Routledge.

Thornham, S. (1997) *Passionate Detachments*. Routledge.

metanarrative. An overarching structure of meaning or 'world view' which helps to explain how society or human nature functions. Religion, or science, are examples. Particularly from a media context, **Marxism** and **capitalism** can be regarded also as controlling metanarratives which define meaning in terms of their own internal logic. **Postmodernist** discourse has been founded on the notion that controlling modernist metanarratives have broken down.

method school of acting. Has come to dominate Hollywood and involves the attempt to become mentally and sometimes even physically like the character the actor is performing. Internalizing their actions and behaviour patterns helps the actors to create more believable and identifiable roles, which satisfies the more naturalistic, identification-driven Hollywood system of filmmaking. This school was run by Lee Strasberg, who adopted the style/theory from the famous Russian theatrical teacher **Stanislavsky**. Hollywood actors who went through this school included Brando, Nicholson, and many major actors/actresses to come out of Hollywood.

Metz, Christian. Investigated the possibility of a 'language', even a grammar of film and audiovisual media, which has lost favour in recent years, being considered overly reductive. Critics argue that film can never be a single comprehensive language because of its multi-sensory, multimedia and hybrid quality which thereby prevented the possibility of having unique rules and a fixed grammar. It is alternatively suggested that audiovisual media contain a variety of often interconnecting languages. The orthodoxy of David **Bordwell**'s classic narrative model of the cinema overtook the over-complicated **semiotic** analysis of Metz. Nevertheless, his influence on film theory and analysis has been immense, with a range of other influential theories.

Gledhill, C. and Williams, L. (eds) (2000) *Reinventing Film Studies*. Arnold.

Metz, C. (1974) *Film Language: A Semiotics of the Cinema*. Indiana University Press.

Metz, C. (1982) *The Imaginary Signifier: Psychoanalysis and the Cinema*. Indiana University Press.

mimetic. Relating to levels of **realism** which a text produces. Mimesis is taken from the Greek, meaning the process of imitation. Audiovisual moving colour images create the most realistic representational art form. **Verisimilitude** is the correlation between how 'realistic' the representation is and the actual reality which is being represented. For example, the word 'tree' is low on the verisimilitude scale (but can be decoded if you understand the English language), whereas a drawing of a tree is higher and more universally understandable, and an actual photograph is even higher. Probably the highest level of verisimilitude is a moving image film shot in colour. Such terms can be used to explore the levels of 'realism' embedded within various mediated texts.

Barthes, R. (1977) *Image, Music, Text.* Fontana.

Berger, J. (1972) *Ways of Seeing.* Penguin.

Burton, G. (1990) *More than Meets the Eye.* Edward Arnold.

***mise-en-scène*.** What is viewed within the frame of a film; it was popularized by French critics in the 1950s. Studying the visual style of film/television involves focusing on how the scenes in the texts are visualized and put together.

The study of *mise-en-scène* helps students to appreciate the aesthetic devices used to visually create meaning in an audiovisual text. Areas which can be focused on include: set, props, lighting, colour, camera angle/lens, framing, **depth of field**, **proxemics** as well as density of image, for example.

Welsch, T. (1997) 'Class-room strategies for Film/Media Teaching Mise-en-Scene Analysis as a critical Tool', *Cinema Journal* 36(2).

mixed ability teaching. Teaching a range of **abilities** of children within a single class. Criticisms of these methods often point out the problems of correct pacing and the dangers of more able pupils not being stretched or challenged, while the less able become confused.

The study of media can function effectively within these constraints since the stimulus used can be read in so many ways, students can 'unpack' and 'deconstruct' texts to reflect their own interests and **cultural**/academic **competencies**. However, this is not to deny that serious difficulties might arise in dealing with a wide range of student capabilities.

moderation. The process by which different teachers, or examiners, agree on marks to be awarded for a particular examination or piece of work. Moderation therefore involves an attempt to achieve conformity with the same standards, usually based on a representative sample of work. A new strategy of **benchmarking** is in the process of being developed in universities to maintain standards across similar subject areas such as media studies.

For example, after A Level exams are completed, examiners are sent a sample of unmarked papers from within a wide range of abilities. After these have been marked 'blind', examiners meet to discuss and agree grades which become the normative criteria for the rest of the assessments to be marked. At degree level also, good practice usually involves a second marker acting as internal moderator together with an independent external moderator, thereby ensuring grading is consistent and at the appropriate level in relation to similar centres and courses.

modules. Short, self-contained, units within a course. These enable flexibility in the teaching and assessment arrangements made for a subject, rather than relying too heavily upon terminal assessment at the end of a course. Many Advanced and Advanced Subsidiary Level (A and AS Level) courses in media are now modular. In the revised specifications produced by awarding bodies in response to the new 'Subject Criteria for A and AS Level' (QCA 1999) modules are termed 'units'. Also many degrees in media adapt a modular system of delivery and assessment.

The opportunity to assess students at times other than the end of their course allows students to assess their progress through the course and learn from their mistakes, which takes pressure off final exams. There are pedagogical dangers, nevertheless, in a modular assessed course, most notably the possibility of fragmentation and compartmentalism, with some students unable to appreciate necessary connections across modules and across various levels of study.

Monroe, Marilyn. A famous **method** film star in the 1950s, who tragically committed suicide after a very volatile career which included scandal involving the American President Kennedy and other famous people. She is probably the most written-about actress of all time, due to her vulnerable persona and engaging acting style. **Madonna** in particular has appreciated her potency for a new generation, as discussed by **Fiske** and other cultural critics.

Dyer, R. (1979) *Stars*. BFI.

Dyer, R. (1986) *Heavenly Bodies: Film Stars and Society*. St Martin's Press.

Fiske, J. (1989) *Reading the Popular*. Unwin Hyman.

montage. Putting two often unrelated images together, creating meaning which is sometimes above and beyond the individual images before they were linked together. The theory was developed by the Russian filmmaker and writer Sergei **Eisenstein**, who exploited the theory both practically and theoretically.

moral panic. Caused by the mass media conspiring to help create fear or contempt in the general public against some elements in society. The term was first suggested in Britain by Stan Cohen in his study of 'mods and rockers' from the 1950s, where such teenage rebels were represented by the mass media as a threat to society and symbolic of dangerous developments in youth culture. Ever since, the mass media in particular are often **scape-goated** for promoting some horrific effects on 'normal' society. While youths have been a constant subject for moral panics, other 'outsiders', including unmarried mothers and gypsies as well as various ethnic minority groups, have been equally victimized. Stuart **Hall** has applied similar techniques, to show how the British working classes are made quiescent and also scape-goated, in his important studies of the representations of racism and violence in British news media in particular (see **crime TV** and **race** in particular).

The media themselves have been the focus of moral fear, with each campaign against the dangers of a new medium always finding reasons to suppose that it is especially dangerous in its new guise. In the nineteenth century, as Martin **Barker** discovered, so-called 'penny dreadfuls' (comics for children) were said to be highly corrupting, particularly because they were the only literature readers could afford. Similarly in the early twentieth century, films had the big screen, which exaggerated the moral dangers created as a result of total immersion in a darkened theatre. Comics could be 'pored over' for hours in private and television was regarded as particularly dangerous because it was viewed in the privacy of one's own home, when one's 'guard' was down. The video cassette recorder (VCR) and pre-recorded videos also carried grave risks, according to self-appointed censors, because children could choose what they watch, without parental control (Barker 1989). More recently the **internet** has come under attack for enabling pornography and other 'non-acceptable stimuli' to become available in the privacy of homes and raising the spectre of it being consumed by children.

Studies by David Morley and others suggest that audiences do not passively absorb inputs from the screen but instead produce **active readings** of what they see. Morley concludes that audiences' actual modes of relating to TV are far more complex than the protocols most researchers presuppose.

A range of ideological positions from extreme left wing (**communist**) to right wing (**fascist**) are often used to exaggerate various social/political problems within a given culture. These mediated positions usually end up scapegoating some minority or other and seek to construct a consensus of ordinary media consumers. For example, moral guardians like Mary Whitehouse rage against the 'filth' in mass media products (i.e. provocative representations of sex and violence) and crusade for stricter codes of **censorship**. This corresponds with right-wing beliefs and perceptions that focus on the decline in the family and the need to preserve 'innocence' in childhood. The 'at-risk' viewer is consequently stereotyped as a passive TV addict, aided and abetted by irresponsible parents. Television as a medium is thereby denigrated as chewing-gum for the eyes, and inferior to a more reflective literate culture.

Barker, M. (1989) *Comics: Ideology, Power and the Critics.* Manchester University Press.

Cohen, S. (1972) *Folk Devils and Moral Panics.*

Hall, S. (1994) *Coercion and Consent.* Polity Press.

Morley, D. (1986) *Family Television: Cultural Power and Domestic Leisure.* Comedia.

multicultural education. A form of education designed to reflect and celebrate the multicultural nature of society. Often the emphasis in multicultural education is placed upon mutual respect, appreciation of varied cultural and religious backgrounds, and communication. Concepts such as social justice, tolerance and co-operation are often stressed within the curriculum in the expectation that the values and attitudes of children will be enhanced. Media education actively supports multicultural approaches to education, both with regard to content and through formal methodologies of assessment and evaluation.

multiculturalism (USA). In America the term literally means the mixing of cultures and espouses the utopic notion that cultures and races can be harmoniously merged together. However, the history of America and the continuing **racial** conflicts tell a different story. The continent has grown and evolved as a result of mass emigration from Europe and around the world to what has been described as the 'land of hope and the free'. Of course such colonization must be placed within the context of usurping numerous tribes of Native American Indians, which were dispatched with often genocidal precision. (See for example many western films which deal in various ways with such racial conflicts over land and the frontier.) As America became more populated and urbanized the greatest multicultural mix continued to be a racial one.

As a progressive academic notion (attacked by critics as overly 'woolly and liberal') the term has achieved important gains within the establishment, particularly with regard to **political correctness**. For example, in 1960, 94 per cent of all American students were WASP (White, Anglo-Saxon Protestants) and over two-thirds were male. By contrast in 1993, 20 per cent of all students were non-white and over 55 per cent were women. Yet the biggest ethnic groups, including Hispanics and Afro-Americans, remain under-represented within educational establishments.

Throughout the Western world, multiculturalism has been put onto the agenda of cultural discourse, particularly within media studies, by focusing in particular on all types of representations.

Shohat, E. and Stam, R. (1994) *Unthinking Eurocentricism: Multiculturalism and the Media*. Routledge.

multimedia. A generic term which tends to focus on new computer media and its interrelationship with other media. In particular multimedia studies looks at the **internet** and **CD-Roms**, as well as various software packages which manipulate text, image and sound.

Murdoch, Rupert. See **ownership and control**.

music industry. Under-researched within media education and even under-used in conventional media studies. While **Madonna** and a few other music icons have been extensively analysed by **Fiske**, etc., nonetheless, the study of music and its effects on society has not been adequately analysed and should become a growth area for academic media research in the future. Ann Kaplan has produced an engaging study of music videos, and Dick Hebdige and Simon Frith in the UK have specialized in (sub)**cultures**, style and music culture analysis. But so much more is needed, and students often want to reflect their new music tastes.

Frith, S. (1988) *Music for Pleasure: Essays on the Sociology of Pop*. Routledge.

Frith, S. (1992) 'From the Beatles to Bros.: 25 years of British Pop', in *Social Changes in Contemporary Britain*, ed. N. Abercrombie. Polity Press.

Frith, S. and Goodwin, A. (eds) (1990) *On Record: Rock, Pop and the Written Word*. Pantheon.

Hebdige, D. (1979) *Subculture: The Meaning of Style*. Routledge.

Hebdige, D. (1987) *Cut 'n' Mix*. Comedia.

Kaplan, E. A. (1987) *Rocking around the Clock: Music Television, Postmodernism and Consumer Culture*. Methuen.

Richards, C. (1998) *Teen Spirits: Music and Identity in Media Education*. Routledge.

myth. Fiction used to explain human existence and tradition. **Lévi-Strauss** the anthropologist asserts that a myth is meaningful to the extent that it engages with the fundamental contradictions of a society and offers a 'solution' or at least mediates the underlying problems of a given society. John Hartley, a contemporary media writer, suggests that myths and **fairytales** allow a society to use factual or fictional characters and events to make sense of its environment, both physical and social. Myths refer to a culture's way of understanding, expressing and communicating to itself concepts that are important to a nation's sense of identity as a unique culture.

According to Umberto Eco, an Italian semiologist and writer, the primal myth of *Superman* involves the retelling of a well-known tale, which is central to myth's function in ritually reaffirming basic cultural beliefs. Roger Silverstone on the other hand suggests that the mythic grows out of our fears of chaos, establishing social solidarities and 'making sense' out of the panic engendered by the unknown. Mythic study has increased in popularity, particularly with the growth of mythic heroic super-heroes in the latter part of the twentieth century.

Roland **Barthes**, in his seminal book *Mythologies*, discovers myths in familiar objects and experiences like newspaper articles, a wrestling match, a film star and so on. All these, he argued, could be critically 'read' as texts, yet their meanings appears 'natural' and beyond question. **Ideological** critics have continued to argue that this remains a key function of myth.

Myth analysis also encourages a **structuralist** approach to the study of culture, since the aim is not to describe the social world as it already exists, but to uncover the processes and rules by which it is created and why people believe what they believe.

Sigmund Freud focused on the power of myths through his dream interpretation and considered that the unconscious contains an (in)accessible store of hidden memories and ideas. In particular, by applying the Greek myth of Oedipus to human sexuality and neurosis, Freud's theories have affected how human nature has been understood and represented in the mass media, particularly film. Freud considered all forms of art as reflections of inner psychological states, which have become very influential in psychological studies of film and media generally.

Barthes, R. (1972) *Mythologies*. Jonathan Cape.

Culler, J. (1983) *Barthes*. Fontana.

Tullock, J. (1990) *TV Drama*. Routledge.

N

narrative/narratology. Narratology looks at how *stories are told*, which includes all media products from fiction to documentary and even print news formats. The study of narratives remains a core preoccupation within media studies. Storytelling is important from childhood, when **fairytales** are narrated both orally and through reading. The mass media continue this process of storytelling for 'children' of all ages, with for example the Cinderella story becoming translated for a modern audience through *Pretty Woman* (1990).

A narrative has the power to position an audience in relationship to the story in opposing ways: either as objective, where audiences are positioned outside the action; or subjective, where the viewer/reader can be drawn directly into the story from the position of one of the characters, adapting their point-of-view (POV) in the narrative and seeing and identifying with the story from their eyes. An 'objective' camera gives the audience a privileged position from which to observe the story, which is often called an omniscient point-of-view – meaning an all-seeing/all-knowing point-of-view. But of course both positions may alternatively occur within the same scene.

The most influential theory concerning film narrative is the '**classic narrative** structure' promoted and consolidated by **Bordwell** using the theories of **Propp** and Todorov. This suggests that there are several rules/conventions which bind Hollywood films together through conventional 'cause–effect, logical and temporal' constructs. As a result the illusion of **naturalism/realism** is maintained by the use of several cues which signal narrative progression from an initial exposition of the story through enigma and disruption of balance towards final **closure** and resolution.

The classic narrative system is considered a chain of events in a cause–effect relationship, occurring in a definable time and space. Narrative structures work as a sense-making mechanism, linking events together so as to make their relationship meaningful and therefore understandable.

Hollywood narratives are not normally designed to confuse audiences, unlike much so-called **avant-garde** cinema of the 1960s and 1970s.

The classic narrative suggests that a fixed reality is simply being expressed and that the viewer only has to evaluate the discourse within the narrative, not the narrative discourse itself. In fact, according to Colin **MacCabe**, narrative remains a major factor in realism's attempt to conceal and even deny its own contradictions of production. This is because it claims a transparency of vision which is determined by a uniform controlling discourse.

According to Bordwell, the classic narrative system, at least in its purest form, ends in the 1960s with the cross-fertilization of European art cinematic techniques like Godard's use of '**jump-cuts**' and the proliferation of more radical yet highly successful youth-cultural texts like *Easy Rider* (1969), which greatly influenced Hollywood. More frequently towards the end of the century, there has been a continuous cross-fertilization of genres and styles which has affected the apparent purity of the classic narrative style. In particular, critics speak of the evolution of **postmodernism**, which promotes a 'mixing and matching' of styles including narrative types.

NARRATIVE EDITING

Continuity editing is organized in temporal sequence which becomes unnoticeable. Classical narrative editing techniques include

- match-cutting of shots linking scenes together;
- cross-cutting for suspense;
- close-up for dramatic focus;
- point-of-view perspectives, such as eye-line matching and the use of shot-reverse-shot.

A primary aim of the classic narrative structure is to encourage audience identification with the main protagonists, which serves to maximize pleasures of audiences, unlike the often alienating effects encouraged within art cinema. (See Peter **Wollen**'s structuralist model comparing the two types of filmmaking, where for example digression is often used to break up the linearity of classic narrative within **avant-garde** cinema.)

Bordwell *et al.* finally suggest that classic narrative promotes film **closure** which is unproblematic and restores the **ideological** status quo, whereas art cinema is bound by more radical devices, according to Peter Wollen, like '**estrangement**, foregrounding and (un)pleasure'.

Bordwell, D. et al. (1979) Film Art. Addison Wesley.

Bordwell, D et al. (1985) Narration in the Fiction Film. University of Wisconsin Press.

Bordwell, D. (1989) Making Meaning: Inference and Rhetoric in the Interpretation of Cinema. Harvard University Press.

Bordwell, D. and Thompson, K. (1994) Film History: An Introduction. McGraw Hill.

Cook, P. (ed.) (1999) The Cinema Book. BFI.

narrative: types of character. Propp, in *The Morphology of Folk Tales* (1968) analysed 100 Russian tales and noted structural similarities which could be condensed into the following groups of characters:

- hero (or apparent anti-hero);

- villain (set in opposition in the text and the struggle over something each wants);

- princess figure;

- subsidiary characters, including the donor, father-figure, etc.

This model can be applied very easily to *Star Wars*, for example. **Bordwell** suggests that narratives are composed in order 'to reward, modify, frustrate or defeat the perceiver's search for coherence'.

Elsaesser, T. (1981) 'Narrative Cinema and Audience-Oriented Aesthetics', in *Popular Television and Film*, ed. Bennett, T. *et al.* BFI.

Fiske, J. (1987) *Television Culture*, ch. 8 on narrative. Routledge.

Wollen, P. (1968) *Signs and Meanings in the Cinema*. BFI.

Wollen, P. (1976) 'Structural Analysis of *North by North-West*', *Film Form* I(I).

naturalism. A form of representing reality explored in painting and literature and continued into film and TV, which gives the illusion of being 'natural' and 'normal' and thereby 'real'.

This form has been strongly criticized by theorists like Lukacs for hiding the true ideological reality of life within the form. Contemporary TV writers like John McGrath and Troy Kennedy Martin (see for example, his cult conspiracy eco-drama series *Edge of Darkness*) often creatively subvert conventional forms of naturalism, thereby creating identifiable characters and places. Yet at the same time naturalism has also been associated with political progressivism, such as the nineteenth-century novels of Zola or Ken Loach's successful polemical film narratives like *Cathy Come Home*. The concept is primarily applied within **realism** and **narrative** debates.

nature/nurture debate. Focuses on whether genetic influences on intelligence, personality and **ability** are stronger than socio-cultural, environmental/educational influences. Keenly discussed among educationalists, psychologists and sociologists, this issue has spawned the creation of extreme **theories** about the development of intelligence within different racial groups.

From a media perspective, this debate feeds directly into **effects theory**. If nature and genetics are relatively more important, then media cannot have as great a nurturing influence as suggested, on children specifically, and vice-versa. Social scientists suggest that bad or aberrant/dysfunctional behaviour can be traced to poor and non-nurturing environments. For example, lots of gangster movies and crime texts try to explain why the criminal has turned out as they have, by focusing on their childhood environment.

new media/technology. Includes all recent technical innovations in the media. It could be argued, however, that all mass media have at some stage been described as 'new media'. In the context of a new millennium, the term is particularly applied to the **internet**, **digital** TV and **multimedia** generally. Debates occur whether such new media are changing society and if so how? For example, J. S. Katz, *Perspectives in the Study of Film* (1971), affirms that new media are not just gimmicks for creating worlds of illusion, but 'new languages' with new and unique 'powers of expression' (p. 23), whereas J. D. Bolter and R. Grusin, with their concept of '**remediation**', counter that there is a powerful interconnectivity between new and old media. New technology most certainly affords a wide range of platforms for audiences to engage with its wider range of services and texts.

But within a media educational context the apparent benefits of increased **interactivity** and communication remain problematic. Marxist critics, for example, apply theories of **technological determinism**, which infer that the growth of technology is consciously designed to control human behaviour and serves to increase consumer spending. In many ways this negates the benefits of interactivity and **empowerment** in particular.

Bolter, J. D. and Grusin, R. (1999) *Remediation: Understanding New Media.* MIT.

Convergence, journal of new media published by the University of Luton Press.

New Right A collective term used to describe Conservative pressure groups and think-tanks in Britain and elsewhere. Many critics suggest that the New Right successfully drove the educational agenda of the late 1980s with their beliefs in educational efficiency bred from competition, privatization, **deregulation** and the promotion of market forces.

new technology. See **new media/technology**.

news agencies. Commercial organizations who gather news stories for the purposes of distributing them to other media for a fee. News agencies are usually used by newspapers and broadcasting clients who require these external sources of information and/or imagery because they do not have or cannot afford to get such stories in-house. For instance, to keep foreign correspondents in every country in the world would be very expensive, even for a major news broadcaster like the BBC. So many foreign stories especially are acquired through agencies to ensure a comprehensive news-gathering capability. The largest news agencies include AFP, AP (Associated Press) and Reuters, who in 1995 had a revenue of £2,703 million with over 2,000 journalists in 90 countries.

Briggs, A. and Cobley, P. (eds) (1998) *The Media: An Introduction.* Longman.

news values. The relative criteria that determine the selection of news stories. Norwegians Galtung and Ruge first identified such values, which are used to decide how much time and space is devoted to the range of stories considered newsworthy by various media industries. Such criteria are used to distinguish the relative importance of news stories across local and national news alongside formal divisions between **tabloids** and **broadsheets**. The criteria used to evaluate news include the following:

proximity – how geographically near the story is to its audience

frequency – how often the news story usually occurs

amplitude – relative size of the story

unambiguity – certainty of events happening as reported

familiarity – ability of audiences to relate to a story

surprise – suddenness of story occurring or breaking

continuity – story's fit into a pattern of related stories

These criteria are used extensively to analyse print media within media curricula.

Curran, J and Seaton, J. (1997) *Power without Responsibility*. Routledge.

newspaper language-(rules). There are a number of common features within the language used in newspapers. Journalists must appreciate the variation in housestyles if they are to move from one newspaper to another. The greatest variations in language can be seen when comparing **tabloid** and **broadsheet** newspapers. Whereas tabloid language must always be simple, provocative and punchy, broadsheet language is often more difficult and sophisticated. However, in general a number of rules can be applied to all good journalism:

1 Go for the shorter word where there are alternatives and use single words. For example, 'near' not 'adjacent to' and 'now' instead of 'at the present time'.

2 Avoid foreign or little-used words. For example, use 'meeting' and not 'rendezvous'.

3 Avoid excessively long sentences and use active rather than passive clauses.

4 Avoid excessive use of adjectives and adverbs.

5 Beware of jargon and banish clichés.

6 Keep punctuation simple and paragraphs short.

(Hodgson, G. W. (1992) *Modern Newspapers Practice*. Focal Press)

niche audience. A highly targeted audience rather than a large undifferentiated group of various types of consumers. Particularly with a proliferation of new media sources, such as magazines, television and radio channels, there is a greater capability of ensuring that the specific needs of interest groups are met. For example, BBC Radio 1–5 have specific styles which conform with a range of age groups and interests that in turn correspond with a carving out of the larger, national radio audiences which could not be satisfied with one radio channel.

non-verbal communication (NVC). The use of hand and other gestures as well as all body movements to create meaning. **Communications** A Level in particular develops the skills of reading human posture and body movement, which can be of enormous benefit both in public and in private life. The importance of NVC is shown with regard to the power of initial impressions in interviews. To analyse star performance as well as more humble media roles it is necessary to fully comprehend the range of signals developed within NVC. Such knowledge can aid students' performance in role-play and can help develop skills which can be used when working in the media.

Price, S. (1996) *Communication Studies.* Longman.

norm-referencing. Finding the appropriate standards and criteria to develop comparative **assessment** standards. For example, a cohort of pupils' marks are placed in rank order and then grades are allocated to divisions of that order. Thus grades are awarded according to ranking rather than based on actual achievement. The assessment of performance is therefore achieved by direct reference and comparison to the performance of one's peers.

For example, the top 5 per cent of pupil marks may be awarded an A grade, while the bottom 10 per cent may be ungraded, whatever the distribution of those marks might be. Here pupils' work is being judged in comparison with that of other pupils and there is no fixed **standard** that has to be achieved to be awarded a particular grade. In general, however, such abstract assessment strategies are often linked with **criterion-referencing**, where benchmarks are used to determine pass levels and grades above, up to A* grades.

NVQ (National Vocational Qualification). A competence-based qualification largely taught and assessed in the workplace as opposed to the **GNVQ (General National Vocational Qualification)**, which is based in the classroom.

OFSTED (Office for Standards in Education). A non-ministerial UK government department, independent of the Department for Education and Employment (DfEE), whose role is to improve standards of achievement and quality in education through inspection, reporting and advice. OFSTED inspects schools on a regular basis and has recently also taken on the role of inspecting further education (FE) colleges, publishing a report after each inspection. Inspections are carried out within a national framework, with teams of independent inspectors contracting for work under a system of competitive tendering.

mail: OFSTED, Alexandra House, 33 Kingsway, London, WC2B 6SE
tel: 020 7421 6800
website: www.ofsted.gov.uk

online. Describes the services available to anyone who is directly connected via their computer and modem to the **internet**. In the UK and elsewhere governments have been actively involved in maximizing the percentage of the population who can go online, affirming that this becomes symptomatic of an educated and communication-sophisticated populace who are empowered by the new technology. New service providers are in a constant competitive war to get as many customers online as possible.

ontology. A branch of metaphysics/**philosophy** concerned with what really does exist, rather than only appears to exist. Ontology is thus concerned with the essence of things and their existence. The nature of being and the relationship of existence to human consciousness is central to its study. Especially through the core concepts of **representations** and **realism**, particularly with a growing preoccupation with **cyborg** theory in film, ontology has become more directly discussed within **cultural**/media studies.

open-ended question. One where the pupil is encouraged to answer in their own words in a reasonably expansive way, rather than by giving a yes-or-no response to a closed question, or responding to a multiple-choice question. In media education the use of open-ended questions is often favoured, as these require pupils to think through media concepts and ideas for themselves; a process that is less likely with the use of closed questioning. Questionnaires seldom use open-ended questions, preferring the use and ease of analysis of closed questions which require simple yes/no/don't-know answers.

other. A very common term within **cultural studies** which often analyses how marginal (outsider) **representative** characters – for example Native American Indians, homosexuals, non-whites and even females – are constructed as in some way deviant or non-normal. **Feminists** and so-called 'queer theorists', together with **race** theorists, speak of how minorities, while represented as being marginalized, nonetheless often simultaneously evoke more 'progressive' and provocative aspects of the dominant culture. Edward Said, an important multicultural theorist and literary critic, speaks of 'Orientalism' – which encourages the stereotyping of the East by the dominant Western culture – as both devious and exotic. Further examples occur in **crime** and science fiction texts where the other is represented as a criminal or monster or alien – often read as symbolic of a feared and repressed aspect of normal or dominant human behaviour and social consensus/conventions.

Said, E. (1978) *Orientalism*. Random House.

Said, E. (1992) *Culture and Imperialism*. Knopf.

Shohat, E. and Stam, R. (1994) *Unthinking Eurocentrism: Multiculturalism and the Media*. Routledge.

ownership and control. A major focus and area of study which looks at how most media organizations are owned and consequently how this might affect their output. Many studies emphasize how media organizations – film companies, TV, press, radio and new media – are first and foremost industrial and commercial organizations that produce and distribute commodities which are designed to maximize return on investment. Where this economic power becomes most important is when media organizations take over a large share of media production.

For example, media critics often cite the Murdoch empire, which controls a wide range of newspapers in the UK, including: the *Sun, The Times,* the *News of the World* and the *Sunday Times.* In particular, the power of the *Sun*, which is the largest-selling daily in Britain at around 4 million, is often analysed to determine its effects on audiences. For instance the *Sun* was a long-term supporter of Margaret Thatcher and the Conservative party, but then suddenly switched allegiance to Tony Blair and New Labour at the start of an election campaign and claims to have been instrumental in eventually bringing the Labour party to power in a landslide victory in 1997. Media analysis has been divided on the relative power of the media to affect political voting swings. Nonetheless, the power of the press to determine and even reinforce the news agenda, as well as affirming pervasive attitudes and values within a society, cannot be underestimated.

Murdoch's empire does not end with newspapers, since he now also has a dominant share in the Sky TV channel, which is becoming very powerful, having succeeded in capturing the viewing rights of British Premier League football. In America, his empire controls *20th Century Fox*, which also has a huge back-catalogue of films that can be shown on his TV channels. He also controls various Australian newspapers, including the *Times* and *Fontana* publishers, together with numerous non-media interests.

Mergers and takeovers have become more and more pervasive within the global economy, with owning and controlling media organizations often representing the 'icing on the cake' within big international deals. Naturally this causes concern for media critics, who try to anticipate the political and economic effects of such deals. If the 'bottom line' is always the share price of the organization, then the content, especially if it is controversial, can always be affected within such multinationally controlled media organizations.

A very good 'fictional' case study of how an American TV news programme might be compromised by such a takeover bid is Michael Mann's film *The Insider* (2000), which looks at the true story of a 'whistle blower' on the tobacco industry in America. In general terms the history of the studio system and film production is a good case study of how ownership and control affects filmic output. Because media industries are an essential part of the capitalist world economy, media analysis tends to foreground the bottom-line economic imperative to make money. Ideological analysis has always privileged this way of looking at the media, yet surprisingly, such a primary influence is sometimes omitted from textbooks and media readers.

Maltby, I. and Craven, I. (1995) *Hollywood Cinema*. Blackwell.

O' Sullivan, T. *et al.* (1994) *Studying the Media: An Introduction*. Edward Arnold.

Skeggs, B. and Mundy, J. (1992) *The Media: Issues in Sociology*. Nelson.

P

paparazzi photography. The activity of highly paid freelance photographers who shoot snapshots of the rich and famous, and sell them to newspapers and magazines. This type of photography has had a very bad press of late with the death of Diana, Princess of Wales.

paradigm shift. A significant change in the way in which a school of thought considers its field of study, theories, methodologies and problems that have to be solved. When the old paradigm no longer meets the needs of a community of scholars a new paradigm arises which is accepted, following a process known as a paradigm shift. Marxist theory can be considered as a paradigm as can a religion or even a language. Historically, critics talk of changes between epochs like the Agricultural age or the Industrial age, with some even talking about the present epoch as an Information age. In particular **McLuhan**, for example, talks about a paradigm shift from a typographic culture, which is driven by the written word and aided by the invention of the printing press, to the electronic mass media, driven by instantaneous visual communication.

parallax. A technical term for the difference between what can be seen through the viewfinder and what is filmed by the camera's lens. In SLR (single-lens reflex) cameras, such distortions are avoided, since what is seen through the viewfinder is what is actually filmed.

participant observation. A **research** technique whereby a researcher joins a group he or she wishes to study and observes the behaviour of the group from a member's viewpoint. This research strategy is often used to bolster a range of **ethnographic** studies on, for example, audience pleasures.

passive learning. A situation where little or no pupil contribution is made to the learning process. Here, pupils are expected to be passive recipients of information given to them in whatever form the teacher feels is appropriate. It is from objections to this form of rote learning that media studies has sought to generate, together with newer interactive styles of teaching, a more engaging approach to education generally.

patriarchy. A male-dominated society, often correlated with a **capitalist** one. Marxist and particularly **feminist** critics infer that the mass media often actively promote a negative attitude and stereotype of women, which helps to reinforce the legitimacy and normalcy of a male-dominated society.

Payne Fund. A financial arrangement which allowed for extensive research in America to determine the effects of the mass media on society. Many critics suggested that much of this research was improperly designed, with faulty methodological measures, and that such studies began with an overriding proposition which sought to prove a direct correlation between the media and its effects on society. Its findings have always been inconclusive, with numerous qualifications which all but invalidated such research.

pedagogical progressivism and media studies. Pedagogy is literally the science of teaching, including curriculum construction and teaching methodology. In essence, pedagogy is concerned with what teachers plan out as the aims of education, and how they select and use certain teaching methods and materials in the classroom to achieve these aims.

Early media writers like Len **Masterman**, in his (1980) study *Teaching about Television*, along with other educationalists, questioned the 'rote' or 'banking' system of knowledge acquisition and learning within a hierarchical teacher–pupil relationship. The open and 'progressive' form of education championed by Masterman and others was conceived in opposition to the **Leavisite** position, which believed in a hierarchical **canon** of valuable texts that needed to be imparted to students to promote a worthwhile culture. Leavis suggested that if anything like a worthy idea of satisfactory living is to be saved, students must be trained to 'discriminate and resist'. He continued in *Culture and Environment* (1933) to argue for the values of an organic 'culture' as opposed to the mass-productive 'culture' of the mass media.

Media texts originally entered the classroom in film appreciation classes in order that they could be used as a bulwark against the influences of inferior and even pernicious popular culture and help to discriminate 'quality' from 'second rate' film texts. Leavis and his purist followers strongly believed that literature must be seen as a social force and a defence against what they regarded as encroaching barbarism, perpetuated no doubt by the growing mass mediated popular culture.

Manuel Alvarado, another founding father of media education, avoids such polarizing attitudes but questions Masterman's assumption that there is 'a best way' to teach and concludes that teaching and learning is a struggle, so that teachers must remain clear about the educational aims and subject areas they are covering. More recently David **Buckingham** has also contested Masterman's crusading rhetoric, emphasizing the need to develop a 'theory of learning' rather than what he deduced was Masterman's agenda of liberating students from the 'false beliefs' acquired from the media. Buckingham suggested that students often try to simply guess what is in the teacher's mind and therefore come up with the 'right answer'. This raises an important pedagogical dilemma, whether what educationalists think they are teaching is really what students are learning.

This educational debate is part of a bigger discussion which, its early antagonists suggest, uses education, in the crudest terms, as a means of saving the 'working classes' from the 'chains of ideology'. The teacher is positioned as moral guardian who almost serves to inoculate students against the pernicious pleasures of the mass media. Media studies as a young pedagogical discipline was considered an important site of cultural and political struggle, to determine *whose* knowledge about the media should be produced and learned, as well as *how* students should be learning the media, and for *whose* benefit. While becoming less contentious, these controversial debates have never been fully resolved, which probably contributes to the growing maturity yet continuing freshness within the discipline.

The theorist **Vygotsky** in particular is applied by Buckingham, to affirm that the 'direct teaching of concepts is impossible and fruitless' (Lusted 1991, p. 218). The aim of media education, according to Buckingham, is not merely to allow children to read or make sense of media texts, or even to write their own; it must also enable them to understand and to analyse their own activity as readers and writers. Language, Buckingham concludes, 'serves as a fundamental tool in developing thought and understanding, to enable students to use language is clearly to empower them. Yet to enable them to understand language itself is to empower them still further' (Lusted 1991, p. 219). Such a strategy corresponds with the fundamental aims of **media literacy** throughout the English-speaking world.

See the wide range of key texts already cited in the Introduction.

Buckingham, quoted in Lusted, D. (ed.) (1991) *Media Studies Book.* Routledge.

Peirce, C. S. An American philosopher who founded the study of pragmatics, which studies knowledge and meaning as mediated by signs. He constructed a model of semiotics which included **icon**, **index** and **symbol,** and he was convinced that signs were more complex than, for example, Saussure suggests, and totally dependent on context for their meaning.

Fiske, J. (1982) *An Introduction to Communications Studies.* Methuen.

Price, S. (1993) *Media Studies.* Pitman.

phenomenology. In particular focuses on the relationship between the perceiving individual and the world of things, people and actions that might be perceived. Reality has no meaning except as individuals experience such phenomena. Even on the basis of the tiniest scrap of information, humans will provide whatever is missing (filling in the gaps) until they have organized their perceptual fields into objects that make sense.

Allen, R. (1987) *Channels of Discourse.* Methuen.

Blackburn, S. (1996) *Dictionary of Philosophy.* Oxford University Press.

philosophy. The study of the nature of knowledge (epistemology), wisdom, behaviour, existence, reality and moral values by the use of reason and argument. More recently, philosophical reasoning has been explicitly used within debates and even within teaching strategies in media education. For example, epistemological debates concerning how we know what we know have continued to inform the core concept of **realism**. They have also been reflected within **representational** debates that have been greatly assisted by the formulation of **cyborg** theory. Most particularly, **ethical** debates have always been at the forefront of media discussions.

Blackburn, S. (1996) *Dictionary of Philosophy.* Oxford University Press.

photography. The use of lens-based cameras to take two-dimensional representations of three-dimensional reality. The practical creation and analysis of black and white and colour still images has remained an important part of teaching and learning **media literacy**. Still images can provide a controlled and relatively cheap medium to explore many major issues concerning all forms of mediation. For example, media studies curricula often analyse the composition and representation as well as the contextualization of such images and how they are **anchored** with captions in photojournalist pieces in newspapers and magazines. Also the switch to **digital** photography within newsrooms and elsewhere has contributed to the growth of the medium.

The aims and objectives of a photographic pathway on the media arts degree at the University of Luton include the following:

- To explore the qualities and properties of the medium in its widest context and allow students to appreciate the range of communication possibilities.
- To teach students how to look at, interpret, understand and critically assess the use of still images as a medium of communication.
- To foster an understanding of the implications of new technology on (still) image production.

Specific objectives include:

- To teach students the basic principles of black and white photographic processing and printing.
- To develop students' ability to plan and visualize a brief and work to complete within both time and technological limitations. (In particular the development of *framing*, *composition* and *planning* skills.)
- To develop students' ability to meet the needs of clients and customers while also striving to remain both inventive and original. (For example the development of *selection*, *editing* and creative *individuality*.)
- Students' learning how to use digital cameras, image manipulation software (such as Photoshop) and outputting and printing.
- Students learning to effectively plan and manage (visual) project work to both present ideas clearly and become confident in justifying and explaining work within the context of media studies generally.

Lister, M. (ed.) (1995) *The Photographic Image in Digital Culture*. Routledge.

Squires, C. (ed.) (1990) *The Critical Image: Essays on Contemporary Photography*. Lawrence and Wishart.

Wells, L. (ed.) (2000) *Photography: A Critical Introduction*. Routledge.

Wright, T. (1999) *The Photographic Handbook*. Routledge.

photojournalism. Puts in practice the old adage which affirms that a picture is worth a thousand words. The ability to capture a decisive key moment for a news story is becoming more and more important in the visually driven media culture. The assumption that the camera tells a more compelling truth, which words cannot grasp so instantaneously, remains one of photography's strengths. Such assumptions are, however, endlessly questioned by media theorists, now that such images can be easily manipulated at the touch of a key on the computer.

In particular, the scavenger, cheque-book journalism of the '**paparazzi**' photographers has been most denigrated in recent years, particularly in relation to the death of the ex-Royal, Diana. Nevertheless, as was well documented, these photographers would not be in business if the public did not have such an insatiable desire for more and more images of celebrities. At the other end of the spectrum would be syndicate photographers, like the famous Magnum company of Harold Evans, Cartier Bresson *et al.*, who were instrumental in capturing some of the most important and influential moments in the twentieth century.

Photography in journalism and elsewhere is often used to illustrate the use of **semiotics** as a tool for decoding such images, as well as the **representational** meaning of images, often **anchored** by headlines and framing.

pilot. A trial run of a new series on radio or more usually TV. Rather than risk investing in a whole new series, media companies often try out new formats and gauge industry or public reaction before completing a full series. This strategy is used extensively in America, where great weight is placed on the success of a pilot. This can result in innovative and creative products not being made, because more time is needed for audiences to warm to the latest forms of innovation. Apologists for the system argue that poor ideas, or 'turkeys' as they are often described in the trade, can be nipped in the bud long before scarce resources are wasted on them.

plagiarism. Using the 'writings' of another without crediting them with it. It is a very serious academic offence and often occurs because students are not fully conversant with **research** conventions. However, with the growth of the **internet**, students are often tempted to 'cut and paste' material directly from web pages and pass it off as their own. Because of the multiplicity of sites, it is sometimes difficult to detect, but remains a high-risk activity. Students can be expelled from courses if they attempt such strategies. See also **copyright**.

Plato's allegory of the cave. The Greek writer Plato is considered the founding writer of modern Western **philosophy** and constructed his theories around 'ideal essences' as expressed in art compared to 'crude reality'. He used the allegory of a cave to illustrate how human perception is controlled/mystified by a false sense of reality. Plato preached how humans metaphorically live their lives in dark caves and only perceive shadows cast by fires on the walls aided by some natural light coming in from the opening of the cave. Consequently they do not see the 'true reality' of life but only a flickering reflection through the shadows cast on the walls of their environment. This metaphor can be used to illustrate the illusion of **realism** presented by mass media which in some ways equates with Baudrillard's notion of the **simulacrum**.

political correctness (PC). A belief and practice of not offending certain minorities, including women and other groups, by using derogatory language, etc. It became popular in the late 1980s and 1990s, especially on American college campuses in support of **feminism** and **multiculturalism** in particular. Critics have argued, however, that there is a danger of this curtailing free speech.

Duchak, A. (1999) *The A/Z of Modern America*. Routledge.

politics and media effects. Politics involve the creation of a consensus in Western democracies so that nations can be both controlled and manipulated by the politicians who are in power. The mass media is considered a major force which both reflects and sometimes questions such use of political power. This is a major **ideological** preoccupation and focuses on how the mass media affects politics and vice-versa. It does this in several ways, including

- how the media set **agendas** for topics. Politicians in particular cannot always initiate or sustain topics without the help of the mass media.
- how the media give form and substance to world events. Through the media we learn what is good and bad, right and wrong, just or unjust. Reporters in particular act as narrators and interpreters for audiences to decode mediated events.
- how the media often reduce abstract or ideological principles to human personal components.

Politicians in particular need a medium to get across their agenda. Without the oxygen of the media, politicians would find it very difficult to get across their message and be heard by the people. However, this in turn also means that politicians and politics often have to comply with the entertainment and commercial constraints of the media. They can also become the target for media investigations to highlight corruption, or simply to expose private sexual deviancy for prurient audience gratification. Especially if the media is a **public service broadcast** provider, then it is incumbent on such media to expose political corruption and act as moral **watchdog** for the general public by remaining an independent investigative power or a '**fourth estate**'. How successful the mass media are in carrying out such duties and responsibilities remains a preoccupation within much media analysis.

Curran, J. and Seaton, J. (1997) *Power without Responsibility*. Routledge.

polysemy. The feature that texts have more than one meaning. Students of the media quickly learn that it is highly dangerous to assume there is ever only one meaning within any mass media text. Especially with such large audiences, there are often many interpretations and meanings constructed as a result. See **Hall**'s explanation of dominant/negotiated and oppositional **meanings**, for example.

popular arts. The book of this title by Stuart **Hall** and Paddy Whannel written in 1964 is often considered an important benchmark in the evolution of media study in the UK and elsewhere. They attempted to widen the canon of education to include new forms of communication, including radio, cinema and recorded music. Yet, surprisingly, the book's premise was based on a fear of commercialization within popular culture. Because of the longer historical pedigree of film appreciation and critical analysis, it has become more quickly legitimized within academic structures and cross-fertilized with aesthetic debates from art and narrative literary debates. Nevertheless, many of the theoretical and methodological strategies used to subsequently analyse film have become filtered and adapted into more mainstream media education in general. (See **pedagogical progressivism and media studies**.)

Turner, G. (1991) *British Popular Culture: An Introduction*. Unwin Hyman.

popular culture. The study of all forms of popular entertainment, from comics, films and TV to dance and music, for instance. The mass media represents a major proportion of what has come to be described as popular culture: TV, film, radio and popular press. Such media are sometimes contrasted with **avant-garde** cinema or even great literature. The most common examples of popular culture which have been extensively analysed in media education include **soap** operas and **crime** dramas, for example. Within the broad umbrella of **cultural studies**, analysts such as John **Fiske** speak of audiences' ability to actively resist and play with the dominant ideology of popular cultural messages. **Feminist** critics, on the other hand, often try to recuperate a denigrated form like the soap opera as being more progressive and radical than it is often considered. All such apologists for the legitimacy of popular culture focus on the valuing of **audiences**' pleasures rather than dismissing them like early **Marxists**, who remained fixated by the dangers of manipulation of mass audiences and the possibility of succumbing to **false consciousness**. Audiences' pleasures can no longer be dismissed out of hand by elitist critics who appear to have a higher order of value built into their analysis.

(See extensive list of references in **culture** sections).

pornography. What outrages contemporary standards of decency or humanity accepted by the public at large. But who defines its apparently common-sense subject matter? Is it the general public, the producers and/or the government authorities?

Whereas the **right wing** regards sex as sacred, and pornography as encouraging the corruption of the young who need protection, the **left wing** is equally worried, especially from a conventional Marxist-feminist position, regarding pornography as contributing to the perpetuation of male domination. For example, Andrea Dworkin presents an extreme anti-pornographic position which defines such representation as positioning women as victims of masculinity. Laura Mulvey developed a more general notion of the male gaze as permeating Hollywood cinema, which serves to objectify women's bodies, thereby exaggerating male power over women. Other post-feminists like Linda Williams came to regard pornography as potentially liberating and even democratizing sexual representation while promoting active female **agency**.

Atkins, T.R. (ed.) (1997) *Sexuality in the Movies.* Indiana University Press.

Dworkin, A. (1981) *Pornography: Men Possessing Women.* Women's Press.

Griffin, S. (1982) *Pornography and Silence: Culture's Revenge against Nature.* Women's Press.

Palumbo, D. (ed.) (1986) *Eros in the Mind's Eye: Sexuality and the Fantastic in Art and Film.* Greenwood Press.

Williams, L. (1991) *Hard Core: Power, Pleasure and the Frenzy of the Visible.* HarperCollins.

portraiture. Involves capturing an image of the human features and personality. It is probably the most enduring form of painting, and has over the last century become applied in **photography**. From the snap images of relatives and friends to the more formal ritualized portraits captured by 'professional' photographers, images of human beings remain our most enduring record. Many of the conventions of representing the human form have evolved aesthetically from the long history of painting portraits. Again, a lot can be learned about the two forms of image-making by comparing and contrasting painting and photography.

Key skills which are usually acquired through the application of portraiture include

- how to approach the making of a self-portrait or a representation of another person;

- use of natural light; and

- using flash and interiors.

Berger, J. (1972) *Ways of Seeing.* Penguin.

Brandt, B. (1982) *Portraits.* Gordon Fraser.

Clarke, G. (1992) *The Portrait in Photography.* Reaktion Books.

Linwood, J. (1986) *Staging the Self: Self Portrait Photography 1840–1980s.* National Portrait Gallery Catalogue.

Sherman, C. (1990) *Untitled Film Stills.* Cape.

Sontag, S. (1977) *On Photography.* Penguin.

Spence, J. (1986) *Putting Myself in the Picture.* Camden Press.

positivist rationality. Suggests that progress is regarded as technological growth and the learning and mastery of skills for solving practical problems. The underpinning models that suggest this include:

Technocratic – which became dominant in America and regarded the notion of schooling as functionally similar to any form of business enterprise;

Interpretative – which focuses on how forms and underlying assumptions contribute to an understanding of life. It is postulated that humans are not passive recipients of information;

Reproductive – such as **Althusser**'s already discussed, which suggest that schools help to reproduce a class society as part of the dominant ideology.

Postman, Neil. In his very readable *Amusing Ourselves to Death* (1995) rightly affirms that 'knowledge' is not just there in a book, waiting for someone to come along and learn it. Rather, true knowledge and understanding is produced in response to questions, and new knowledge results from asking new questions. His ideas are often based on the notion of the 'three-minute culture', which suggests that the mass media perpetuates a superficial culture which demands instant gratification in audiences.

Mass media, he claims, have promoted this ultra-fast, stimulus-driven culture, which results in students being unable to focus and concentrate on literate culture for any length of time. They therefore find it difficult to learn and assimilate knowledge. Postman used grand generalizations which asserted that Western society has moved out of a 'literary culture' that privileges patience, complexity and sophistication, towards an 'electronic' one, which privileges speed, shallowness and vacuousness. While his writings may appear to be somewhat crude and polemical, he inspires debate and discussion which helps students engage with major issues concerning the potency of the mass media.

postmodernism. Based on scepticism of all grand **theories** or metanarratives, such as modernism, which ostensibly believed in the possibility of progress, coherence and scientific rationality. Postmodernism attempts to describe and explain contemporary human existence from perspectives different from those of modernist and post-Enlightenment thinkers.

While conservatives and even **Marxists** regard this most slippery of concepts as the confirmation of the dead-end of the old democratic routes and thus a confirmation of the status quo, more radical critics regard the phenomenon as helping to unfold and stimulate new openings and fractures within conventional discourses alongside the break-up of existing stultifying **metanarratives** such as Marxism. Optimistic critics affirm that the umbrella discourse allows for more space within the otherwise homogeneous discourse of critical study, especially through a greater appreciation of the range of pleasures media texts can provide. Instead of always questioning and deconstructing media texts (which is relatively easy to carry out from the academic heights of media theory), more democratic space is afforded for **liminal**/excessive/counter positions to be proposed. Instead of having to decide between one reading position and another, postmodernist discourse promotes a pluralistic 'both–and' approach rather than an 'either–or' polarized position, so that the interpretant does not have to choose a given strategy and stick to it. Nevertheless, there remain serious dangers of degenerating into relativistic slippage and endless ambiguity.

From a pedagogical position it is usually better for students to become proficient with metanarrative debates, particularly Marxism and other 'modernist' theories, before engaging with postmodernist theory. Otherwise students at best become overly confused, while more frequently they become blasé and cannot appreciate the purpose, much less the function, of 'old' and 'difficult' modernist metanarratives. It seems much easier to 'wallow' in vague, relativistic postmodernist discourses, where the rules are somewhat ambiguous. Yet it must be appreciated that most of the great postmodernist critics – Jameson, Lyotard, Harvey, *et al.* – are also Marxist thinkers. As a phenomenon, it is extremely difficult to periodize and tease out this very problematic but most rewarding series of debates and ideas.

Bertens, H. (1995) *The Idea of the Postmodern*. Routledge.

Best, S. and Kellner, D. (1991) *Postmodern Theory: Critical Interrogations*. Macmillan.

Docherty, T. (ed.) (1993) *Postmodernism: A Reader*. Harvester Wheatsheaf.

Sarup, M. (1988) *An Introductory Guide to Post-Structuralism and Postmodernism*. Harvester Wheatsheaf.

post-structuralism. See **structuralism**.

power. Central to an understanding of how social structures function; media studies deals a lot with the **representations** of power. Political theorists speak of the use of power within a social system and **ideological** critics speak of the way power is mediated within mass media texts.

practical application in media studies. Many critics suggest that practical work allows students to interrogate their own positions. But this can lead to the 'technicist trap', by focusing on the promotion of product and technology over process and ideology. The great risk with practical work is that the student will simply learn to copy the professionals at the expense of acquiring a more critical and analytical perspective. The major difficulty for media teachers in particular is how to find ways of validating what students already know, while at the same time enabling them to move beyond this.

Masterman suggests that by allowing students to work/play with new technology as soon as possible within a curricular timetable, ignorance and fear of technology can be overcome (the process of **demystification** as it is called) more quickly. However, before a 'hands-on' session in a TV studio, or within any practical technologically driven areas of the media, it generally 'works' better to provide an overview of the interrelationships between the constituent elements of the process to be used. This helps students to appreciate the significance of the process and helps contextualize the practical exercise which is to follow.

Some media practitioners suggest that practical 'chaos' is a necessary antidote which helps to dramatize the process of production as opposed to the illusory professional mythology of a smooth translation from script to screen on radio and TV. The underpinning philosophy of practical teaching supports the truism that 'It is easier to oppose and deconstruct than to construct', which John Berger asserts in his classic *Ways of Seeing*. Practical work is necessary to appreciate both the relevance and the application of theoretical concepts, and these remain interconnecting halves of the process of media education.

Berger, J. (1972) *Ways of Seeing.* (BBC series) Penguin.

Jarvis, P. (1992) *Editing for Film and Video.* BBC.

Millerson, G. (1989) *Effective TV Production.* Focal Press.

Wayne, M. (1997) *Theorising Video Practice.* Lawrence and Wishart.

preferred (dominant) reading. The assumption that media texts are meant to be read in a certain way, which usually supports the **dominant ideology**. This type of reading is often compared with the 'oppositional' and 'negotiated' as defined by Stuart **Hall**.

prejudice. A preconceived, often negative, **attitude** or set of attitudes towards an individual or group of people. It is literally a pre-judgement, revealing intolerance and discrimination, often based on characteristics such as **race**, colour, ethnicity, sex, **age** and/or **class** and often arising out of ignorance and fear of the unknown.

presentations. Used extensively in media education to assess students' abilities to present information and a persuasive argument through a formal, oral session, often using audiovisual material to back up and exemplify the exercise. Within media education in particular it is important to develop a wide range of communication skills, as well as the more conventional writing and report capabilities. For example, a group presentation might involve simulating an advertising agency brief, which involves presenting ideas for a future campaign. Each member of the team would take on a certain role to help convince the client (assessors) that their worked-out ideas have been fully researched and would be successful. An accompanying report often has a similar structure to the presentation with the following sections:

> Title page; table of contents; summary of brief; introduction; findings; conclusions and recommendations; appendices.

All good presentations are well researched, have a coherent structure and inspire confidence in the range of abilities demonstrated by the students and use audiovisual aids effectively. For example overhead transparencies (OHTs) should be well designed. They should not look cluttered with too much text and be used to punctuate the presentation – not to slavishly read out everything on it. Like all skills, practice is needed to build up student confidence. Finally, and most importantly, good presentations are able to handle a wide range of questioning which, for example, often seeks to find difficulties with the methodologies used. Employers in particular speak of the need to develop students' communication skills, and presentations are a good way of doing this.

Hague, P. and Roberts, K. (1994) *Presentations and Report Writing*. Kogan Page.

press as public watchdog. The notion is similar to the **fourth estate** concept of the press. This considers that the primary function of the press is to protect the general public by always remaining vigilant and highlighting any forms of corruption by government or other powerful agencies, which may not always be working with the best interest of the people in mind. Investigative journalism remains the ultimate expression of this function of the press, and is a major aspect applied through the ethos of **public service broadcasting** in particular.

Common-sense assumptions regarding press and media debates, adapted from Curran and Seaton, include:

* Freedom of expression should not be taxed.
* The voice of the people should be heard.
* Truth would confound error in open debate and would emerge in the interplay of the free marketplace of ideas.

Hence the function of media as a public watchdog can be summarised as:

* *Agency of social reform*, designed to liberate, educate and inform.
* *Forum for exchange of ideas*, which reflects the democratic notion of the media as a public sphere.
* *Purveyor of public information*, which correlates with the notion of service to the general public.
* *Checks on government abuses*, by being a mouthpiece for the general public etc.

But there are downsides to such benevolent and positive attributes of press power and responsibility. For example:

* The growth of salacious 'investigations' in the **tabloid** press in particular which become sources of diversion and entertainment (often dismissed by **Marxist** theorists as similar to Roman 'bread and circuses' designed to keep the masses quiescent).
* The press is sometimes allowed to become a personal platform for politicians who require the oxygen of publicity, and for other powerful figures who control their advertising revenue, to have an unlicensed access to the general public.
* Powerful press owners can used their vested interest and power to promote their commercial and political agendas.

Curran, J. and Seaton, J. (1997) *Power without Responsibility*. Routledge.

Negrine, R. (1989) *Politics and the Mass Media in Britain*. Routledge.

press complaints. The **Calcutt Committee** in the UK proposed a voluntary code of practice for the press which focused on 16 areas of agreement where they accept restrictions and obligations and which was ratified by the Guild of Editors on 26 November 1997.

1 Accuracy

2 Opportunity to reply

3 Privacy

4 Harassment

5 Intrusion into grief or shock

6 Children

7 Children in sex cases

8 Listening devices

9 Hospitals

10 Innocent relatives and friends

11 Misrepresentation

12 Victims of sexual assault

13 Discrimination

14 Financial journalism

15 Confidential sources

16 Payment for articles

(www.ukeditors.com)

Complaints about breaches of the code of practice should be made to the Press Complaints Commission, 1 Salisbury Square, London EC4Y 8JB. email: pcc@pcc.org.uk.

Of course there are ways around these codes, especially when certain stories or subjects are deemed to affect the 'public interest'. This includes detecting or exposing a crime, protecting public health or safety, or preventing the public from being misled by some statement or action of an individual or organization. All of the above codes, however, must be stringently enforced where children/minors are concerned.

primary source. A source of information which is collected as raw data from the field (general public), and which is often used in practical media projects. For example, students might design **questionnaires** on the targeted **audience** to investigate their attitudes, values and beliefs so that subsequent programmes can meet their needs. They then have to make sense of their findings. In contrast, secondary sources are where someone else has done the primary research and made their presentations or findings in journals/books/internet, etc.

problematic. A term often used in media and elsewhere to mean a system of thought which needs to be explained. Like deconstruction, problematizing a debate or question means looking 'beneath the surface' and often attempts to discover an **ideological** subtext in a media text. Media teachers and assessors continuously call upon students to problematize various media text issues and discover new meanings or at least question more easily established existing assumptions.

product placement. A more discreet form of advertising, where the advertised product is positioned for instance within a film or a TV programme without drawing unnecessary attention to itself. For example, the Bond films often use multinational logos and advertise brand names on a wide range of luxury products and services. It is suggested that such 'discreet' advertising can be most effective. There are codes restricting it, but companies pay large sums to get round these, and even programmes on **public service broadcasting** stations have been accused of using such advertising strategies.

production values. Reflect the relative costs of adding quality and technical excellence to a media product. The phrase 'high production values' implies that great care and expense has gone into the product, unlike the opposing notion of 'low production values'. However, with regard to so-called B pictures – especially *film noir* from the 1940s – it can be argued that their so-called 'low production values' allowed directors to be more inventive and creative while not being bound to follow formulaic expensive conventions.

progressive education. A term that has gained a variety of meanings over the years and is therefore difficult to define succinctly. Originally it referred to a form of education espoused by educationalists who felt that the traditional methods of education used in the nineteenth century – typified by rote learning, teacher-centred education and corporal punishment in schools – were in need of reform. In the 1960s and 1970s, progressive education was attacked by various right-wing groups and academics in the belief that the ideas underlying it were causing a decline in educational standards. These so-called progressive styles of education have remained a term of abuse, particularly in the popular press in the UK, ever since.

The use of the label 'progressive', applied to a school, an educational **theory**, or a person, is problematic since it usually contains elements of both traditionalism and progressivism. The term is usually applied to a form of broad general education, based largely on humanities and the liberal arts, but with elements of science and technology, which utilizes child-centred approaches. In media education in particular, progressivism has been witnessed within humanistic and behavioural approaches to media, which have encouraged both a people-centred perspective and the use of enquiry learning methods.

proofreading. Checking the copy of a book/magazine or any draft broadcast text for language errors or other forms of mistakes. Media students who produce journals or other print-based media products should be able to proofread copy to a professional standard.

propaganda. See **German propaganda** and **war and propaganda**.

Propp, Vladimir. A Russian, author of *The Morphology of Folk Tales* (1928), which looked at a wide range of folktales (see **fairytales**) and discovered patterns within their narratives which remained consistent. His theories have become very influential within **narratology**, where his ideas are discussed in more detail.

proxemics. The study of the physical distance between people during various forms of public interaction. The more 'intimate' people are the more they allow their friends to invade their public space. However, generally within various cultures there are unwritten rules of the distance maintained between individuals during various social/business communications. This is particularly important for the study of performance in all aspects of the media.

psychoanalysis. The study of mental and subconscious elements within the human condition. The scientific discipline began through investigating illness by looking into the patient's past, usually through hypnosis. The first exponent of this technique was Sigmund Freud, who discovered that a common cause for such ills was due to unconscious sexual traumas. Sexual difficulties were caused as a result of an unresolved Oedipus complex (wishful fantasy of a son unconsciously desiring to sleep with his mother) or an Electra complex (ditto for a girl). Such theories have caused major disagreement and debate ever since – especially among **feminists** who take issue at his suggestion that women suffer from 'penis envy'. No wonder many critics often considered him to be a woman-hater or misogynist. But such a glib summary does a major disservice to the theorist who, together with **Marx**, is considered one of the most influential minds on the twentieth century.

What has all this got to do with the mass media? Critics suggested that film in particular is reminiscent of a dream, and the darkened space of a theatre is reminiscent of the process of going to sleep. Freud suggested that dreams manifested the unconscious desires of the dreamer – releasing the irrational *id*, which is usually counterbalanced by the moralistic *superego*, to express the most repressed desires, hopes and fantasies of the individual. Horror films in particular serve to expose the repressed id, which is often accompanied by various screaming girls!

Psychoanalytic analysis, aided by many theorists after Freud, especially Lacan with his various stages of human development – particularly the 'mirror phase' of childhood – has been used by feminist theorists to uncover the deepest recesses of human nature as expressed on film. Especially since the 1970s some of the most engaging if also jargon-ridden film and media theoretical analysis has been written using various psychoanalytic methods of analysis.

Stam, R. and Miller, T. (2000) *Film and Theory: An Anthology*. Blackwell.

public access TV. Most common in America, it is designated for the use of the general public and is usually non-commercial. With the growth of **digital**

TV and the increase in the number of channels, particularly with the increase in cable, public access TV is becoming more commonly available. However, many argue that within such a proliferation of media channels, its democratic function is being marginalized even ghettoized. Also in Britain, cable companies find it difficult to get material to fill their local TV channels and often turn to local media education providers to get material.

public service broadcasting (PSB) (UK). A form of broadcast media which usually is not determined by commercial factors and has statutory obligations to fulfil with regard to both content and audience profile. The social responsibility model of the media infers that mass audiences need a diet of education/information and entertainment which is guided by a strict ethical framework to promote the best attributes in human behaviour, rather than pandering to the worst. As a philosophy of broadcasting it contrasts with the **free press model,**which came to be prevalent in America in particular, and which promoted the notion that audiences should get what they wanted with little regulation of standards and quality, since programming would naturally gravitate towards maximizing the satisfaction of audience needs and demands.

Back in the 1920s the first director general of the **BBC**, John Reith, stamped the ethos and values of the organization which has remained as a controlling ethos ever since. In particular, the evolution of television is often focused around PSB issues of *quality* and *accountability*, which have remained both contentious and endlessly ambiguous and problematic within radio and TV to this present day. The concept of quality in particular keeps changing over time. For example, when the highly successful *EastEnders* was introduced in the 1980s, there was a serious debate over whether the BBC should reduce its threshold of quality to include more commercially driven products like soaps. Yet by the 1990s the programme was considered an essential part of the BBC's striving for high-quality programming. The same debates occurred with regard to the purity and quality of **docu-soaps** and the rise of many other hybrid forms which are often imported from America, the home of commercial broadcasting.

The other major issue of accountability has remained equally contentious and is tied to **ideological** and party political debates over access during election periods. In particular, the handling of contentious political issues from the General Strike in the 1920s to the Northern Ireland 'Troubles' in the latter half of the century have been very difficult for the BBC. Lord Reith neatly sidestepped the first test of the BBC's impartiality by endorsing the government's stand during the strike, inferring that since the government was elected by the people, then it was they whom the BBC should pay allegiance to.

The BBC maintained a monopoly in broadcasting until the 1950s, when ITV, financed by commercial advertising, began broadcasting. This initiated the high/low debate over quality and cultural standards, with ITV appealing to a more populist audience and successfully buying up American popular programmes for a British audience. By the 1960s a new, more highbrow BBC2 was introduced, allowing BBC1 to compete more directly with ITV. Many critics suggest that in spite of such competition, a cosy cartel evolved, with the BBC and ITV achieving almost equal shares in the UK audience, and ITV acquiring a monopoly on advertising revenue. The British broadcasting template was later extended with the introduction of a new publisher style of broadcasting through Channel 4, which bought in the majority of its programming from new independent TV companies. Now at the turn of the century there is a further terrestrial channel, Channel 5, which so far has only captured a very small percentage of the UK audience.

The BBC remains forever protective of its non-commercial status and of not being controlled by 'big business' or other advertising interests – unlike its main rival, ITV, who many forget is also a public service provider even though it is made up of commercially independent companies and financed through advertising. The BBC is owned if not controlled by the general public and financed by the annual licence. However, with the share of audiences decreasing, the BBC is finding it increasingly difficult to hold on to market share, which serves as justification for the general populace paying a licence fee. Many critics believe PSB, as defined by Reith, to be at an end, and that soon more commercial pressures will be forced on the BBC with governments demanding even greater economic viability.

All these changes in public service broadcasting have been driven by government commissions (listed under **BBC**), which were set up to determine changes needed and make recommendations, which are usually followed through. Now in the reign of a new Director General, Greg Dyke (2000), the BBC is a much more confused organization and has been forced down the route of becoming more and more commercialized, yet at the same time trying to remain a flagship of public service broadcasting.

Curran, J. and Seaton, J. (1997) *Power without Responsibility*. Routledge.

Goodwin, A. and Whannel, G. (eds) (1990) *Understanding Television*. Routledge.

Hartley, J. (1982) *Understanding News*. Methuen.

Slattery, M. (1999) *Key Ideas in Sociology*. Macmillan.

public sphere. First suggested by Habermas in *The Structural Transformation of the Public Sphere* (1962). This is a site where social meanings are generated, circulated, contested and reconstructed. It is a primary arena for the making of **hegemony** and the promotion of cultural common sense. Habermas regarded culture as the reservoir of knowledge, from which participants in communication about the world take their interpretations. Society represents the legitimate order, through which participants secure their membership in social groups and affirm their solidarity and personality. The public sphere, according to its admirers, provides an ideal forum for citizenship or the 'social glue' for society to 'speak to itself'. The mass media, if only ideally, can be considered as a potential site for this public sphere.

Habermas's model of the public sphere, it is claimed, promotes a neutral zone where access to relevant information affecting the public good is widely available and where discussion is free from domination by the state, with all participating in public debate on an equal footing. The media thereby facilitate this process by providing an arena of public debate. While traditional societies use **myths**, magic or the authority of God to maintain a public sphere, modern societies use the mass media.

publishing. Includes all areas of print publications including magazines, newspapers, journals and of course books. Media studies is often accused by **Postman** *et al.* of promoting 'superficial' visual literacy at the expense of books and 'typographical' culture. Nonetheless, a core strand of media education involves the historical study and appreciation of all types of textual publications and how they create meanings.

Practical exercises in design skills for the publishing industry would develop

- creativity in approaches to the design problem,
- accessibility of the design,
- technical proficiency,
- coherence of copy and quality of editing,
- appropriateness of links,
- research into similar authors/publishers/bookshops/websites,
- selection of typefaces and illustrations,
- uniqueness of material.

(Adapted from Alexis Weedon's Publishing pathway on the media arts degree at the University of Luton.)

Butcher, J. (1992) *Copy-editing: The Cambridge Handbook for Editors, Authors and Publishers.* Cambridge University Press.

Clark, G. (1994) *Inside Book Publishing.* Routledge.

Feather, J. (1998) *A Brief History of Publishing.* Croom Helm.

Finberg, H. (1990) *Visual Editing: A Graphic Guide for Editors.* Wadsworth.

Lewis, J. (1996) *Typography, Design and Practice.* Studio Books.

Owen, W. (1991) *Magazine Design.* Laurence King.

Palmer, J. (1991) *Potboilers: Methods, Concepts and Case Studies in Popular Fiction.* Routledge.

Tschichold, J. (1995) *The New Typography.* University of California Press.

Tufte, E. (1997) *Visual Explorations: Images, Quantities, Evidence and Narrative.* CT Graphics Press.

Q

qualitative/quantitative research. Qualitative research involves the use of detailed primary research strategies, for example to investigate media audiences. The research methods used are largely adopted from the social sciences, which make frequent use of observation and individual interviews. Previously, much educational research was *quantitative* in nature and while such work is still carried out, many researchers now prefer qualitative methods like in-depth interviews and **focus groups**, believing that they provide a greater depth of understanding.

Quantitative research on the other hand broadly concerns ascribing numerical values to observations, behaviours and outcomes. It is largely based on scientific approaches and statistical methods which are often in direct contrast to qualitative methods of research. The use of structured interviews and **questionnaires** are favoured techniques. Such approaches are heavily reliant on observation and careful creation and measurement of questionnaire results, to produce laws or generalizations that are observable under similar conditions elsewhere. In particular, media students must learn to design and carry out a range of questionnaire projects which comprise a series of logically sequenced questions designed to be used as a method of collecting information.

questionnaire. A formal, progressive set of questions which hope to abstract from respondents specific social/cultural beliefs and attitudes. Such a method is used extensively in practical media projects to help produce relevant primary research on some pre-given hypothesis or to match audiences with media texts.

A good questionnaire should be relatively short, clear, unambiguous and logical and

- should be designed specifically to suit the study's aims and objectives and the nature of the respondents;
- must have a clear idea of what is expected from the respondents. So before any audience research is carried out you should define in detail

why you are doing this form of research and what specifically you need to discover from it.

A rationale for each question asked must be worked out in advance, together with a justification for the sequence of questions. A major mistake students often make is assuming they can leave questions open and ambiguous – such as 'What type of television do you like?' Such a question would be more useful and easier to quantify afterwards if options were provided for respondents to tick, like comedy, current affairs, sport, etc. Furthermore, it would be even better if respondents were asked to prioritize their likes, using a format like 1 = most liked and 6 = least liked. Always leave a box for 'other' – to allow respondents not to be tied down by your fixed list. Different strategies are used for postal, phone and face-to-face questionnaires.

Farthing, M. et al. and Newbold, C. et al. (1996) Media: Communication and Production, 2 vols: Intermediate Level GNVQ and Advanced Level GNVQ. Longman.

R

race. A defining term together with **class**, **age** and **gender** which categorizes **audiences**. It is often used to categorize or classify people who share broadly similar ethnic, physical, social and cultural characteristics, as well as geographical origins. In their definition of a 'racial group' the Commission for Racial Equality (CRE) make reference to:

- colour
- nationality
- ethnicity
- a long shared history
- a cultural tradition of its own
- a common geographical origin
- descent from a small number of common ancestors
- a common language
- a common literature
- a common religion
- being either a minority or a majority within a larger community.

Commission for Racial Equality (CRE) (1989) *Code of Practice for the Elimination of Racial Discrimination in Education.* CRE.

Racism is a term which refers to prejudicial thoughts and actions resulting in the unequal treatment of a particular racial group. A racist assumption often made is that a person's characteristics, behaviour or intelligence are determined by their race and that one race is superior to another. Often the terms race and ethnicity are used interchangeably to describe the characteristics of a perceived group of people. However, race is a broadly biological definition whereas ethnicity is culturally determined.

Nevertheless, race remains a controversial social concept and has become a central debate within the broad field of media representations. **Marxists**, for instance, suggest that language becomes embedded in the unconscious of individuals, where it becomes an organizing principle for interpreting the world and for individual self-identity. When minorities refuse to accept the identity or coding of being inferior, they oppose not only established patterns of interaction but also the structure of oppositions within the dominant ideological system.

A popular film to study which explicitly deals with this issue and provides good source material for student analysis is: *Do the Right Thing* (1989) directed by Spike Lee. Poster (1995, pp. 126–31) has an informative textual analysis of Lee's film.

Daniels, T. and Gerson, J. (ed.) (1989) *The Colour Black: Black Images in British TV*. BFI.

Friedman, L. D. (ed.) (1990) *Unspeakable Images: Ethnicity and the American Cinema*. University of Illinois Press.

Gilroy, P. et al. (1994) *The Empire Strikes Back: Race and Racism in 70s Britain*. Centre for Contemporary Cultural Studies/Routledge.

Hall, S. (1990) 'The Whites of their Fyes: Racist Ideologies and the Media', in *The Media Reader*, ed. M. Alvarado and J. Thompson. BFI.

Poster, M. (1995) *The Second Media Age*. Polity Press.

Shohat, E. and Stam, R. (1994) *Unthinking Eurocentrism: Multiculturalism and the Media*. Routledge.

Snead, J. (1994) *White Screen, Black Images*. Routledge.

radio. One of the major media investigated by media studies and in fact the oldest electronic mass medium. Historically radio was the chief medium which was used to mobilize public opinion and ensure information/ propaganda was disseminated which connected with the needs of the allies. Ever since, radio has remained a mainstay for popular culture. By the mid-1990s there were 160 local radio stations in the UK and 3 national networks with advertising revenue over £300 million and growing (Briggs and Cobley, p. 203). Even among students there has been a growth in interest in the work of DJs and the power of radio to communicate, from pirate radio to more mainstream fare.

Particularly in Britain, with the huge popularity of celebrities like Chris Evans and Zoe Ball for example, radio has been able to compete with TV as a popular medium. The BBC has always placed great importance on radio, and the medium has remained a particular favourite for politics and political debate. Similarly journalist students often learn their craft moving from print to radio and into TV journalism.

One of the most celebrated presidential debates between Kennedy and Nixon in America served as a touchstone of the relative benefits of TV broadcasting compared to radio. Extensive research has shown that the TV debate was 'won' by Kennedy who 'performed' in a calm manner and looked convincing in his nice well-pressed suit and appropriate body language. Nixon on the other hand was said to be very tired (he looked haggard and even slightly unkempt with his creased suit). Also Nixon was suffering from a discomforting ailment which meant he kept fidgeting in his seat and sweating profusely, denoting a lack of confidence and believability. However, the radio research group were receiving none of these visual signifiers and could therefore concentrate on the language of the argument.

This focus group was not as convinced by Kennedy's rhetoric as the TV control group, who were swayed by the confident visual signification of Kennedy. Ever since, politicians and the media have appreciated the power of the media to create impressions by the way they are presented. In particular overall looks, first impressions and 'sound bites' are essential cues for effective communication within the mass media.

RADIO DRAMA

As a medium, radio is very effective for innovative drama, since it can exploit audiences' enormous imaginative potential. The truism often used in radio advertisements that 'the pictures are better on radio' is particularly relevant to radio drama. One of the most cited examples of radio drama is Orson Welles' *War of the Worlds*, which mixed in non-fictional newsreading conventions to dramatize an alien invasion back in the 1930s. The broadcast was so effective and realistic that many listeners did not realize it was a work of fiction, and panic ensued.

TEACHING RADIO: AIMS AND OBJECTIVES

For example, the aims of the radio pathway in the media degree programme at University of Luton include:

- To enable students to discover and develop their own strengths and interests in the medium of radio.
- To allow students to use technical skills creatively and to apply them to different production contexts.
- To teach students the essential professional ethos of the broadcasting industry.
- To enable students to appreciate the various uses of sound in radio broadcasting.
- To enable students to produce radio programmes which conform to the needs and practices of the industry.
- To enable students to appreciate the essential needs of the radio industries so that they can seek employment in radio if they choose to do so.
- To introduce students to the working practices of the radio industry through activities such as an RSL (Restricted Service License) station.

The objectives include the following:

- Students will become critically aware of the range of broadcasting output.
- Students will learn the fundamental technical skills of radio, for example the use of portable and studio equipment.

- Students will be able to interpret their ideas creatively to make material suitable for radio.

- Students will acquire the research and communication skills needed to set up and conduct radio interviews.

- Students will learn the creative use of sound in a dramatic context.

Boyd, A. (1993) *Broadcast Journalism: Techniques of Radio and TV News.* Focal Press.

Briggs, A. and Cobley, P. (1998) *The Media: An Introduction.* Longman.

Crissell, A. (1996) *Understanding Radio.* Routledge.

Crook, T. (1998) *International Radio Journalism: History, Theory and Practice.* Routledge.

Training videos: from the BBC on broadcast journalism, interviewing, news reporting and the law. Produced at Borehamwood and marketed through BBC Worldwide, Woodlands, 80 Wood Lane, London W12 OTT.

Useful radio websites include:
Australian Broadcasting Corporation – www.abc.net.au
Boston Radio Archives – http://radio.1cs.mit.edu/radio/whatfiles
British Broadcasting Corporation – www.bbc.co.uk
Broadcast Education Association – www.usa.edu
The Broadcasting Archive – www.oldradio.com
Canadian radio stations on the internet – www.breaktech.com/ca_radio
CBC Radio Network – www.radio.cbc.ca
CBS Radio Network – www.cbsradio.com
Radio Services at ABC, Australia – www.otr.com/main

ratings. The aggregate audience/readers for a given media product/service. Such figures are very important for the success of the media organization since they help determine the amount of advertising revenue for example, which is often related to independently validated ratings. See **audience** and **advertising** in particular.

rationalism. A philosophy based on scientific reasoning for the acquisition of knowledge. Here the rational mind is itself thought to be a source of valid knowledge, beyond that of the world of experience and perception, which can be deceptive. Rationalism argues that knowledge and education based on the senses and empiricism are flawed, as the senses can be deceived, while reason cannot. It also has a clear view of what constitutes truth and states that there are significant amounts of knowledge that are certain.

Such a philosophy has somewhat contradictory implications for media analysis, since students are expected to apply subjective textual analysis, for example, which explores how the media text affects them. At the same time students have to construct and apply pseudo-scientific language and measures to ensure such analysis does not degenerate into relativistic sensory perceptions.

readability. Describes how easy a text is to read and comprehend. Some of the factors used to assess readability scores are sentence length, sentence construction and numbers of syllables in each word or sentence. All media students, who have to write essays as well as other types of writing, including reports, logs and diaries, must develop the appropriate skills to express themselves clearly. Often this process is made more difficult by the variable jargon and often difficult language register of many of the textbooks students have to use. Note several wordprocessing packages, such as Word, have a readability check which can be useful.

realism. A primary **key concept** in media education, which focuses on the level and degree of 'construction' which is embedded within media representations. Almost all students begin with a common-sense notion of 'realism' and what is 'realistic', in the process of evaluating media products, especially film and TV programmes. However, what students have to learn is how such surface realism is constructed and how notions of what is realistic have evolved and changed over time. Such changes are particularly noticeable when students contextually compare texts from a long time ago – which are more easily codified as being constructed and more unrealistic – with contemporary media products.

From a media education perspective, realism debates have historically focused on the **ideological** ability of realist texts to engage the audience as opposed to the mystification effect of so-called **naturalist** aesthetic strategies embedded in **classic narrative** texts.

Art theory and discussions of **mimesis** and **verisimilitude** in particular are terms most frequently used to appreciate and understand levels of realistic construction in mediated texts. The hierarchy of verisimilitude (pertaining to the real) embedded in a range of representational forms help explain the concept. For example, four letters making up the English word 'tree', is relatively low on the verisimilitude scale (in one sense at least) and cannot be understood if you do not know English, whereas drawings are higher in the scale, so that the representation of a tree is more universally recognizable. By adding colour and sound and even movement, in a film for example, the representational scale can get even higher with regard to the representation of a three-dimensional living tree.

Nevertheless, representations of the world always remain a set of codes and visual tools which the creator uses, and which changes over time with changes in tastes and the creation of new technologies to replicate reality. The formal codes of the medium can be used to represent reality in differing ways, depending for example on the lighting, camera angles, framing, etc. Whereas with film/television documentary, realistic representations are not always an optional extra, with fictional narratives they can be. Nonetheless, all forms of media representations call on audiences' knowledges of 'reality' in their quest to inform, educate and entertain.

recuperation. A term used to demonstrate how some otherwise negative attribute can be reconstituted to project a positive position. It often works in oppositional ways by changing some idea into a critique of the system. **Feminists**, for example, sometimes speak of the way a female character in a **melodrama** overcomes the dominant **patriarchal ideology** and subverts it. However, a similar term, 'incorporation', can also have connotations of oppositional ideas being recovered or taken over by the dominant ideology, so that such 'active' or 'resistant' female representations can also serve to reaffirm the status quo.

references. Usually secondary sources used to illustrate or back up an essay/research project. The references cited in a piece of work demonstrate the influences which have affected the creation of the finished product. There are at least two standard ways of citing references. Students must apply the standards used in their curriculum and remain at all times consistent. For example in the Harvard system, the author, date and page number of the quotation are put in closed brackets directly after the citation. Then at the end of the essay, the full bibliography is written up in author-alphabetical order with full details of title of source book, publisher and year of publication. Another common system is the use of end/footnotes after each quote, with full details placed in these notes.

reflection theory. A dominant theory in the study of media texts over time and throughout history. As a common-sense assumption it suggests that media artefacts reflect the social, cultural and historical culture from which they come.

The roots of the theory and its application for media analysis could be said to have begun with Sigfried Kracauer's *From Caligari to Hitler* (1947), which suggested that the rise of fascism could be uncovered, even predicted, within the German expressionist film movement of the 1920s, especially through films like *M, The Cabinet of Dr Caligari, Metropolis*, etc. The excessive style and (over)acting with its painted sets and obtuse angles dramatized the psychic tensions inherent in German culture in the 1920s which effectively symbolize the country's rampant inflation and political upheaval. Kracauer spoke of how these films highlighted the stark solutions facing Germans: either 'tyranny or chaos', which was also reflected in these films. However, unable to cope with the latter, they chose the former. Ever since, media studies has remained preoccupied with how cultural texts echo, comment on and even directly reflect issues which are current in the culture at the period. Cultural critics often speak of what are called **zeitgeist texts**, which most directly capture the temperature and mindset of a historical period.

Nevertheless, cultural historians remain resistant to such crude comparisons, suggesting that such excavation is often validated only in retrospect, which makes it difficult to prove any direct causal connection. For instance, Kracauer's thesis regarding **German propaganda** was written with the benefit of hindsight in 1947 after the Nazi experiment had reached its conclusion.

reflective journal. Usually used to underpin and comment on a production project. There are various forms of reflective journal which are used by media students to interrogate the process of production which they are involved in. They are often used particularly for 'final projects' at A Level and degree level so that students can connect various underpinning theories within their practical project.

Generally such reflective journals are seen as having value in helping the writer reconstruct **knowledge**, clarify thinking and express feelings. Practical media students use such journals to connect theory and practice, which underlines the importance of research within the creative process.

regulatory bodies. They set or approve national educational standards and monitor the quality assurance and assessment arrangements of awarding bodies to ensure that they work fairly and effectively. In England, Wales and Northern Ireland the regulatory bodies are the Qualifications and Curriculum Authority (QCA), the Qualifications, Curriculum and Assessment Authority for Wales (ACCAC) and the Northern Ireland Council for the Curriculum, Examinations and Assessment (CCEA).

reification. The process by which a subject is objectified, which often results in what **Marx** and others describe as **alienation** from society. In Marxist theory this process is caused by the exploitation of the worker by capital. This notion is transcribed by media theorists to include the mass media apparatus.

remediation. Remediation is a term used to illustrate the interconnections between various media as they cross-fertilize each other. Bolter and Grusin suggest that it is the guiding principle behind all new media forms which simply refashion old ways of communicating. The authors continually assert that all new media simply refashion older media, citing for example the revolutionary computer software package, aptly titled 'Windows', whose goal is to make the interface itself 'transparent' (p. 34). While the term is very useful and educationally helpful for students to appreciate the continuity of new media with the evolutionary trajectory of all media forms, there is a danger of oversimplification and reductivity.

Bolter, J. D. and Grusin, R. (1999) *Remediation: Understanding New Media.* MIT.

Brereton, P. (2000) review of Bolter and Grusin (1999) in *Convergence* (Summer). University of Luton Press.

representation: female/male. 'Twentieth century critics have taught generations of students to equate popularity with debasement, emotionality with ineffectiveness, religiosity with fakery, domesticity with triviality and all of these implicitly with womanly inferiority' (Gledhill, p. 28).

Gender representations present the most complex, controversial and possibly the most important issue/debate within media education. We are all defined by our gender. From the Christian 'myth' of Adam and Eve, Western art in particular has sought to represent the sexes as symbolizing the primary division within human nature. The dominant theoretical consensus promoted by **Marxist** critics suggests that the **classic narrative** structure of Hollywood cinema, in particular, serves to 'naturalize' and render invisible the dominant ideology of **patriarchy**.

Focusing on how media texts position their audiences with regard to gender representation has become of primary importance – for example, the so-called female preoccupation of genres like **melodramas** and **soaps** compared to the 'male-addressed' genres of **news**, action dramas and sport.

Almost all media texts can be analysed by focusing on how they represent their protagonists: as male/female, young/old, native/alien, etc. Especially within a mass media which has become dominated by representations of human beings, it has become a prerequisite of analysis to focus on how such characters are represented.

(See also **race, class, age**.)

Gledhill, C. (ed.) (1987) *Home Is Where the Heart Is*. BFI.

repressive state apparatus. See **Althusser**.

research. Looking closely into some aspect of investigation either using primary research (first-hand techniques) or secondary (looking at how others have produced some relevant evidence) to discover a response to some issue being investigated. All preparatory work including reading books, magazines, looking at the internet and TV/film programmes can be regarded as secondary research which involves increasing amounts of time as students progress up the educational ladder and become more self-motivated. Primary research is more often connected with audience research in media education, which involves defining a problem and forming a hypothesis, which in turn requires audience research to prove/disprove or at least question the assumptions implicit in the original hypothesis. For example, do females prefer 'passive' rather than 'active' media texts, such as melodramas and soap operas?

Planning and presentation of research usually follow a set series of steps which include:

- statement of the research problem;
- literature review, including a statement of the location for the investigation within the current body of knowledge and research paradigms;
- creation of a possible hypothesis;
- research design and methodology, outlining a justification for its use and the proposed means of analysis;
- collection of research evidence, always remaining aware of possible bias;
- discussion of results; analysis and conclusions;
- critique of research undertaken, statement on how ethical issues were handled in the research, possible future research, implications of research.

Essential for media student projects are:

British Film Institute Film and Television Handbook (formerly 'Yearbook').

Morrison, D. E. (1998) *The Search for a Method: Focus Groups and the Development of Mass Communication Research*. University of Luton Press.

Peak, S. and Fisher, P. (eds) (2000) *The Media Guide*. Fourth Estate.

Also useful are:

Calvert, S. and P. (1992) *Sociology Today*. Harvester Wheatsheaf.

Kent, R. (ed.) (1994) *Measuring Media Audiences*. Routledge.

May, T. (1993) *Social Research: Issues, Methods and Process*. Open University Press.

right of reply. Usually refers to media organizations allowing the general public access to express their views concerning some media product. Media organizations often want to involve their audiences to ensure there is a dialogue and/or because it is enshrined in their **public service** ethos. Consequently, they allow individuals the right of criticizing broadcast programmes and encourage producers to respond – like in Channel 4's weekly *Right of Reply*, which responds to viewers' comments and complaints. Also an unwritten convention within journalism involves contacting the person named in a story before it is printed to allow them the right of reply to the points made in the article.

right wing. A shorthand expression which reflects a political/ideological position which leans towards **fascism** and extreme forms of individualism, often with little time for the social welfare of others.

role-play. More and more prescribed as a teaching strategy/assessment methodology for engaging with the complexities of media issues. It can also help to explore and tease out a range of debates, and often encourages students to overcome their specific prejudiced positions or points of view. On a practical level, group projects help to develop confidence and vocational skills that allow students to take on specific roles which replicate the professional workplace. For example, in a video production, there might be a scriptwriter, camera person, sound technician, editor and director, who all must work together if the project is to succeed.

rote learning. Learning 'by heart', usually through repetition and practice. It is considered a traditional approach to learning which relies heavily on memorizing core information. Learning by rote ensures that pupils can recite whatever it is that has been 'learnt', but they may not necessarily understand the concepts or ideas that surround what they have memorized. See **progressive education** for a critique of such learning, by media practitioners.

S

sampling. The process and method of taking a representative number of people which can accurately reflect the chosen target audience as a whole. In statistics it defines the selection of a part of the population in order to make an evaluation of the whole population. A variety of sampling methods exist for different forms of data and different purposes, each designed to have various levels of validity and reliability. A sampling strategy has to be decided upon when carrying out primary audience research, such as issuing **questionnaires**.

scapegoating. When some individual or group is accused unfairly of some misdemeanour. Such individuals/groups are often demonized in the mass media as part of a **moral panic** in that society. For example, in UK, the striking miners, at least initially, were used in this way as have been blacks, single mothers and more recently refugees.

scheduling. The mapping-out of a list of programmes on a given channel/frequency, together with the times at which they will be broadcast. Scheduling is a very important institutional and business structuring device within media broadcasting. Finding programmes that work well together on given days, and compete well with other channels, is central to the success of any broadcasting company. Techniques such as 'hammocking' – where less well-known programmes are sandwiched between more popular ones – are used to try to sustain audiences over longer periods. Balance has to be maintained to maximize audiences, especially since ratings often determine the profitability of the whole organization. However, with VCRs and the ability to 'time shift' programmes (i.e. record them and see them later), audiences have greater control of their viewing habits, and are less controlled by the schedulers. Nevertheless, the placement of programmes in a schedule remains a highly contentious and complex game of managing audiences' tastes. For example, axing ITV's flagship news programme, *News at Ten*, because it interfered with the uninterrupted showing of films, has not been universally popular, with continuous critical comments displayed in other media.

scopophilia. Suggested by Freud as taking other people as objects and subjecting them to a controlling and curious gaze. In essence it includes the pleasure in using another person as an object of sexual stimulation through sight. The term became popularized by Laura Mulvey in her seminal 1975 thesis 'Visual Pleasure and Narrative Cinema'.

self-actualization. Used by Abraham **Maslow** in his 'hierarchy of needs' as the highest point when an individual fulfils their full potential. His theory is particularly relevant to **advertising**, which tries to tap into audience motivations so that they will buy the product/service advertised.

self-reflexive. See **documentary**.

semiotics (denotation/connotation). The science of reading visual and other signs within society. See Saussure, **Peirce** and **Barthes** in particular, who are key theorists and founders of the discipline. Barthes developed the clear difference between **denotation** and **connotation**, which has become the most basic difference regarding the multiple or **polysemic** meanings within all sign systems. Where denotation is considered the surface, unchanging and generally agreed meaning of an image, the connotative level of meaning is often more ambiguous and open to interpretation – often dependent on cultural and other factors. For example, a photograph of a woman can easily be decoded as such. However, when such an image is used to evoke 'beauty' or 'femininity', such connotations are dependent on cultural and historical associations. In previous centuries women who would now be considered fat were then looked on as beautiful and painted as such by classical artists. By the 1960s, the 'twiggy' or skinny look, in the UK at least, became the norm for females to aspire to and was very fashionable. What is considered 'beautiful' depends on which magazines are looked at and when they are published and for what audience. Hence the connotation of beauty is subjective and open to interpretation. The mass media and the film industry in particular use connotations of beauty to cast female and male actors in films to maximize their effectiveness in such films. The star system can be seen to demonstrate changing connotations of beauty. However, specific aspects of the face and the body must be addressed rather than vague generalizations. Semiotics as a tool of analysis helps such discussion acquire more specificity and coherence.

Fiske, J. (1982) *Introduction to Communication Studies*. Methuen.

Price, J. (1993) *Media Studies*. Pitman.

Simpsons. Probably the most successful animated comedy series, according to the *Guinness Book of Records*, *The Simpsons* is the longest-running primetime series on TV. It has been a regular TV series since 14 January 1990, and broadcast its 225th episode on 16 May 1999. Originally, the series was designed as a set of inserts for *The Tracey Ullman Show* and has made its creator Matt Goening a multi-millionaire. The highly identifiably family characters, Lisa, Homer, Bart, Marge and Maggie, have become household names, and the storylines encourage repeated viewings for their comic and contextual references.

Guinness World Records: 2000

key websites:
www.incsite.com
www.foxworld.com
www.snpp.com
www.springfield.simplenet.com
www.simpsondirectory.com

simulacrum. A term used by Baudrillard to explore how distinctions between an original and a copy become blurred. He has become convinced that life for modern Western audiences has become 'hyper-real'. The lack of 'originality' and the growth of 'pastiche' embedded in this notion of a simulacrum has become important for understanding a postmodernist aesthetic. **Disneyland**, in particular, provides a fascinating example of this phenomenon and can help to critique notions of **realism**. See also **Plato's allegory of the cave**.

Baudrillard, J. (1979) *Seduction*. Macmillan.

Baudrillard, J. (1993) *America*. (Trans. C. Turner) Verso Press.

Baudrillard, J. (1994) *Simulacra and Simulation*. (Trans. S. F. Glacier and A. Arbor) University of Michigan.

skills. A diverse range of physical, social or mental abilities, usually achieved through practice. Skills are often placed alongside knowledge, understanding and attitudes, forming a broad range of educational objectives for the learning process. There may be considerable overlap between the skills in each of these areas. In practical media education in particular, there is a strong emphasis on group skills, together with presentation and other skills.

Skillset. The national training organization for broadcast, film, video and multimedia in the UK. At present they are attempting to create vocational standards that map onto existing practical degree programmes in the media.
tel: 020 7534 5333
email: info@skillset.org

soaps. The **melodramatic** dramas that appear very frequently on TV and radio. As a serial form they do not have narrative **closure**, and have multiple plot-lines with an emphasis on talk and 'female gossip'. They had their origins in American radio in the 1930s and 1940s and have become the most popular and most analysed genre on TV. Yet at one stage they were the most despised form on TV. Soaps have now become the most academically valued, especially with the rising dominance of **feminist** discourse and **audience studies**. The genre traces its roots from afternoon mini-drama series which were used as a vehicle to advertise products sponsored by soap companies, to later 1950s film melodramas which were equally despised as emotional weepies for women. With huge weekly audiences, soaps provide an immediate and relevant source for extensive discussions regarding **representations**, **realism** and **ideological** and contemporary social issues.

Ang, I. (1985) *Watching Dallas: Soap Opera and the Melodramatic Imagination*. Methuen.

Buckingham, D. (1987) *Public Secrets: EastEnders and its Audience.* BFI.

Dyer, G. (1987) *Boxed In: Women and Television.* Pandora.

Dyer, R. *et al.* (1981) *Coronation Street.* BFI.

Geraghty, C. (1991) *Women and Soap Opera: A Study of Prime Time Soaps.* Polity Press.

Geraghty, C. and Lusted, D. (1998) *The Television Studies Book.* Arnold.

Gitlin, T. (ed.) (1987) *Watching Television.* Pantheon.

Morley, D. (1986) *Family Television: Cultural Power and Domestic Television.* Comedia.

social realism. A term which privileges a film/video style of production and acting which strives to capture the 'true' political reality of life as depicted for the protagonists on screen. Such an **aesthetic** was regarded as an alternative to the artificiality portrayed in Hollywood fiction in particular. Two notable national movements which promoted such a radical agenda for filmmaking were Italian neo-realism in the 1940s and the British new wave (or kitchen sink) social realism in the late 1950s and early 1960s. The latter was started by 'northern' writers who captured the raw reality of working-class life. In turn these 'gritty' narratives were made into famous theatre productions and feature films like *Saturday Night, Sunday Morning* (1960) and *A Kind of Loving* (1962).

John Hill suggested that there were several criteria which explained the success of social realism in such films; these included place, character, class and sexuality. No longer was the artificiality of studio sets used but actual streets and landscape. Similarly with regard to character and class, real three-dimensional working-class heroes were forged out of these stories, which rang true for the mass audiences who clearly identified with the protagonists. Most important from a commercial perspective, the films dealt explicitly with sexual and relationship issues which included abortion, homosexuality and relatively explicit sexual representation, which audiences found engaging and provocative while also being 'realistic'. Cultural historians suggest that while the movement ended in the mid-1960s, it fed directly into the social realism of soaps like *Coronation Street*, for example, and the growth of **documentary** realism on television.

Hill, J. (1986) *Sex, Class and Realism.* BFI.

social responsibility model. Asserts that the media cannot be totally free and must be careful in exercising their benevolent function for all citizens. It feeds directly into the UK model of **public service broadcasting**. Britain and many other European countries in particular rejected a fully fledged **free press model** for the media because they saw the possibility of **fascist** and other radical influences succeeding in co-opting the media for their own ends. Nazi Germany in particular is often cited as a media example, which illustrates the need for the media to be independent of the state, yet remain tightly regulated. As Curran and Seaton suggest, post-war governments could not accept that in a free flow of information, audiences would always choose the 'correct' or appropriate 'democratic voice'. Consequently, the media was considered to have the added responsibility of being 'socially responsible' and always vigilant for what was considered the 'common good' of society.

Such debates can be illustrated by the media coverage of the conflicts in Northern Ireland and the **Thatcher** administration in particular, who believed that the IRA and other paramilitary organizations should not be given 'the oxygen of publicity' for their pernicious activities. By definition, terrorism feeds off publicity. But by not affording them access to the broadcasting media, many commentators, even those within the BBC and ITV, believed such terrorist organizations were winning a major **propaganda** coup, since they could always cite **censorship** as one of their grievances and even use it as justification for their actions.

Curran, J. and Seaton, J. (1997) *Power without Responsibility*. Routledge.

socialism. A political, social and economic concept which expresses the **ideological** struggle for 'equality of opportunity' and as such is opposed to **capitalism**. Various forms of socialism exist, but traditionally its doctrine has sought the collective ownership of the means of production, the contribution of each individual to the society in which he or she lives and in return the receipt of protection, education and care from that society. Forms of socialism such as **Marxist** socialism or **communism**, democratic socialism and Christian socialism each vary in the emphasis they place on economic, political and social aspects of their doctrines. While the achievement of social justice and equality remains the primary objective of all forms of socialism, there is less consensus on the means to this end.

Sontag, Susan. A very influential writer for cultural and media studies generally. Her seminal *Against Interpretation* (1961) critiqued established ways of deductively analysing literature and signalled a movement away from 'over interpretation', which was elitist and often prescriptive.

She argued in her seminal *On Photography* that a **capitalist** society requires a culture based on images for it to succeed. This image-based culture is needed to furnish vast amounts of entertainment in order to 'stimulate buying and anaesthetise the injuries of class, race and sex'. Consequently, it needs to gather unlimited amounts of information to exploit natural resources, increase productivity, keep order, make war and give jobs to bureaucrats. This provocative assertion remains a cogent starting point for an **ideological** approach to media/cultural studies, particularly her conclusion that communication forms are not 'innocent' and transparent carriers of meaning, because they are 'impregnated with values' which actively shape the message(s) they communicate.

More recently she analysed the cultural meaning of diseases such as cancer and AIDS. In *Illness as Metaphor* she questions why Western society is preoccupied with thinking metaphorically concerning illness.

website: www.bemorecreative.com/cqctdemo/one

soundbite. A short piece of speech which encapsulates an important and often provocative piece of information. Soundbites are often produced by

politicians who want to capture the public consciousness but accept **McLuhan**'s notion of the short attention span of audiences. Consequently, they try to get across some message in as engaging a way as possible within the shortest time-span. Radio and TV journalists in particular have to learn to write and produce good soundbites if they are to communicate effectively.

spatial. Anything that relates to space; something that is subject to or controlled by the conditions of the space it occupies. Film, for example, can be defined as the manipulation of time and space. Spatial analysis involves an **aesthetic** appreciation of the *mise-en-scène* and the way elements in the frame are arranged.

Space is often connected with place in **cultural** analysis. Where space is related to an abstract notion, place is a more particular and identifiable notion. Cultural studies, drawing on geographical analysis, has been greatly influenced by the proliferation of spatial analysis, which in some ways has superseded the primacy of ideology and helps to legitimize and consolidate **postmodernist** discourse, for example.

special effects. Used to make film and radio sound-effects more spectacular. Study of 'SFX', as they are known, has become a growing consideration, especially with new media. The whole history of cinema could be considered as one long experiment in a range of special effects. Whereas a majority of critics dismiss SFX as empty spectacle and part of the commodified element of capitalist enterprise in film, more recently effects are seen as central to the sublime and excessive nature which often engenders spectacle above all else.

Barker, M. (1998) *Knowing Audiences: Judge Dredd, its Friends, Fans and Foes*. University of Luton Press.

Hayward, P. (1990) *Culture, Technology and Creativity in Late 20c*. John Libbey Press.

spectatorship. The condition or state associated with viewing by individuals who are brought together to witness an event. Almost all audiovisual media consumption involves some form of spectatorship. **Psychoanalytical** theories are closely associated with issues around spectatorship. See also **voyeurism**.

spin-doctor. A media expert often associated with a political party, whose job involves dealing with the mass media and trying to get a 'positive' message across using whatever tactics are necessary. The major criticism of such 'spinning', as it is called, is that information is massaged and manipulated so that the full details are not always communicated. In many ways style and surface gloss are used rather than the full details of any given story. Of course it makes journalists' lives easier to be given stories pre-digested, but good journalists always want to get beneath the surface and determine the full picture for themselves.

standards. Levels of performance or quality, as defined by professionals within a given field. Standards in education are now usually considered as being maintained partly by means of public examination and league tables, on which different educational institutions can be compared. The role of inspections undertaken by **OFSTED** has also been recognized as instrumental in establishing and maintaining public perceptions of standards in education.

Standards can also be statements against which individuals can plan and monitor their achievement, as well as providing professional recognition of expertise and attainment. Within media studies, especially at undergraduate level, there is a firm move towards **benchmarking**, which lays down minimum standards for each subject area.

Stanislavsky, Constantin. A Russian performance theorist and writer who invented a style of acting which made the performance more real and identifiable for an audience. Actors had to 'become' the role by internalizing the persona of the character they were performing. The technique became known as the **method school** in America, under the tutelage of Lee Strasberg, who made it particularly popular with a wide range of Hollywood actors.

Stanislavsky, C. (1990) *An Actor Prepares.* Methuen.

Star Wars. Has become a phenomenon now for over 25 years, since the first film directed by George Lucas appeared on cinema screens. The success of the film is due to its use of **special effects** (SFX) which were ahead of their time when the film first came out. Also the creation of mythic heroes/villains helped capture a world audience which has not waned over the years. The **representation** of alien planets often conforms with conventional Western stock imagery of the '**other**' or third world. This is further illustrated in the 1999 sequel, with aliens displaying 'humorous' counter-cultural attributes which are at best patronizing if not **racist**. This representation seems to reinforce attitudes regarding the worship of the hi-tech, Euro-American mythic hero as against the repulsive, evil, irrational creatures of other worlds, extending Turner's famous American 'frontier thesis' into space.

Intertextual reference: President Reagan adapted Lucas's potent signifier for his aborted satellite air nuclear defence strategy – much to the annoyance of the director.

Star Wars is one of the few filmic phenomena that, when re-released 20 years later, again became a major hit for a new generation in preparation for a fresh sequence of films in the ongoing saga. The use of universal heroic myths and excellent special effects ensure the stories' continuing success. Consequently, the series provides effective material for teaching and illustrating the potency of ancient heroic **myths** within modern culture.

Steadicam. A special harness for a camera which when strapped to the operator allows fluid movement within the shots. The method opens up a much 'freer' style of movement and in many ways replicates a 'watcher's movements'. For example, the child's-eye view in Kubrick's *The Shining* (1980) was one of the first films to effectively use the technique.

stereotypes. Group concepts held by a social group about a social group and which are based on 'inferior judgement processes', which can often be irrational.

General common-sense statements about such types in the media:

- They are false/untrue/unreal;
- They are always derogatory;
- They are aimed at subordinate/minority groups;
- They reinforce prejudice against these groups.

However, as Tessa Perkins incisively asserts:

1 Stereotypes are *not* always 'false' in content.

2 They are *not* always negative.

3 They *can* be held about one's own social group.

4 They are *not* always concerned with minority/oppressed groups.

5 They are *not* simple because they lack depth or complexity – they are simple and complex (their ability to 'work' so directly in a mass-media culture implies complexity).

6 They are *not* rigid/unchanging.

7 We do not simply 'believe' or 'disbelieve' in stereotypes, since they may 'work' for us and communicate with us without our necessarily 'agreeing' with them.

8 They do not *necessarily* influence our behaviour/attitude/practices.

Stereotypes often encourage sexism and racism. Simple social categories do not do justice to complex human individuals, but stereotyping is a basic fact of human nature. Making categories and drawing relationships of similarity and difference is an inescapable part of the process of constructing mental worlds that guides our thinking and predicts our actions. What is important is where these categories are used and to what purpose they are put. Stereotypes are dangerous when they provide a false and misleading picture of what people actually are like. (pp. 2–10, cited in Tessa Perkins' chapter in Michele Barrett *et al.* (eds) (1979) *Ideology and Cultural Production*. Croom Helm.)

Most drama depends on a kind of instant labelling of characters – 'stereotyping'. In Hollywood films of the 1930s, black actors were usually asked to play comic and foolish cowards while women were generally the objects of male desire.

We refer to a sign as a stereotype when the signifier and signified merge to reinforce in the audience a belief that the signifier necessarily embodies this concept: that women are *always* weak and unreliable, that black people are *always* foolish cowards. Doctors, however, seldom complain about being represented as good and wise.

Morgan, J. and Welton, P. (1986) *See What I Mean: An Introduction to Visual Communication.* Edward Arnold.

still photography. Can be defined as a two-dimensional representation, either in black and white or colour, of a three-dimensional reality. The medium provides a convenient practical means to illustrate theoretical models in connection with the wider audiovisual media industries as well as developing students' visual literacy and aesthetic sensibility.

For example, the use of lighting on an image can help illustrate the aesthetics of *film noir*, dramatizing how the meaning of an image changes with the use of low and obtuse streaked lights. For instance, lighting under the chin can make the subject appear sinister with strong shadows.

Also the comparative benefits of **montage** versus deep focus can be explained more easily using the mechanical/aesthetic functions of aperture, using a range of different **F-stops** and deep focus in an SLR camera.

Both the form and aesthetics of film and mass media generally are difficult to explain, since they appear natural and easy to understand; still image analysis in particular can help to break down these illusions by slowing down the process, and can help to demonstrate how images actually create meaning. Consequently for many media educationalists, still photography serves as a primary tool for illustrating the basic 'alphabet' of visual literacy.

storyboard. A sequence of images and accompanying sounds/dialogue which detail how the narrative will progress visually, giving information on camera angles, special effects, etc. Such detail is often demanded even before practical production shoots can take place within students' projects, to ensure that all aspects have been considered towards visualizing the entire production.

Hart, J. (1999) *The Art of the Storyboard: Storyboarding for Film, TV and Animation.* Focal Press.

structural film. A term often applied to a particularly American kind of **avant-garde** or experimental film. A famous example is Michael Snow's *Wavelength* (1967), which simply involves a camera tracking 360 degrees around a loft room for the length of its performance. Such films are non-representative, non-narrative exercises, which are often concerned with ideas concerning perception and vision.

Sitney, P. A. (1976) *Structural Film Anthology.* BFI.

structuralism. A wide-ranging and influential theory which focuses on the underlying building blocks of any aesthetic form, including the media. Ferdinand de Saussure is a very important structuralist theorist regarding language and the development of communication. Saussure is the founder of what he describes as linguistic structuralism, which includes the following elements:

- *Langue/parole*: language is a whole system: words and rules which are historically given, upon which speakers are forced to draw. A word, an utterance (*parole*) is defined by its position in language as a whole.

Langue, then, is a system of rules, which makes *parole* possible. Speech or *parole* exists in the here and now and is experienced in linear form, as one word follows another. It is an event made concrete in space and time. Language (*langue*) has no such linear form and is never visible but an abstract whole. *Langue* is the system, *parole* is any realization (or expression) of that system. For example, a football match is the *parole*, whereas the rules by which we know how to interpret the game are the *langue*.

- Signifier/signified: the signifier is the sign itself – word, letter, sound – which is the vehicle of meaning; the signified is the idea or meaning conveyed by the signifier. Meaning, for Saussure, derives from a system of '*langue*', from its formal relationship and rules, and not from its relationship to an outside or independent world. Semiotics is therefore a science which studies the life of signs and what governs them.

Also **Lévi-Strauss**, the anthropologist, helped develop primary binary opposition structures to understand culture, particularly the opposition between 'nature and culture'. Such binary oppositions have been effectively used by Kitses, **Wollen**, **Williams** and many other critics to analyse films and media in general.

Lévi-Strauss asserted that meaning arose out of oppositions and differences in particular contexts. He posited this central opposition between nature and culture. He regarded myth's primary function as serving to reveal and overcome such contradictions as life/death, this world/other world, humans/gods, sex/virginity. Media theorists began to apply these mythic roles most effectively onto mass media to explain how they are structured and the forces which maintain their primary conflicting tensions.

Structuralism became a very influential movement which affected much of the humanities as a way to connect meanings and suggest links between elements. At the heart of the idea of structuration is the idea of a system: a complete, self-regulating entity that adapts to new conditions by transforming its features while retaining its systematic structures.

However, with the rise of so-called **post-structuralism**, such certainties were very much called into question. *Post-structuralism elements* include:

1 A stress on closed systems.

2 Plurality of meaning.

3 Impossibility to claim truth.

4 Impossibility of meaning itself.

Peter **Wollen**'s very effective model to differentiate Hollywood film from the more highly valued **avant-garde** is used extensively in film theory:

Hollywood/classical film:	*Modernist/art film*:
Narrative transitivity	Narrative intransivity
Identification	Estrangement
Transparency	Foregrounding
Single diegesis	Multiple diegesis
Closure	Aperture
Fiction	Reality
Pleasure	Un-pleasure (Bliss)

Similarly John Ellis's divisions between TV and cinema as contrasting media apparatuses and formats for audience pleasure are also frequently used for comparative analysis:

Cinema:	*Television:*
Unitary text	Segmented series
Narrative image	Flow
Sustained/intense	Casually domestic
Gaze	Glance
Complex sound/	
image balance	Simple balance
Mise-en-scène	Character
Photo effect	Live effect
Closed coherence	Continuous update
Impersonal narration	Direct address
Sexual difference	Family

Such structural models provide very useful educational frameworks for students to begin to appreciate the complexity and interconnectivity of various media formats and help problematize various issues. Students are encouraged to unpack and find contradictions with such models, which ensures that they actively learn and maybe even critique such provocative but always incomplete models of media analysis.

Cook, P. (ed.) (1999) *The Cinema Book*. BFI.

Ellis, J. (1982) *Visible Fictions: Cinema, Television, Video*. Routledge.

Wollen, P. (1972) 'Counter Cinema: Vent d'est', *Afterimage* 4.

Wollen, P. (1982) *Readings and Writings: Semiotic Counter Strategies*. Verso.

summative assessment. Occurs at the end of a course with the purpose of identifying a pupil's level of attainment within a subject. Such assessments are regularly used to rank or grade pupils for comparative purposes.

surrealism. An art movement which art critics suggest began with André Breton and his first manifesto in 1924. It encourages the juxtaposition of objects/artefacts which do not usually appear in the same frame of reference and look odd and out of place. Its founders spoke of the important influence of Freud in tapping the unconscious of dreams and the human psyche and used his ideas within art to undermine traditional conventions. The most famous film director to use surrealistic techniques was Luis Bunuel, who began with experiments like *Un Chien Andalou* and *Age d'Or* and continued to direct some very provocative and accessible surrealistic films including *The Discreet Charms of the Bourgeoisie* and *The Obscure Object of Desire*. Surrealism continues to influence media production, although maybe not as in previous times, when there was apparently more to react against, within more defined social constraints.

surveillance. Watching intently; it has become a preoccupation within Western culture. From the police security cameras designed to watch public spaces and protect against crime, to individuals being closely observed for investigation or sexual gratification, this mode of observation pervades popular cultural representation. A major theorist, **Foucault**, in *Discipline and Punish* (1977) applied Jeremy Bentham's design for a prison known as a 'panopticon' to explain how society works. With the prison guards in the centre observing all the prisoners in cells around them, the panopticon serves as a metaphor for modern society, where 'we' are all potential 'prisoners of a system' with public officials able to observe through closed circuit television cameras as well as other surveillance methods. The recent film starring Jim Carrey in a real-life soap-opera, *The Truman Show*, where his whole life has been relayed as a soap, without him realizing it, provides an interesting example of the phenomenon.

Major civil rights issues such as freedom of expression, free association and freedom of information have been brought into question by the growth of a surveillance culture which legitimizes invasive security powers to control and manipulate the use of a range of hi-tech media devices.

syllabus. An overview, or outline, of a course of study, particularly relating to the subject content to be taught. In contrast to a curriculum, which embraces an entire set of subjects and cross-curricular activities, a syllabus is primarily designed to explain the content of an individual subject.

symbol. Where a sign has some relation to the object of interpretation or 'interpretant'. See **Peirce** and **semiotics**.

T

tableau. A scene from a film or TV programme where the actors remain silent and freeze their actions. The technique was often used for symbolic effect in ancient theatre, and is still used to striking effect, for example in the closure of *Grand Canyon* (1991), when all the characters look out into the sublime space at the end of the film.

tabloid. A style of media production which is usually associated with the print industry and is often used as a reference to popular **journalism**. Characteristics of tabloid journalism include brevity – not wasting words and detail – along with an emphasis on large headlines. Provocative and emotional language is often used to communicate more directly with audiences. Critics often suggest that such language encourages extreme forms of **jingoism** and panders to audiences'/readers' **racial**, sexual and other **prejudices**. Tabloid styles of journalism – as opposed to **broadsheet**, or 'quality' – is also becoming more popular within other media, including radio and television.

taxonomy. A classification of some kind. In education, taxonomies have been used to classify levels of thinking and reasoning skills into hierarchies, such as **Bloom**'s (1956) taxonomy.

Bloom, B. S. (ed.) (1956) *Taxonomy of Educational Objectives: Handbook 1: Cognitive Domain.* Longman.

team teaching. Any teaching where two or more teachers plan and deliver some aspect of education to a group of pupils in the same classroom. In media this may be used when a game, **role-play** or simulation is undertaken that requires the presence of more than one teacher, often for management purposes. In media education team teaching is particularly effective where different skills – particularly with regard to the theoretical and the practical – can be brought together within the same teaching situation.

technological determinism. When technology is regarded as the prime guiding force for change in media and communications generally. It suggests that change does not simply happen as a result of some boffin creating a eureka moment, thereby transforming all our lives with substantial change for the better. Instead, **Marxist** critics like Herbert Schiller suggest that big business finally determines which piece of new technology gets produced and becomes promoted, and thereby allowed to succeed. This is primarily determined by the profit motive. Consequently if an innovation is not going to make money, it will be less likely to be developed. Surprisingly, lots of innovation in the West has occurred as a by-product of space travel and military research and development, which is later used for civilian applications. The development of the **internet** is an unusual example of this pattern: it was designed as a means for the armed forces to access databases and not for profit-making purposes. Nevertheless, the normative trajectory of new digital technology is usually driven by the economic imperative.

technophobia. The fear of using technology like computers. Many media theorists such as Len **Masterman** speak with regard to teaching practical media courses of the need to **demystify** new technology before learning can take place.

telephony. Telephony is the use of all types of phones to communicate between humans and machines. How meaning is created through the growing use of telephones and mobile phones in particular, as well as their social and cultural effects, is underdeveloped as a media subject, while becoming highly lucrative as a distinct media industry.

Professor M. Alvarado questions why it is that the social analysis and understanding of the most important form of individual human communication over large distances has been so totally ignored.

Communication models like Shannon and Weaver's are drawn directly from how telephony functions as communicative devices.

television: UK share of audience. ITV (Independent Television) is made up of a number of major holding companies which control various regions in the ITV network. (Note: various mergers are imminent, which may mean a reduction of key players within the ITV network in particular.)

Company	Audience
United News and Media (Meridian, Anglia, HTV and C5)	9%
Carlton (Carlton, Central and West Country)	8%
Granada (Granada, Yorkshire, LWT, Tyne Tees)	11%
Other ITV companies	6%
BBC (British Broadcasting Corporation)	39%
Channel 4	10%
Channel 5	5%
Satellite (BskyB) and cable	14%

Source: ITC press release of 28/4/2000.

text. Any mediated product or cultural artefact – film, television/radio programme or any printed material like a newspaper, book, etc. Describing this wide range of mediated products as 'text' helps to legitimize other forms of visual literacy and the need to 'read' images/sound/movement, for example, alongside more traditional written language.

textual analysis. The process of identifying and evaluating the meaning of a text, primarily through the study of its form, such as its internal structure which serves to create meaning. At a basic level this can be regarded as a type of content analysis, using a **semiotic** model of investigation. In more advanced levels, the social/political/ideological and historical context in which the text is constructed is also taken into account.

Techniques used for media textual analysis are often copied from literary study and involve a close investigation of the conventions to discover how the text can be regarded as individualized. For example, film studies place great emphasis on the ability of students to develop sophisticated skills of textual analysis. These might include differentiating and articulating why various elements are foregrounded and dramatized; for example, *mise-en-scène* (colour, lighting, sound, framing), editing (montage, deep-focus), performance (linguistics, address, commutation test, star study, etc.). Textual analysis skills are essential for all media students to find their 'voice' and acquire the confidence to read and even critique other analyses. Almost all media education is underpinned by textual analysis, so it is essential to develop a range of skills in this area which allow students to express their often unique interpretation of media texts.

Thatcherism. A cultural concept applied to the reign of Margaret Thatcher as prime minister in the UK. The notion was promoted by Stuart **Hall**, who suggested that her right-wing ideology destroyed the residual idea that there was any kind of correspondence or direct connection between economic class and either political or popular culture, or indeed between the identification of class interests and the state. She went so far as to assert that there was no such thing as 'society'. Thatcherism, according to Hall, redefined the idea of culture primarily within economic terms. The Thatcher era promoted a *laissez-faire* attitude towards **public service broadcasting** (PSB) in particular, demanding that they become more competitive and economically viable, rather than hiding behind what was considered an elitist ethos. The overall political strategy of **deregulation** and privatization of a range of public services from telephony to water (and even, some argue, education) has continued in the UK and elsewhere. Many media critics find such a strategy highly contentious, particularly with regard to press freedom and its effects on the overall quality of media production.

theory. A set of ideas or sometimes rules which are intended to provide an explanation for some behaviour, or other 'raw data'. In media education, a great number of theoretical perspectives have been applied. The range includes **psychoanalytical, effect, feminist, structuralist, semiotic, ideological, postmodern**, etc., which are all dealt with in this Guide. From a teaching perspective, theory must have some bearing on practice and should be made to appear relevant to the study of the media, otherwise students will rightly reject it. In particular, students often have an aversion to 'grand theory' which appears to be constructed from its own rules and language with apparently little connection with 'the real world'. Making theory both relevant to their needs and understandable is the endless challenge for teachers if they are to connect with their pupils. At the same time, students must make an effort to understand and avoid dismissing such theories out of hand, without first understanding and appreciating how meanings are created. A rule of thumb used by David **Bordwell** suggests that theory is like a black box: if it gets the job done, you do not have to look that close inside the box. Making theories function and 'work' by relating them to practical applications is the primary aim of theoretical media analysis. Acquiring the motivation and acumen to engage with theory for its own sake, like a philosophical discourse, remains the 'icing on the cake' for more advanced study.

third cinema. Third cinema is a term used to distinguish cinema made in the less-developed world. Usually such films deal with subjects ranging from the effects of colonialism, class, sexual politics, otherness and poverty. For example, filmmaking in the Indian subcontinent, affectionately described as 'Bollywood', constitutes an even bigger film industry than the more conventional Western Hollywood model. Yet the Bollywood aesthetic and output is seldom analysed, much less recognized, in the West.

Pines, J. and Willemen, P. (eds) (1989) *Questions of Third Cinema*. BFI.

time-shifting. A term used to relate to the use of VCRs to copy television programmes and view them at leisure. See also **scheduling**.

TV and effects theory. Many people criticize TV as 'junk food'. This panders to the general attitude of perceiving the medium as an anaesthetizing, addictive narcotic which conforms with what has been called the **hypodermic needle model**. It implies a direct causal relationship between the medium and its effects on audiences. For example, Marie Winn speaks of the 'plug in drug' in her book of the same name. In many ways, media education has evolved from the **Frankfurt School** and their research from the 1940s onwards on the effects of the mass media on audiences. Enormous amounts of research, particularly under the auspices of the **Payne Fund**, were executed especially in America, to gauge the connections and correlations between representational and 'real' sex and violence. Such research was almost always driven by a predetermined **ideological** agenda, which sought to scapegoat the media and deflect attention away from more 'complex' root causes of social problems. This can be appreciated through research like Martin **Barker**'s preoccupation with the creation of **moral panics**, especially through the evolution of 'comic violence' and social censure in Britain. These effects debates are endlessly analysed, especially with the apparently increasingly violent society which is 'echoed' through mediated violence.

Effects theories provide a major crossover with social science, where the majority of this type of research takes place. An example is the famous research in the early 1960s which involved plastic 'Bobo' dolls, devised by the psychologist Albert Bandura, to test the influence of violent stimulation on children. The study found that children exposed to a film clip of an actor 'beating' the doll were more likely to play in an equally 'aggressive' manner than the control group who had not seen the film stimulus. Distinguishing between 'play' and 'violence' within children's behaviour, after observing controlled stimulus, remains a contentious methodological subject for debate. Just because children act out behaviour which appears to replicate performance on screen, does not necessarily prove a connection, especially when the 'victims' used to suggest an increase in so-called violent behaviour are inanimate dolls! A major assumption has to be made that children do not consciously recognize the difference between 'human' and such inanimate objects and that behaviour patterns can be decoded independently of the context of 'violent' attacks. Such research begs important questions like, 'Would kids behave differently if behaviour was not circumscribed by codes of "play" using playful objects?'

These debates became highly problematic when examining case studies like recent killings of schoolchildren in America; or the Hungerford massacre in the UK, when it was alleged that the killer was stimulated to go on a shooting spree after viewing violent movies; or the killing of the four-year-old Jamie Bulger by two ten-year-old children which traumatized the UK and was widely reported throughout the world media. By uncovering a tenuous yet unproved linkage of the crime to the stimulus of viewing *Child's Play 3* – which had a similar method of murder to the horrific real event – the media whipped up a frenzy of attack, scapegoating this film and others, describing them as 'video nasties'. Again the media was scapegoated through a serious moral panic debate, especially in the tabloid press.

But scientific research into such effects remains highly inconclusive and often uses questionable methodology. It is also mostly carried out on what are considered the more vulnerable elements in society, particularly children of the lower classes, with the implicit assumption that more settled middle-class sections of the community are less likely to be similarly affected.

Biggs, A. and Cobley, P. (1998) *The Media: An Introduction.* Longman.

Morrison, D. E. et al. (1999) *Defining Violence: The Search for Understanding.* University of Luton Press.

U

uses and gratification theory. Starts with the view that for the audience, the mass media is a resource that is drawn upon to satisfy a range of needs unlike the more straightforward stimulus/response **hypodermic needle model**. The reader/viewer is seen in a more active role. For example, boys read comics to fulfil desires for action and adventure, whereas girls read comics like *Jackie* to indulge their romantic instincts. This theory tends to promote a more active approach to the study of audiences and the reception of media texts generally.

utopia. An idealized environment where evil is banished and all humans live in perfect harmony with each other. Sir Thomas More's famous treatise constructed a planned, rational society of human beings. The opposite of utopia is a dystopic environment as represented in science fiction texts like *Blade Runner*, which reflected a 'hell-like' society and environment. According to Marcuse, of the **Frankfurt School**, the goal of oppositional culture is, or ought to be, the unification (or perhaps the reunification) of art and labour. In other words, the activation of utopian values.

V

validity. The extent to which a test, or other form of assessment, accurately measures what it is intended to measure. As such the results of a test may look plausible but may not actually reflect what the test has been designed to find out. For example, it may simply be assessing knowledge, rather than understanding or skills. Therefore it will not give a full picture of a student's attainments within a subject. Consequently, media syllabi encourage a variety of assessment methods, including comprehension exercises, practical projects and presentations, as well as more rigid academic essays, and timed or computer exams, to affirm a wider appreciation of attainment.

value added. The additional educational value gained by children by virtue of their experiencing an educational process. Such additional 'value' cannot be easily measured, particularly through simplistic approaches such as the creation of league tables of data.

In an attempt to gain more valuable and accurate indications of quality measurement, the use of value-added statistics have been analysed, such as the rate of conversion of 'poor' GCSE grades into 'better' A Level grades. Complicated multi-layered models exist that give a more accurate indication of the nature of the value added to students. More open-access universities, with large numbers of students from minority groups and often with 'poor' grades, seek to focus on value added as an extra measure for legitimizing the educational value of higher education.

DfE (1995) *Value Added in Education.* Briefing paper.

Goldstein, H. (1987) *Multi Level Models in Educational and Social Research.* Griffin.

verisimilitude. See **mimetic** and **realism**.

Vertov, Dziga. An early pioneer in the Russian film industry who regarded the medium as a pro-social propaganda tool. He developed a theory called 'kino-eye' during the 1920s, which is best illustrated by *The Man with a Movie Camera* (1929). He regarded the camera as more perfect than the human eye to perceive the chaos of reality. Vertov presented everyday life occurrences as the camera perceives them. The camera itself became the star of the film. He drew comparison with the human eye by applying basic functions like focusing. Throughout the film there is a superimposition of a camera lens with a human eye which effectively symbolizes the kino-eye principle.

Paul, D. (ed.) (1983) *Politics, Art and Commitment in the East European Cinema*. Macmillan.

video games. Have moved out of the public arcade and become a central part of home entertainment. They are now probably the biggest growth industry in media entertainment. **Interactive** games are played on conventional TVs as well as more sophisticated box-top consoles connected to the TV and even stand-alone pocket-size game consoles like Gameboys. The games industry has grown enormously over the last number of years from the primitive ping-pong tennis simulation game, with a white dot moving across the screen, to recent highly sophisticated interactive games like the Japanese multimedia craze Pokémon, with cinematic quality graphics and special effects. With such games costing £20–£50, it is little wonder that the industry is becoming more important financially than conventional cinematic releases. Conventional blockbuster film releases are more and more being tied into games franchises, so that advertising and tie-in possibilities are maximized and several markets can be saturated at the same time.

For **McLuhan**, games can function in much the same way as the **fairytales** do for Bettelheim – as a way of bringing meaning to life. Games are a sort of artificial paradise like **Disneyland** or some **utopian** vision by which we interpret and complete the meaning of our daily lives. Yet most video games are not educational in any sense, and often involve simple problem-solving, with chasing and destroying games built into the endlessly repeated narratives. Marina Warner in a Reith Lecture on childhood myths suggests that video games are not necessarily 'narratives' but reductive ways of telling stories (cited in *The Media Education Journal* 16 (Summer 1994)).

Some research suggests that over 90 per cent of players are male, compared to the representations of women in such games which stereotypically are acted upon, rather than initiating action like most melodramatic victims. However, of late more active, if still highly sexual female agents like 'Lara Croft' are being created for the games market.

Nintendo, one of the biggest brand names, for example, has donated £3m to research to investigate the educational possibilities of video games, which should become an increasing focus for media research.

Provenzo, E. F. (1991) *Video Kids: Making Sense of Nintendo*. Harvard University Press.

video nasties. A press nickname for videos which are deemed totally at odds with normal values in society, and which often include elements of gratuitous violence, sadism, etc. As part of a **moral panic** debate, they are cited as helping to cause many of the horrific copy-cat acts of violence in Western society. In particular, films like *Child's Play 3*, *A Clockwork Orange* and *The Texas Chainsaw Massacre* are often scapegoated as directly causing acts of violence and affecting civilized human values.

Barker, M. (ed.) (1984) *The Video Nasties. Freedom and Censorship in the Media*. Pluto.

Barker, M. and Petley, J. (eds) (2000) *Ill Effects: The Media/Violence Debate*. Routledge.

video skills. Involve learning the basics of using cameras and basic editing to produce a finished product. How to shoot video and edit sequences together, using various formats from basic VHS to professional broadcast quality work, is what many practical media students want to learn. Such skills require extensive hands-on use of cameras by students working on individual/group exercises and small video projects. Managing all the elements of the audiovisual process demands extensive tutorial assistance. Exercises include camera movement, manipulating narrative time and space, using natural and artificial lighting and, in particular, managing actors. Such projects also require the development of group management skills, together with proficient technical skills to use equipment confidently and successfully.

Croton, G. (1989) *From Script to Screen*. BBC.

Ferncase, R. (1992) *Basic Lighting Worktext for Film and Video*. Focal Press.

Hodges, P. (1994) *The Video Camera Operator's Handbook*. Focal Press.

Jarvis, P. (1988) *Shooting on Location*. BBC.

Millerson, G. (1989) *Effective TV Production*. Focal Press.

Millerson, G. (1991) *Television Lighting Methods*. Focal Press.

Millerson, G. (1993) *Television Production*. Focal Press.

Nisbett, A. (1989) *The Uses of Microphones*. Focal Press.

Reisz, K. and Millar, G. (1968) *The Techniques of Film Editing*. Focal Press.

Schihl, R. (1989) *Single Camera Video*. Focal Press.

Watts, H. (1982) *On Camera*. BBC.

Wayne, M. (1997) *Theorising Video Practice*. Lawrence and Wishart.

video technology: the future? The growth of video technology, according to utopic optimists, helps promote a democratic society and improves communication while at the same time keeping the money men satisfied with increased productivity and profitability. Proponents of the benefits of new technology naturally include Bill Gates, who because of such new technology has become one of the richest men in the world. As founder of the giant Microsoft Corporation, he proposes in his polemic, *The Way Ahead*, that competition driven by such innovation is intrinsically good and leads to a greater level of 'democracy' of the media. Computers and **digital** recording and editing in particular can of course decentralize work, which can feasibly promote a more democratic media.

Jane Root, who now works in the BBC, affirmed in *Open the Box* (a book and TV series) that new technology like the fax and **internet** cannot be **censored** even within high-conflict situations like wars. We (i.e. the audience) can acquire uncensored information and therefore know what is happening, therefore new technology can serve as a powerful antidote to censorship and political corruption.

However, **Marxists** like Herbert Schiller on the other hand remain cynical towards the beneficial effects of new technology like video, describing them as 'technologies of oppression'. They suggest that competition always favours the giants who define and determine media memory of what is right and beneficial. The evolution of technology is, Schiller argues, always in the end affected by **technological** and economic **determinism**.

Armes, R. (1988) *On Video*. Routledge.

Hartley, J. *et al.* (1985) *Making Sense of the Media*. Comedia.

Pool, I. de S. (1983) *Technologies of Freedom*. Belknap Press.

violence (representation of). Violence and more specifically the representations of violence have remained a primary area of study within the media. In particular, the role of 'violent images' and so-called **video nasties** in socializing children and promoting various forms of deviancy have remained a primary concern for media debates.

There is a commonly held assumption that TV turns children into passive, unthinking zombies. Ignorance and innocence are characteristics assumed essential for the existence of childhood, a view also promoted by **Postman** (1987). This idea of the child as a 'tabula rasa', an open book and totally innocent, often remains unquestioned, a preconceived assumption at the heart of much of the debate about media 'effects'.

Buckingham, D. (1996) *Moving Images: Understanding Children's Emotional Responses to TV*. Manchester University Press.

Gunter, B. and Mcleer, J. (1990) *Children and TV: The One Eyed Monster*. Routledge.

Hill, A. (1997) *Shocking Entertainment: Viewers Response to Violent Movies*. University of Luton Press.

Morrison, D. E. *et al.* (1999) *Defining Violence: The Search for Understanding*. University of Luton Press.

Postman, N. (1987) *Amusing Ourselves to Death*. Methuen.

vocational education. Embraces the different types of strategies used to prepare pupils for the world of work. More and more education is being developed which combines skills development alongside the social and group skills necessary to survive in the world of employment. Media education in particular promotes the strategy of developing key skills for future employment which include group, communication and literary skills.

voyeurism and pornography. Related strands of **spectatorship** and representation which conspire to produce sexual gratification for audiences. When a person derives gratification and pleasure from watching sexual acts or objects, they are said to be engaging in voyeuristic activity, much like a peeping Tom, who is defined as one who takes morbid interest in sordid sights. However, it is argued that the very act of watching a film encourages a form of voyeurism, since it involves audiences looking behind closed doors into the lives of fictional protagonists.

Laura Mulvey's seminal article 'Visual Pleasure and Narrative Cinema' (1975) attacks the way the dominant system of film presents only certain types of pleasure. She argues that the **classic narrative** fiction film created images of women that were used for the gratification of audiences. The Hollywood style arose largely from its skilled manipulation of visual pleasure. Mainstream Hollywood film took the pleasure of watching erotic images and transformed them into a reflection of the dominant system. Cinema produced (male) fantasy in which the audience observed from a darkened auditorium. It is the (active) male look which determines what we see on the screen most of the time. She defines such voyeuristic pleasure as '**scopophilia**' – subjecting other people to a controlling and curious gaze. The interests, obsessions, fantasies and so on which we see on the screen will be those of the dominant males who control Western society.

Mainstream film, according to hardline feminists, appears unable to represent women as anything other than the objects of the male gaze. This major debate within media is often illustrated through Alfred Hitchcock's voyeuristic filmic output which provides a fruitful battleground for such debates.

For example, in *Rear Window* (1954), the camera seldom strays from inside Stewart's apartment, and every shot is closely aligned with his point-of-view as he uncovers a murder. Hitchcock usually took women as 'objects' as well as subjects in his films, yet audience identification is generally aligned with the imperilled woman, which may problematize Mulvey's thesis.

Pornography, on the other hand, is determined by the historical context in which it arises and is often evidenced by looser definitions in contemporary times that in the past. In broad terms pornography is defined as sexual representations which objectify the characters represented in purely sexual terms. Differentiating between pornography, erotica and more conventional voyeuristic film leads to provocative debates within media studies.

Hargrave, A. M. (1992) *Sex and Sexuality in Broadcasting*. John Libbey Press.

Hill, A. (1997) *Shocking Entertainment: Viewer Response to Violent Movies*. John Libbey Press.

Kappeler, S. (1986) *The Pornography of Representation*. Polity Press.

Mulvey, L. (1989) *Visual and Other Pleasures*. Macmillan.

Tester, K. (1994) *Media, Culture and Morality*. Routledge.

Watney, S. (1989) *Policing Desire: Pornography, Aids and the Media*. Comedia.

Vygotsky, Lev (1896–1934). A Russian psychologist whose research addressed questions concerning children's mental development and theories of learning. His findings were at odds with those of Piaget's stages of development. Vygotsky believed that children learn most effectively when supported by an adult. Perhaps his best-known work was in the field of language and thought development, where Vygotsky believed that children's intellectual growth was dependent on their mastery of language. He identified three stages of speech development: external, egocentric and inner. Vygotsky wrote over 200 works, including *Thought and Language* (1934) and *Mind in Society* (1978). His theories have been most particularly applied by David **Buckingham**, within media education.

war and propaganda. Many historians and media analysts have explored
representations of war in the mass media. Such study has become extensive
when connected with propagandistic effects. The flowering of propaganda
has intensified since the Second World War, when all sides became masters
in using the media. With the Vietnam War, it is often claimed that nightly
coverage on American TV helped to turn public attitudes against the war,
and fuelled massive anti-war demonstrations and student revolts. It is
claimed that the **Thatcher** government, appreciating the power of
broadcasting media in particular, was very conscious of the 'oxygen of
publicity' in dealing with all forms of opposition to the state. Consequently,
they ensured a more tightly censored broadcasting regime for conflicts like
the Falklands War.

The Gulf War and the recent protracted Balkans conflicts were mediated
in many ways like 'hi-tech' video games as the Allies focused on 'precision
bombing' – which has recently been exposed by the **BBC** as highly
inaccurate – and avoided the necessity of costly conventional land battles.
CNN in particular dramatized the Gulf War live for Americans and the rest
of the world as events were occurring simultaneously on the battlefield.

The moral/ethical and political dilemmas for media investigators –
particularly those which espouse **public service broadcasting** and **fourth
estate** values – involve making decisions between demands for propaganda
as opposed to democratic values and truth. Notions of truth become very
unclear during times of conflict and war, when the media is marshalled as
another necessary ideological state apparatus in the battle for hearts and
minds against the 'common enemy'. The notion of **jingoism** was invented
to reflect the extreme patriotism which especially affected the British
Empire. Such jingoism was more recently in evidence after the sinking of the
Argentine battleship, the *Belgrano* in the Falklands War, which was reported
in the *Sun* with the single-word, triumphant headline 'Gotcha'. A large
number of Argentinean lives were lost on that ship, which was later
confirmed to have been moving out of the area of battle. How to record

public dissent and opposition to the war, for example, or how to voice the often legitimate issues raised by an enemy, become very difficult for media organizations.

For example, back in the Crimean War, *The Times*, in spite of government opposition, reported details of the disastrous campaigns, which were mismanaged, together with the horrific state of medical aid. Such reports led to a change in personnel in the execution of the war and Florence Nightingale set up a nursing fraternity to aid the sick and wounded.

Film, Radio and TV (1994) journal (often has feature articles on war reporting).

Hall, S. (1981) *The Manufacture of News*. Owen and Young.

Harris, R. (1983) *Gotcha! The Media, the Government and the Falklands Crisis*. Faber and Faber.

Jowett, G. S. and O'Donnell, V. (1986) *Propaganda and Persuasion*. Sage.

McLennan, G. (ed.) (1991) *The Power of Ideology*. Open University Press.

watchdog. See **press as public watchdog**.

Watergate scandal. Happened in America and led to the downfall of an American president. Admirers of the **free press model** point to the example of the *Washington Post* journalists whose investigation of an illegal entry and bugging in a government building led to the impeachment of President Nixon. Others, however, cite the abuse of such democratic powers, which are often driven by financial and other concerns. European countries, especially Britain, did not adopt such an open model, preferring what has come to be described as a **social responsibility model** instead.

See the film which deals with the scandal: *All the President's Men* (1976).

web design. Involves the creation of web pages for the **internet**. Creating pages for the internet has become one of the biggest growth areas in **multimedia** over the past number of years. For a basic course, students need to be proficient in using Photoshop, preparing images for the web, creating animated images, capturing sound, as well as manipulating conventional text. Building and structuring a website involves manipulating all of the above.

As well as learning the technical skills required to manipulate information using various software packages on their computer, students also come to appreciate the need for and the development of appropriate design skills that will help create effective web pages.

Photoshop skills which must be appropriated include:

* scanning, saving and storing work;
* selecting and editing using the toolbox with various options and palettes;
* using filters and brush modes, etc.

DiNucci, D., Giudice, M. and Stiles, L. (1998) *Elements of Web Design*. Peachpit Press.

Miletsky, J. (1999) *Web Photoshop 5 to Go*. Prentice Hall.

web pages. Internet sites and locations which contain information that has been designed and entered by the owners of the site. This has become a major growth area, with 'surfing', as it has come to be known (looking at various sites and jumping from one to another in quick succession), becoming the most exciting new research source for media studies in the last few years. So many sites are becoming invaluable for acquiring information about a wide range of subjects for media analysis. A danger, however, which must be accepted, is not always being sure of the authenticity of entries and sites. Unlike the academic fraternity, which is more strictly patrolled and marshalled by a strong editorial and peer review systems of checks and balances, the internet is open to numerous abuses. Especially in the hands of inexperienced students, hunting for 'quick' summary pieces to assist with essays, there is a growing danger not only of **plagiarism**, which is increasing as an academic problem, but equally significantly misquoting and using faulty, inadequate and often third-rate citations. There is no substitute for reading conventional books and authenticated journal articles. However, that said, surfing the internet is invaluable for 'topping-up' information, getting leads for other sources of information as well as getting a variety of numerous other opinions on an apparently unlimited range of media subjects.

The following sites are particularly invaluable for research on a wide range of media areas.

Librarians in particular recommend the BUBL link for all manner of authenticated research; its film pathway is particularly good: http://bubl.ac.uk/link/filmstudies.htm. There are also valuable connecting 'hot-spot' links (by double-clicking on the blue web address) to the American Film Institute, BFI, scriptwriting pages and numerous film review and journal pages.

www.bfi.org.uk – is a very detailed site for the **BFI** which can link up to research areas essential to the study of film.

www.mailbase.ac.uk/lists/film-philosophy – is a very good site for culture/film essays and debates which have become most popular, especially within film studies.

www.skillset.org – links into the **Skillset**, which is the national training organization for film, video and multimedia in the UK.

www.filmsite.org – has reviews and analysis of many of the greatest films of all time.

www.mediachannel.org – is a fantastic American site which can access reviews of books and films as well as highlighting how media is being manipulated, etc. It is maintained by a charity left-wing group and is a very useful starting point for any investigation.

www.aber.ac.uk – has assorted links which look at various media and film issues. It contains excellent work-notes for undergraduate media students, including for example essays on 'The Grammar of Television and Film' and notes on 'Why do People Watch Television?', www.newmediastudies.com – is a related site.

www.ctheory.com – is a very good if often heavily theoretical cultural site (but unfortunately appears not to have been maintained recently) with excellent essays and reviews by top-rate theorists from all over America and elsewhere.

http://eee.uci.edu – provides an interesting model for a web page film studies course led by Professor Ann Friedberg.

www.mecfilms.com/critic – again looks particularly at film issues, especially film history.

www.cyberfilmschool.com – provides some worthwhile information on film/video making and lighting, etc.

www.culturegov.uk – provides information on regulations for media ownership, etc.

www.fcc.gov/ – Federal Communication Commission. Provides information on regulation and licensing of broadcasting in America.

www.bbc.co.uk – main address for access to the BBC.

www.newscorp.com – for access to Murdoch's global media empire.

www.educationunlimited.co.uk/specialreports/universities2000 – If you want to look at the *Guardian/Observer*'s ranking of media studies institutions in the UK, this is a good site.

http://eserver.org/theory/need – looks again at some very wide-ranging cultural topics.

Otherwise use the wide range of search-engines, typing in a key search word, and you should come up with appropriate sites for your investigation.

western. The western film seeks to resolve in its own way the conflicts between 'key American values like progress and success and the lost virtues of individualism, honour and natural freedom' (Frayling, p. 26). The western is set historically between 1860 and 1890 and explores a series of narrative resolutions of contradictions in American society. As a **genre**, the western has been extensively studied, particularly with regard to its demise or transformation into related genres such as urban detective and revenge stories, or westerns in space, like *Star Wars*, which produced a new frontier to fight for. Westerns have been the most popular genre, particularly among male audiences, since they dealt particularly with **gender** issues of masculinity and violence.

Jim Kitses has produced a very useful **structural** list of binary oppositions using **Lévi-Strauss**'s model to explain the primary tensions and conflicts in a western:

The wilderness	Civilization
The individual:	*The community:*
freedom	restriction
honour	institutions
self-knowledge	illusion
integrity	compromise
self-interest	social responsibility
solipsism	democracy
Nature:	*Culture:*
purity	corruption
experience	knowledge
pragmatism	legalism
brutalism	refinement
savagery	humanity
The west:	*The east:*
America	Europe
the frontier	America
equality	class
agrarianism	industrialism
tradition	change
the past	the future

(Cited in Short, R. (1991) *Imagined Country*. Routledge.)

Channel 4 (1995) *The Wild West: The Way the American West was Lost and Won 1845–1893*, series.

Cawelti, J. (1971) *The Six Gun Mystique*. Bowling Green University Press.

Frayling, C. (1981) *Spaghetti Westerns*. Routledge.

Frency, P. (1973) *Westerns*. BFI.

Kitses, J. (1969) *Horizons West*. BFI.

Wright, W. (1975) *Sixguns and Society: A Structural Study of the Western*. University of California Press.

whiteness. As a representational issue, it is rarely addressed, with the majority of **race** analysis focusing on non-white, usually minority representations. Possibly as a by-product of the Nazi belief in Aryan purity, discussions of whiteness have remained affected by such connotations, consequently race analysis has remained preoccupied by more politically correct treatments of minorities and **multiculturalism** within a dominant white culture.

For example, Richard Dyer's 1997 study, *White*, suggests that the android/**cyborg** in *Blade Runner* has become an important progressive representational icon in Hollywood films and provides a new definition of whiteness. The replicants are described by the 'racist' chief of police as 'skin jobs' which need to be exterminated. Yet the film in many ways eulogizes them, with many critics going so far as reading their 'ethnicity' in 'post-human' terms. Even the hunter-hero, Harrison Ford, is inferred to be a replicant by the end of the film, which certainly questions his 'whiteness'.

Hill, M. (ed.) (1997) *Whiteness: A Critical Reader.* State University of New York Press.

Why study the media? This question remains the most frequently asked of this subject. Len **Masterman**, one of the founding fathers of the subject in Britain, poses several general but interconnecting reasons for its study, which include:

- High rate of media consumption.
- Ideological importance of media influences in the conscience industry.
- Growth of management and manufacturing of information.
- To educate students for the future and thereby help to promote a democratic structure.
- The privatization of information and consequently the need to expose this.

Masterman idealistically asserts that the teacher and pupil should jointly 'challenge the inequalities in knowledge and power' and affirms that the *raison d'être* of media studies is to show the 'constructed' nature of reality by the media rather than merely innocently 'reflecting' it; consequently, teachers must question underlying assumptions of the media which help to 'demystify' the world (see *Teaching the Media*, 1985).

Together with Masterman's utopic and ideological *raison d'être*, more recent justification tends to focus more on visual and **media literacy** demanded by general education and the need to develop such key skills, not just from a purely vocational perspective.

Williams, Raymond. An important Welsh writer who became highly influential within literature and media studies in the UK and elsewhere. He developed numerous core media theories including:

- Residual, dominant and emerging **meanings** and modes of production.
- TV as 'flow'.

For example, Williams suggested that audiences simply 'plug-in' television like other home conveniences such as water or electricity. This idea has important implications when explaining broadcasting **schedules**, for example. TV companies want audiences to stay with their channel for as long as possible. Consequently, if Williams's notion of flow is accepted, then audiences turn on/off TV, not necessarily individual programmes, which makes it easier for branded schedules like the BBC to maintain large audiences. However, the notion loses some of its potency with the development of VCRs and **time-shifting** for example, alongside the evolution of more discriminatory audiences. Audiences can take a more active control in their consumption of media products by choosing to view TV not as 'flow' but in discrete units at their convenience.

Eagleton, T. (1989) *Raymond Williams: Critical Perspectives.* Polity Press.

O'Connor, A. (ed.) *Raymond Williams on Television: Selected Writings*. Routledge.

Williams, R. (1989) *The Politics of Modernism: Against the New Conformism*. Verso.

Wollen, Peter. An influential theorist who has produced a very useful structuralist model to compare classic Hollywood films and **avant-garde**. He has written extensively on film and popular culture generally and has even made avant-garde films. See also **structuralism**.

Wollen, P. (1972) 'Counter Cinema: Vent d'est', *Afterimage* 4.

Wollen, P. (1982) *Readings and Writings: Semiotic Counter Strategies*. Verso.

Wollen, P. (1993) *Raiding the Icebox: Reflections on Twentieth Century Culture*. University of Indiana Press.

women's magazines. Have remained very popular in the print industry as a source of media analysis, particularly with regard to representation, ideology and journalistic conventions. In spite of the phenomenal growth of the new unisex and 'lads' magazine market, women in the UK, according to Naomi Marks, spend around £230 million every year on their monthly glossies, with advertising revenue exceeding £190 million in 1999. So it is no wonder that the top five, *Cosmopolitan* (1972), *Marie Claire* (1989), *New Woman* (1991), *Elle* (1985) and *Red* (1998), are all doing very well (the *Independent on Sunday*, 9 July 2000).

Braithwaite, B. (1985) *Women's Magazines*. Kogan Page.

Davis, A. (1988) *Magazine Publishing Today*. Focal Press.

Hermes, J. (1995) *Reading Women's Magazines*. Polity Press.

Owen, W. (1991) *Magazine Design*. Lawrence King.

Winship, J. (1987) *Inside Women's Magazines*. Pandora Press.

More recently there has been a huge growth in specialist men's magazines in the UK, with *Loaded* and *GHQ* in particular.

Z

zeitgeist media text. A text which evocatively and accurately captures the mood that encapsulates the attitudes, values and beliefs of a period. Historians and film theorists often read films as directly reflecting the political and historical sensibilities of a nation. Films which most accurately and directly embody and reflect such connections are often described as zeitgeist texts.

For example, Stephen Prince's *Visions of Empire* (Praeger, 1992) provides a fascinating analysis of *Back to the Future* (1985) and *Field of Dreams* (1989) as effective zeitgeist films for contemporary America. Such films are said to accurately reflect the social, political, ideological and most particularly cultural specificities of the society they emanate from.

At one extreme movies are considered ideological formations which primarily reflect political controls. Popular film nevertheless can be read, using both right- and left-wing values; for example, for the **left wing**, *Bonnie and Clyde* (1967) was a story of martyrdom, whereas for the **right wing** it remains a cautionary tale. For **myth** study, the shapes of individual movies arise from the rules of transformation; for **psychoanalytical** theory, movies are dreams, screened and reshaped by a culture's collective unconsciousness.

List of Headwords

A Level (Advanced Level)

aberrant decoding

ability

accent

access course

access TV

active learning

active reading

adaptation

address

addresses

advertising

Advertising Standards
Authority (ASA)

aesthetics

Affective Fallacy

affective learning

age

agencies

agenda-setting

agents

alienation

Althusser, Louis

American Culture Association
(ACA)

American mass media

anchorage

animation

anomie

anthropology

anthropomorphism

aperture

AS Level (Advanced
Subsidiary Level)

assessment

assessment criteria

assessment opportunities

attainment

attitude

audience (general)

audience ratings

audience research

Australian media

auteur theory

avant-garde

awarding bodies (UK)

back to basics

BARB (Broadcasters' Audience
Research Board)

bardic TV

Barker, Martin

Barthes, Roland

base

baseline assessment

BBC

behavioural studies

benchmarking

BFI (British Film Institute)

bias

bibliography

Bloom, Benjamin

Bordwell, David

brainstorming

Brecht, Bertolt

British Educational
Communications and
Technology agency (BECTa)

broadsheet

Buckingham, David

Calcutt Committee

Campaign for Press and
Broadcasting Freedom (CPBF)

Canadian media

canon

capitalism

career

cartoon

catharsis

CD-Rom (Compact Disk Read
Only Memory)

censorship

censorship in the UK: film

Channel 4

chequebook journalism

chiaroscuro

child-centred education

Chomsky, Noam

Cinéma Vérité

cinematography

circulation

citizenship

class system

classic narrative cinema

clip art

Headwords

closure
CNN (Cable News Network)
code
cognition
cognitive development
cognitive film analysis
Cold War and McCarthyism
comedy
comics
commercial
commodification
communication
communication models
communism
commutation test
competence
computer aided design (CAD)
computer literacy
concept mapping
connotation
conspiracy theory
constructivism
contact sheet
content analysis
context
contextualize
continued professional development (CPD)
continuity editing
continuous assessment
convention
convergence
copyright
core concept
core curriculum
core subject
costume
counter-culture
coursework
crime TV
criterion-referencing
critical language studies (CLS)
critical theory
cropping
cross-curricular

cultural competence
cultural imperialism
cultural literacy
cultural studies (American)
cultural studies (UK)
culture
curriculum
curriculum development
cyberspace
cyborgs
data
data protection
Dearing Report (National Curriculum and its Assessment)
decision-making
decisive moment
decoding
deconstruction
demystification
denotation
depth of field
deregulation
determinism
developing media in education
development education centres (DECs)
dictionaries
didactic teaching
diegesis
differentiation
digital
digital photography
direct address
discourse
discovery-learning
discrimination
Disney
documentary
docu-soaps
dominant ideology
dumbing down
economic imperative
education
Education (Schools) Act (1992)

effects theory
Eisenstein, Sergei
electronic media
electronic news gathering (ENG)
ellipsis
empiricism
empower
encoding
encryption
environmentalism
equilibrium/disequilibrium
essay
estrangement
ethics
ethnography
evaluation
examination
exemplar
experiential learning
exposé
expressive language
extra-personal communication
F-stop
fairytales
false consciousness
fantasy
fascism
feminism
film A Level syllabus
film noir
fine grain
Fiske, John
fitness for purpose
focus groups
formative assessment
Foucault, Michel (1926–84)
fourth estate
Frankfurt School
free press model
Freire, Paulo
functionalism
functions of the media
game show
gate-keeping

THE CONTINUUM GUIDE TO MEDIA EDUCATION

gender

genre

German propaganda

Glasgow Media Group

globalization

GNVQ (General National Vocational Qualification)

grammar of film/TV

group work

Hall, Stuart

Hawthorne effect

hegemony

hermeneutics

hidden agenda

high-order questions

history of newspapers in Britain

horizontal/vertical integration

hot-spot

house style

hypertext

hypodermic needle model

hypothesis

iceberg principle

icon/iconography

identification

ideological state apparatus

ideology

IMAX

in-camera editing

Independent Television Commission (ITC)

index

information and communications technology (ICT)

infotainment

in-house

Intentionalist Fallacy

interactive

internet

interpellating the audience

interpersonal communication

intertextuality

interviews

intra-personal communication

Irish identity on film

jargon

jingoism

journal

journalism

jump-cut

Jung, Carl

juxtaposition

key concepts in media education

key light

key skills

key stage

King, Rodney

knowledge

Kulshov effect

league tables

learning style

Leavis, F. R

left wing

leitmotif

Lévi-Strauss, Claude

library footage

lighting

liminal/outsider

linguistics

literacy

MacCabe, Colin

Madonna

male gaze

mark scheme

market research

marketing

Marxism

Maslow, Abraham

Masterman, Len

McLuhan, Marshal

meaning

media education versus media studies in Britain

media ethics

media literacy/education (Australia)

media literacy/education (Canada)

media literacy/education (Ireland)

media literacy/education (UK)

media literacy/education (USA)

melodramas

metanarrative

method school of acting

Metz, Christian

mimetic

mise-en-scène

mixed ability teaching

moderation

modules

Monroe, Marilyn

montage

moral panic

multicultural education

multiculturalism (USA)

multimedia

Murdoch, Rupert

music industry

myth

narrative/narratology

narrative: types of character

naturalism

nature/nurture debate

new media/technology

New Right

new technology

news agencies

news values

newspaper language-(rules)

niche audience

non-verbal communication (NVC)

norm-referencing

NVQ (National Vocational Qualification)

OFSTED (Office for Standards in Education)

online

ontology

open-ended question

other

ownership and control

Headwords

paparazzi photography
paradigm shift
parallax
participant observation
passive learning
patriarchy
Payne Fund
pedagogical progressivism and media studies
Peirce, C. S.
phenomenology
philosophy
photography
photojournalism
pilot
plagiarism
Plato's allegory of the cave
political correctness (PC)
politics and media effects
polysemy
popular arts
popular culture
pornography
portraiture
positivist rationality
Postman, Neil
postmodernism
post-structuralism
power
practical application in media studies
preferred (dominant) reading
prejudice
presentations
press as public watchdog
press complaints
primary source
problematic
product placement
production values
progressive education
proofreading
propaganda
Propp, Vladimir
proxemics

psychoanalysis
public access TV
public service broadcasting (PSB) (UK)
public sphere
publishing
qualitative/quantitative research
questionnaire
race
radio
ratings
rationalism
readability
realism
recuperation
references
reflection theory
reflective journal
regulatory bodies
reification
remediation
representation: female/male
repressive state apparatus
research
right of reply
right wing
role-play
rote learning
sampling
scapegoating
scheduling
scopophilia
self-actualization
self-reflexive
semiotics (denotation/connotation)
Simpsons
simulacrum
skills
Skillset
soaps
social realism
social responsibility model
socialism
Sontag, Susan

soundbite
spatial
special effects
spectatorship
spin-doctor
standards
Stanislavsky, Constantin
Star Wars
Steadicam
stereotypes
still photography
storyboard
structural film
structuralism
summative assessment
surrealism
surveillance
syllabus
symbol
tableau
tabloid
taxonomy
team teaching
technological determinism
technophobia
telephony
television: UK share of audience
text
textual analysis
Thatcherism
theory
third cinema
time-shifting
TV and effects theory
uses and gratification theory
utopia
validity
value added
verisimilitude
Vertov, Dziga
video games
video nasties
video skills
video technology: the future?

violence (representation of)
vocational education
voyeurism and pornography
Vygotsky, Lev (1896-1934)
war and propaganda
watchdog

Watergate scandal
web design
web pages
western
whiteness
Why study the media?

Williams, Raymond
Wollen, Peter
women's magazines
zeitgeist media text

Glossary of Educational Abbreviations

A4E   Arts for Everyone

ACCAC The Qualifications, Curriculum and Assessment Authority for Wales

ATQ   Additional Teaching Qualification

BBFC   British Board of Film Classification

BECTa British Educational Communications and Technology agency

BFI   British Film Institute

BTEC   Business and Technician Education Council

CCEA   Council for the Curriculum, Examinations and Assessment

DCMS Department of Culture, Media and Sport

DfEE   Department for Education and Employment

FE   further education

FEFC   Further Education Funding Council

FEWG   Film Education Working Group

GCE   General Certificate of Education

GCSE   General Certificate of Secondary Education

GNVQ General National Vocational Qualification

HE   higher education

HND   Higher National Diploma

ICT   information and communications technology

ITT   Initial Teacher Training

INSET in-service training

LEA   local education authority

NCC   National Curriculum Council

NCET   National Council for Educational Technology

NCVQ   National Council for Vocational Qualifications
NVQ   National Vocational Qualification
PGCE   Post-Graduate Certificate in Education
QCA   Qualifications and Curriculum Authority
SAT   Standard Assessment Task
SCAA   School Curriculum and Assessment Authority
SEAC   School Examination and Assessment Council
TTA   Teacher Training Agency

Bibliography

A selection of key texts and readers.

(Note: publication dates may vary between initial publication and later editions used.)

Alvarado, M. and Thompson, J. (eds) (1990) *The Media Reader*. BFI.

Bell, A., Joyce, M. and Rivers, D. (1999) *Advanced Level Media*. Hodder and Stoughton.

Briggs, A. and Cobley, P. (eds) (1998) *The Media: An Introduction*. Longman.

Branston, G. and Stafford, R. (1997) *The Media Student's Book*. Routledge.

Burton, G. (1990) *More than Meets the Eye: An Introduction to Media Studies*. Edward Arnold.

Cobley, P. (ed.) (1996) *The Communication Theory Reader*. Routledge.

Cook, P. (ed.) (1999) *The Cinema Book*. BFI.

Corner, J. and Harvey, S. (eds) (1996) *Television Times: A Reader*. Arnold.

Curran, J. and Seaton, J. (1997) *Power without Responsibility*. Routledge.

Dimbley, R. and Burton, G. (1998) *More than Words: An Introduction to Communications Studies*. Routledge.

Goodwin, A. and Whannel, G. (eds) (1990) *Understanding Television*. Routledge.

Fiske, J. (1987) *Television Culture*. Routledge.

Fiske, J. (1994) *Introduction to Communications Studies*. Routledge.

Fiske, J. and Hartley, J. (1978) *Reading Television*. Routledge.

Geraghty, C. and Lusted, D. (eds) (1998) *The Television Studies Book*. Arnold.

Hart, A. (1991) *Understanding the Media: A Practical Guide*. Routledge.

Hartley, J. (1982) *Understanding News*. Routledge.

Lusted, D. (ed.) (1991) *The Media Studies Book*. Routledge.

Marris, P. and Thornham, S. (eds) (1996) *Media Studies: A Reader*. Edinburgh University Press.

Masterman, I . (1980) *Teaching About Television*. Macmillan.

Masterman, L. (1985) *Teaching the Media*. Comedia.

McLuhan, M. (2000) *Understanding Media: The Extensions of Man*. Routledge.

McQuail, D. (1993) *Mass Communications Theory*. Sage.

McQueen, D. (1998) *Television: A Media Studies Guide*. Arnold.

Morley, D. (1986) *Television Audiences and Cultural Studies*. Routledge.

Negrine, R. (1994) *Politics and the Mass Media in Britain*. Routledge.

O'Sullivan, T. and Jewkes, Y. (eds) (1997) *The Media Studies Reader*. Arnold.

O'Sullivan, T. et al. (1998) *Studying the Media*. Arnold.

Postman, N. (1987) *Amusing Ourselves to Death*. Methuen.

Price, S. (1993) *Media Studies*. Pitman.

Price, S. (1996) *Communications Studies*. Addison Wesley Longman.

Schlesinger, P. (1992) *Putting Reality Together*. Routledge.

Selby, K. and Cowdery, R. (1995) *How to Study Television*. Macmillan.

Storey, J. (1993) *Cultural Theory and Popular Culture*. Harvester Wheatsheaf.

Strinati, D. (1995) *An Introduction to Theories of Popular Culture*. Routledge.

Turner, G. (1999) *Film as Social Practice*. Routledge.

Williams, R. (1983) *Keywords: A Vocabulary of Culture and Society*. Fontana.